Praise for *Success: It's A Beautiful Thing*

"Tony Conza has shown, time and again, the vision to make Blimpie grow and the courage to make changes along the way. When he speaks about success, a lot of people would be well served to listen."
—M. Douglas Ivester, former Chairman and CEO
The Coca-Cola Company

"It's about time someone demystified the path to success. The beautiful thing about Tony Conza is how he inspires others to see their own potential greatness."
—Rick Goings, Chairman
Tupperware Corporation

"This is a beautiful book about passion in business. anyone looking to enhance the satisfactino they derive from life both on and off the job can learn valuable lessons from this book."
—Roxanne Spillet, President
Boys & Girls Clubs of America

"Tony Conza's new book is a must-read for all aspiring entrepreneurs and those who lead companies, both large or small. Conza gives his formula for success in business as well as life."
—W. W. Allen, Former Chairman & CEO
Phillips Petroleum Company

"Tony Conza tells all who read his story a meaningful insight on how to succeed. A beautiful book by one of America's best."
—Harvey W. Schiller, Chairman & CEO
YankeeNets

"Tony Conza exemplifies the American dream of becoming successful. A great story of accomplishment, passion, and wonderful anecdotes. This is a must read for any individual desiring to succeed."
—Jerry Colangelo, Owner
Arizona Diamondbacks

SUCCESS

IT'S A BEAUTIFUL THING

SUCCESS

IT'S A BEAUTIFUL THING

LESSONS ON LIFE AND
BUSINESS FROM THE
FOUNDER OF BLIMPIE
INTERNATIONAL

TONY
CONZA

John Wiley & Sons, Inc.

New York • Chichester • Weinheim
Brisbane • Singapore • Toronto

ISBN 0-471-38147-0

Printed in the United States of America.

10 9 8 7 6 5 4 3 2 1

To my wife, Yvonne, whose friendship, good sense of humor, and love remind me every day what success means.

ACKNOWLEDGMENTS

To my collaborator, Ken Bookman, who made sure this book was readable.

To my agent, Jane Dystel, without whose guidance and wisdom there would be no book.

To Ruth Mills of John Wiley & Sons for believing in my book.

To my daughter and best buddy, Debra, who has brought so much joy and happiness into my life.

To my Mom and Dad, who inspired me, taught me life's lessons, and provided the foundation for my success.

To my partner, David Siegel, whose smarts and sense of humor helped me get through the hard times, and enjoy the good ones.

To my partners and friends, Pat Pompeo and Chuck Leaness, whose dedication and commitment have been with me every step of the way.

To my brother Joe for his love and friendship and because he has contributed more to my success than anyone realizes.

To my sister Carol, my biggest fan.

To Angelo Baldassare and Peter DeCarlo, without whom Blimpie would never have happened.

To Joe Morgan, who makes me feel good about the future of Blimpie International.

To Nichole Mayers and Maureen Foppiano, my assistants, for putting up with my scribbling.

To all those who have touched my life, supported me, and provided me with wonderful memories.

CONTENTS

INTRODUCTION

What is success? The answer may be a lot simpler than you think: It's whatever you want it to be. The trick is getting there.

I know some folks who are passionate about certain things in their life. Maybe it's cooking or golf or running or religion. These people may ask me, "Tony, what makes you successful at what you do?" Well, there's no mystery here. I'm motivated by what I do—whether it's preparing to run a marathon, playing the piano, or running a worldwide chain of sandwich stores.

Nineteen ninety-nine was a good year for me. I was honored to receive the Boys & Girls Clubs of America President's Award and, a short time earlier, the Ellis Island Medal of Honor. It made me wonder: "How did I get here? How did I achieve such success? I'm just a guy from Jersey City. I'm just a sandwich man!"

The answer is that it has nothing to do with sandwiches. It has to do with setting goals and reaching them. What is it that we are trying to accomplish as we go through life? Wealth, fame, winning admiration from others, a good marriage, freedom from failure? Maybe. The point is that everyone wants the best this life has available. Yet all of these things are just a means to what should be your ultimate goal: enjoying life.

I had always planned to write a book. I just didn't think I'd be writing it now. I always figured that I'd write it when I was finished accomplishing my goals. But when I realized that I would *never* be finished, because there is always another goal that I'll aspire to, I decided not to wait to pass onto others what I've learned.

It took a long time, and a lot of dumb mistakes to learn what I know. A lot of my knowledge is specific to becoming an entrepreneur or running a good business, but the most important thing I want to share is how the principles for achieving success in life are generally the same as they are for business. I want to be able to share my insights and my experiences with others. I want to inspire people and let them know that they can reach their dreams so long as they have the passion to pursue them. And I figured I could take a very common-sense approach in talking to my readers, because I come from a very modest background. I was very shy, I had no money, no connections, no mentors. I dropped out of college after only one year, yet I was able to achieve success because I surrounded myself with good people, applied basic principles, and followed my dreams.

You can, too. Get passionate. Whatever's important to you, get passionate about it, love it, and be inspired by it. The rewards will follow. And if you can't get passionate about something, do something else.

CHAPTER 1

ENTREPRENEURSHIP IS EVERYBODY'S BUSINESS

> Twenty years from now, you will be more disappointed by the things you didn't do than by the ones you did do. So throw off the bowlines. Sail away from the safe harbor. Catch the trade winds in your sails. Explore. Dream. Discover.
>
> **—Mark Twain**

A glaring morning sunlight made its way onto my face, waking me up. For a second or two, I gazed around the room, not certain where I was. Then I remembered: Dormitory. Boston University. My daughter, Debra, a student at BU, was still asleep in the next bed.

College dorm? I was forty years old, for goodness' sake. No, I didn't end up there after a drunken stupor the night before. It was part of a plan: I was trying to capture an experience—the college experience—that I had never had. It was like all those times I walked around a college campus after visiting a Blimpie store in the area.

Even though I had attended college briefly, I always knew that I had missed an experience, but I never thought I had missed an education. My life probably would have been different if I had gone away to college, but I'm positive that I would not have learned a thing about being an entrepreneur. Back then, business schools considered *entrepreneurship* a dirty word. They looked down on people who started their own business, catering instead to the needs of the country's giant corporations and consulting firms. Entrepreneurial skills? You learned them through self-teaching, trial and error, and getting help and advice from mentors. You probably couldn't find an Ivy League MBA who could run a sandwich place like Blimpie.

It's a little better today and I'm glad of that. As head of the Blimpie chain, I work in a world that needs a constant crop of entrepreneurs. Without them, Blimpie and a lot of the rest of the world just wouldn't work.

I look at people like Joe S. Nye, the dean at the John F. Kennedy School of Government at Harvard University who had

---

Entrepreneurial skills? You learned them through self-teaching, trial and error, and getting help and advice from mentors.

---

the vision to seek an entrepreneurial perspective for the school's Dean's Council. I'm proud to have been selected to join the council and share my ideas with them because entrepreneurs should be encouraged as early as possible.

Removing the Roadblocks

Becoming an entrepreneur starts in your gut, not in a classroom. You feel it. You know you want to control your own destiny, and you're fed up with people placing roadblocks between you and success. So, you start to dream. Then you make something happen.

That's how it happened for me, just not very quickly.

After graduating from St. Peter's Prep in Jersey City, New Jersey, I enrolled in St. Peter's College to study accounting. It felt too much like more high school: I was in the same town, lived at home, commuted every day, and quickly got bored, so I dropped out after just one year. I was confused. I got a job as a shipping clerk at a knitwear manufacturing plant in Union City, New Jersey, only to get a pink slip after about three months. The company was cutting back, I was told. And, no, it wasn't interested in hearing my ideas about how to improve the department. That dismissal, a decision made by the company's owner, set the stage for the longest vacation of my life—about four months. I was young enough to enjoy the free time, but I also came to understand that free time wasn't much fun if you were poor.

I was poor. I didn't like not having an income. From the time I was fourteen, I had always worked, first at a grocery store, then at a liquor store. The salary and tips I earned from my bicycle deliveries enabled me to buy my first car, a red Ford convertible, when I was eighteen. I loved that car but now, with no income, I might not be able to keep it. I had to get a job, so I turned to Dad.

My father was neither rich nor well connected. Dad worked for the New York Stock Exchange as a reporter, a position that has vastly changed in today's computerized world. A reporter recorded transactions between brokers and made sure that they appeared on the ticker tape. Dad made a very modest living and spent every penny supporting his family. He managed to get me an interview with Maurice Sommers, the head partner on the trading floor for E.F. Hutton & Company, a firm that long ago became part of the Solomon Smith Barney family. Sommers hired me and put me to work as a floor clerk, scribbling out buy-and-sell orders as they were shouted over the phone by staffers in the order room several blocks away. I enjoyed the frenzy of the trading floor, and was fascinated to watch fortunes being made and lost overnight. I also noted how Wall Street could depict a company as "the growth stock of the century" one day, only to treat it like a dog the next.

I enjoyed being in the center of this financial capital and I learned a lot, but those roadblocks started getting in the way again. It became pretty clear to me that to make any real money on the floor of the New York Stock Exchange, you had to be a broker or partner, and I just didn't see that happening for a kid from my background.

The funny thing is that, back in the neighborhood where I grew up, in many ways I was insulated from my heritage. Dad made a point of dressing in a suit and tie every morning, so people thought we had money. I was always led to believe that our family was doing well and that I should strive to do even better. My parents and grandparents never taught me, my sister, or my brother their native Italian, nor did they even speak it around the house. They just wanted us to be American. Rarely did they even refer to the old country and the early struggles they must have endured.

Later, I came to know about their struggles. When I received the Ellis Island Medal of Honor in 1999, I became more aware than ever in my life of how proud I was of my grandparents. How difficult it must have been for them to leave home, travel to a new world, hear a different language, and do it with no money and little more than the clothes on their backs. How strong they must have been to set such ambitious goals. How driven by hope they had to be, the hope of building a new and promising future for themselves, their children, and their children's children.

My folks made sure I dressed up, too, and they sent me to good schools, including St. Peter's Prep. I had never felt or even thought about class differences until I arrived at 11 Wall Street. That's when I began to feel different. It was like failing the ID check at a dance club and being refused entry. No one said anything, and I certainly could work there. I just couldn't mingle with the crowd. It's probably like what women contend with in today's old boy's network.

One place on the Street wasn't so clubby—the over-the-counter market. I requested and was granted a transfer to the OTC trading desk, the precursor to today's NASDAQ. If the New York Stock Exchange was wild, this was the Wild West. The traders seemed to do pretty much whatever they wanted. My enthusiasm was renewed. I met Frank Figueroa, a great guy. Frank, in fifteen years, proved a loyal, excellent trader who consistently made

---

Becoming an entrepreneur starts in your gut, not in a classroom. You feel it. You know you want to control your own destiny.

---

money for Hutton. Frank was a Puerto Rican and a Jehovah's Witness, and he felt like a misfit. He didn't socialize after work with the Connecticut-martini-WASP crowd that controlled things. Frankie accepted this as his fate but warned me that, if I was expecting anything different, I had better remove the rose-colored glasses. Again, because of my ethnic background and class difference, it looked like no one was going to open any doors for me. The roadblock that I thought I left on the New York Stock Exchange floor continued at 61 Broadway.

I knew that if there was any hope of creating a future for myself, I had to get out of there.

I began searching the help-wanted listings. One day, I found an ad in *The Wall Street Journal* for an over-the-counter trader with a much smaller firm. I brought the ad and a handwritten résumé into Hutton's offices and asked a secretary on another floor to do me a favor and type it for me. She did, but I was away from the trading desk when she delivered it to me, so she left it in full view. Bad career move. When I returned, the other traders were staring at me, and I was told that the boss wanted to see me in his office.

"Sit down," he said, tossing some papers in my direction. "Would you care to tell me what this is?" What could I say? I was caught. "Maybe you should go ahead and send it out," he said. I wasn't fired, but it was pretty clear that that little episode did not enhance my future with the firm.

A Dream

Peter DeCarlo and Angelo Baldassare were the central people in my business life. The three of us met at St. Peter's Prep. Peter and I became very close friends, hanging out on street corners together, working on our cars, spending time with each other's families, and occasionally talking about the possibility of starting a business. I didn't realize it at the time, but we were doing something that would-be entrepreneurs usually do. We thought about starting a business. Entrepreneurs usually want to go into business before they figure out what they would actually do once they got there. People often say to me, "Tony, I have this idea. What do you think of it?" Well, that's not what entrepreneurs do. "I want to go into business" comes before "I have an idea."

I'm not sure why that's so. In my case, the urge to become an entrepreneur was triggered by the roadblocks in my path. You can have a million-and-one ideas but, unless you're first saying to yourself, "I never want to work for a corporation" or "I'm not going to let others stand in my way" or "I'm going to create my own success," those ideas will never materialize.

So, Peter and I, armed with our business itch, started buying women's hosiery wholesale and selling it to family members and friends. Peter even started selling pots and pans door-to-door, something I couldn't get myself to do. He was always the consummate salesman. I was the quiet thinker. The prospect of starting a real business repeatedly came up in conversations—even as he began advancing his sales career in the garment industry and I tried to bust down the barricades on Wall Street.

One day, we ran into Angelo, who invited us and our wives to a Halloween party, where Peter and I once again found ourselves talking about starting a business. This time, Angelo joined in. If there was an entrepreneur among us, it was Angelo. As a teenager, he ran "Angelo's Dances" at the local church hall. For a few years, the dances were *the* place to be seen, and Angelo was raking in the bucks. Strangely enough, though, while I dropped out of college after one year and Peter never even attempted to go to college, Angelo got his degree and went to work at the Federal Reserve Bank of New York, of all places. That's like Bill Gates working in a steel mill. No wonder he was itching to do something.

Then, Angelo asked what would prove to be a fateful question about the Jersey Shore. "Hey, have you guys heard about those sandwiches they call submarines?" Peter and I had spent many a teenage day lying on the beach and many a night cruising the boardwalks up and down the shore. Arlene, my wife at the time, and her family rented a summer place there, where we spent weekends and vacations with our daughter, Debra. So, yes, we had heard of submarine sandwiches, but none of us had ever eaten one. "Tomorrow's Saturday," I said, "Why don't we take a ride and try one?" "Let's do it," said Peter.

The next morning, hangovers notwithstanding, we left our homes in North Jersey and headed down the Garden State Parkway to Point Pleasant, to a little shop that served submarine sandwiches. It was lunchtime and the place was packed, so we queued up at the end of the line. By the time we got to where the slicer was, we had begun to understand what all the fuss was about. A young man behind a slicing machine was taking orders, cutting fresh French-Italian bread down the middle, and placing freshly sliced meats on the bread before passing the sandwich on to the dressing station. There, another guy added shredded lettuce, sliced tomatoes, shredded onions, oil, vinegar, and spices. We stood there and our mouths were watering. We couldn't wait to chomp on these so-called subs.

At that moment, we knew we were on to something special.

What about Money?

On the way home, we began doing what entrepreneurs do: dream. Our words filled the car:

"People up north would love this sandwich."

"A salad on a sandwich is brilliant. What person who likes ham and cheese on a roll, or a veal parmigiana hero, wouldn't go nuts for this sandwich?"

"It's such a simple menu, we can open a chain of these."

"What have we got to lose; none of us are happy with our jobs anyway."

Then reality began to set in.

"None of us have any money. How are we going to do this?"

"I have a family to support. I can't just quit my job."

"What the heck do we know about the restaurant business? About any kind of business?"

However, this group was not about to be stopped. Despite lots of obstacles and challenges, we dreamed of starting our own business, and now we had the other necessary ingredient, an idea. We were excited, enthused, and inspired, and we had the motivation to pursue our dream. Peter, Angelo, and I were just a group of average guys. We weren't born entrepreneurs or highly educated. We just knew that we didn't want to leave our futures to bureaucratic corporate managers with their own agendas. We were driven by the roadblocks we had faced, by frustration, and by a desire to accomplish something.

So, a few days later, we were back at it, trying to figure out how to make this happen. "Hoboken would be a great place to open a store," said Angelo. "My wife's father, Mr. Milo, has a record store there, and he can help us find a location. He would also talk up the place and get people to try us. People in Hoboken love to try new things."

"Sounds good," I said, "but we still need money." This was maybe the first time, but certainly not the last, when I would be the one who seemed most concerned about our finances. Peter and Angelo were both great salespeople, and I've never considered salespeople the ones who worried about money. So I did.

Borrowing from a bank was out of the question. There wasn't a banker around who would even consider making a loan to inexperienced youngsters like us for a high-risk venture like a submarine sandwich restaurant. No, we needed to tap our creative juices if we were going to raise the money to get this business started. Sure, we could probably have convinced our parents to lend us the money, but we didn't want to do that. Whatever assets our parents had came from lots of their blood, sweat, and tears. We would have felt guilty putting them at risk.

We needed to strategize, and, if you want to start a business but don't have enough money, you need to do the same. Doing so might even demonstrate how badly you want to be in business.

Your search for financing can begin with banks that often can get 90 percent guarantees from the Small Business Administration on loans to small businesses. Venture-capital firms may also be an option, as may be lenders accustomed to taking high risks. There are always family and friends, too, but remember, the only thing that might destroy a family or a friendship quicker than lending to one of them would be to borrow from one of them.

Perhaps the easiest way to finance a small business today is by using credit cards. A third of businesses with fewer than nineteen employees fund themselves simply by getting money from their no-questions-asked cards. That's today, though. Back then, we didn't have credit cards, so we had to figure out something else.

"What about Vartan?" asked Peter. Vartan Keshishian was a guy in the garment business who had family money. Everyone agreed that Vartan was a good candidate to be an investor, so we decided to offer him 15 percent of our net profits for a $2,000 investment.

That $2,000 didn't do it all, but it got us started.

After we expanded our business and began to feel confident that we could repay any loans, my parents took out a mortgage on their home; Angelo's parents and a relative would tap their savings to help us with financing.

It wasn't until about seven years later, when I met a young banker named Carl Chirico, that we actually got our first bank loan. Carl was a junior officer at a new branch of National Community Bank of New Jersey, and was looking to build the bank's business. I submitted a loan application to Carl. He reviewed it, placed on his desk in front of me, looked me in the eye, and said, "Tony, your application's okay, but that's not why I'm going to make this loan. I think you are sincere. I believe you will make sure the bank gets paid back." We paid back the $10,000 and would go on to borrow hundreds of thousands of dollars from Carl and National Community Bank (which was eventually acquired by Bank of New York). Later, Carl and I became good friends, and I would invest as a shareholder when he started his own bank.

While Peter prepared to propose the deal to Vartan, we identified a site on Washington Street in Hoboken. The rent was $200 per month. The location helped sell Vartan, and we were on our way. We still had to learn about going into business in general and about the sandwich business in particular but, now, we were inspired, really inspired.

Today, at Blimpie International, we're always having franchisee meetings or employee meetings and we're always trying to motivate people. We hire speakers, we bring in celebrities, and we have successful Blimpie operators tell their stories with the hope of inspiring others. But the truth is that entrepreneurs have to be passionate on their own. From top corporate celebrities to very successful corporate executives to the local Blimpie franchisee, these folks make it happen without any outside influence. No one else can make them do something they are not already itching to do.

I know some folks who are passionate about certain things in their life. Maybe it's cooking or golf or running or religion. These people may ask me, "Tony, what makes you successful at what you do?" It's simple. I'm motivated by what I do. It's no different from the enthusiasm that these folks get from whatever it is that they are passionate about. There's no mystery here. Get passionate about your work, love it, and be inspired by it, and the money will come. And if you can't get passionate about your work, do something else.

Two thousand dollars may not sound like a lot now, but it was then. Even so, it still wasn't enough. Just to get our store built, we had to buy used equipment, beg physical help from friends and

> **Entrepreneurs have to be passionate on their own. From top corporate celebrities to the local Blimpie franchisee, these folks make it happen without any outside influence.**

relatives, and learn how to use a hammer and a paintbrush ourselves. Then we borrowed from the vending-machine man, who gave us an advance on jukebox sales.

Now we had the store built, but we still didn't know how to make these sandwiches. Remember, though, an inspired entrepreneur always finds a way. Why not go directly to the source? we thought. We visited Mike, the owner of the sub shop in Point Pleasant. "Mike, we promise not to open and compete with you. We just need some advice." Mike gave us advice, and we never competed with him.

On April 4, 1964, we opened for business. Peter manned the slicer, I worked the dressing station, and Angelo took the cash. We had one employee. Thanks to Mr. Milo and his word of mouth, customers lined up immediately and kept coming all day long. By the time we closed the doors at 9 P.M., $295 had been rung up—with sandwich prices that ranged from thirty-five to ninety-five cents. Although we were exhausted, we still had to clean up and get ready for the next day. That's when I realized something I now preach to our franchisees all the time. This was not a mutual fund. It was more like having a baby.

When you invest in a mutual fund, you give your money to some financial outfit, then sit back and hope that it makes money for you. Having a baby, of course, is different. Once that baby comes into your life, it never goes away. If you get tired, it doesn't go away. If you want to take the weekend off, it doesn't go away. If you want a vacation, it doesn't go away. However, if you nurture the baby, care for it, and help it grow, one day it will take care of itself—and maybe even take care of you.

Blimpie? What's a Blimpie?

Although the word *sub* is pretty well known today as the term for our type of sandwich, in 1964, people in Hoboken, New Jersey, didn't know what a sub was. The closest thing was a *hero,* generally identified as meatball, chicken parmigiana, or ham and salami on Italian bread. We needed another name.

Our research consisted of visiting all the sub shops we could find—Mike's in Albany (no relation to Mike in Point Pleasant),

---

Get passionate about your work, love it, and be inspired by it, and the money will come. And if you can't get passionate about your work, do something else.

Hoagie Hut in Caldwell, New Jersey, and various other places that called their sandwiches *grinders, wedges, heroes,* or *poor boys.* We learned two things. First, there was no name that was readily identifiable with the sandwich. Second, although some operators had very successful local chains, no one had a business that could be considered a regional, never mind a national, chain.

The name that seemed most compelling to us was *hoagie,* a word from Philadelphia, where the sandwich was very popular. *Hoagie* is a good word, we thought. Let's call our sandwiches *hoa-*

gies. We realized that people in Hoboken were no more familiar with the word *hoagie* than with the word *sub.* If we're going to teach people a word, we thought, why not make it *our* word?

One night Peter, Angelo, and I sat in Peter's apartment and started thinking about what to call the sandwich. We began to thumb through a dictionary, first the A's, then the B's. We stopped when we got to the word *blimp.* A blimp is a dirigible, an airship. That kind of described the sandwich. We added a couple of letters of our own, and Blimpie was born. Big market research.

I love the postscript to that story. In 1992, I volunteered to serve on the board of the Management Decision Laboratory, a program at New York University's Stern School of Business, where I met a woman named Edith Weiner, who is a *futurist,* someone hired by big companies who advises them about what to expect in the future. When I told Edie the story of how we came up with the name Blimpie, she said, "Oh, I use the dictionary all the time to invent words." My response: "You mean that for thirty years I thought this was a dumb idea, and now you're telling me it was brilliant?"

I Gotta Do What I Gotta Do

Before we opened our first store, the three of us agreed that Angelo would quit the Federal Reserve Bank and work days in the restaurant, while Peter and I would keep our jobs and share the nights and weekends. Of course, it didn't always end up that way. Peter and I would often find ourselves in the store together and Angelo, well, Angelo is one of those obsessive types. He'd show up at all times, and he'd call Peter and me at all hours of the day and night to discuss a problem. Often, he'd sleep in the back of the restaurant because "if I fall asleep at home, I may never wake up and make it back here."

Overnight, my life had been transformed. No longer could I sit at home after work and watch *Batman* with Debra or spend some peaceful hours on the sofa reading a good novel. Now my life was oil, vinegar, and oregano, and when I finally got to sleep at whatever time I hit the sack, the clothes I left on the floor smelled of it.

I adjusted well to my new work schedule, however, probably because I knew about sacrifice and hard work from my family. Both my grandfathers immigrated from Italy and worked long, hard hours, one selling candy, ice cream, and newspapers in lower Manhattan, the other laboring for the Erie Railroad (which has since become New Jersey Transit). Dad sometimes worked three jobs to save enough money to buy the materials to build his own home. And Mom was a dressmaker ("Don't call me a seamstress") at Bergdorf Goodman on Fifth Avenue, where she made wedding dresses for the wealthy. Even after she retired to raise three children, she earned some money designing patterns, doing alterations, and making dresses at home for neighbors and family.

I'll never forget the first time my mother visited me at the Blimpie in Hoboken, right after we opened. I was behind the counter in a pullover shirt and a white butcher's apron. A tear welled up in her eye when she spotted me. I knew what she was thinking: "First my son drops out of college, now he gives up a nice job on Wall Street to make salami sandwiches." But Mom just took my hand and said, "Anthony, work hard, work really hard, and you'll be successful."

Mom knew what so many people refuse to accept in this age of instant gratification. Success doesn't just happen. *It ain't easy.* Many, many factors contribute to success, but whether you're building a business, climbing the corporate ladder, selling cars, or making your way through college, you'll beat 50 percent of the

---

Forget those books that tell you that working smart beats working hard. Believe me, success is much more perspiration than inspiration.

---

people all the time if you just work hard. That's what success takes. Even without special skills or smarts, hard-working people can beat out their competition. Forget those books that tell you that working smart beats working hard. Believe me, success is much more perspiration than inspiration.

In the late 1960s, a few years after the birth of Blimpie, we awarded a franchise for a location in East Orange, New Jersey, to two partners—a real-estate salesman and the owner of a travel agency. I thought they were excellent prospects. They even chose the name Success Enterprises, Inc. for their franchise corporation, conveying their goal of having a winning restaurant. There was one big problem. These guys were unwilling to put in the hours, make the sacrifices, and do the hard work necessary to run their business. Though the location opened with high sales volumes, the numbers quickly declined as customers turned their backs on the poor service. Management not only avoided spending enough time in the store, it neglected to exercise the leadership of the staff. Failure was imminent.

Along came a guy named Jorge Figueroa. Jorge was an immigrant from Guatemala who had very little money. He had something much more important—fire in his belly. He wanted desperately to succeed in his own business. He had a passion. We arranged to save the East Orange store—and the owners' investment—by having Jorge take it over in exchange for notes. Jorge not only turned this store around, he used it to launch a long-term successful future for himself as, over the years, he continued scooping up problem stores from poor operators.

No, calling yourself Success Enterprises isn't good enough. These guys wanted to be big shots, but they weren't willing to do what was necessary; they weren't really challenged by the idea.

I'm constantly amazed by prospects who seem to have the desire to become successful franchise operators, successful entrepreneurs. And they put their money—often their life savings— where their mouth is. Then, their restaurant opens and they fail to apply themselves to the task at hand. Our company spends a lot of money training staffers, on training courses, and on field personnel and other support services. In the end, however, it's really the franchisee's hard work that becomes the absolute competitive factor.

I can't prove it, but I'm convinced that hard work has a multiplier effect. I think franchisees who put in twice the effort of typical operators will probably accomplish four times as much. Maybe it's because they are so focused on their tasks, or maybe they are so much more passionate, more interested in what they do. Or maybe their work inspires their employees and those around them, but it always seems to happen.

There's no easy way in business or in life in general to achieve success. It takes commitment, hard work, sacrifice. Or, as we used to say back in Hoboken, "I gotta do what I gotta do. Waddaya gonna do?"

A Little Luck Always Helps

After about three months, Peter and I, encouraged by Hoboken's positive reception, decided to quit our regular jobs and, with Angelo, open two more places. Each of us would run one restaurant. Capital was still a problem, but now we had momentum. By delaying payment to our food suppliers, we used cash flow to pay for carpenters, plumbers, and electricians, thus managing to get our second and third stores open in Jersey City. And the magic continued. Customers came in droves and the popularity of Blimpie sandwiches grew.

Then, something interesting started to happen. Friends, relatives, even strangers began to inquire, "How can I get my own Blimpie store?" A lot of today's state and federal laws and regulations didn't exist back then, nor did most people, including us, know much about franchising. What we did know about was a 150-store chain called Chicken Delight that was franchised through the Northeast. Its jingle, "Don't Cook Tonight, Call Chicken Delight," filled the airwaves in New Jersey and New York. Someone had written a book about the chain, and we got our

---

Franchisees who put in twice the effort of typical operators will probably accomplish four times as much.

---

hands on it. Attempting to model our system after that one, we had our lawyer put together franchise agreements, and we awarded our first franchise for $600.

Chicken Delight's system had one serious flaw that didn't become apparent for a while. The parent company generated revenue by requiring its franchisees to buy paper goods from the company at marked-up prices. We considered the same thing, but we couldn't work the kinks out of our system. So, instead, we simply charged a 6 percent royalty on sales. Talk about luck. Soon after, some lawyers got a number of Chicken Delight franchisees together and started a class-action lawsuit against the company, claiming an antitrust violation. Forcing franchisees to buy from the company was illegal, they said, and the franchisees started buying paper goods elsewhere. Of course, these folks overlooked one problem. If the company couldn't sell its goods, it had no income. No income meant no operating company. No company meant no brand value. Soon, franchisees had businesses that they thought were worth $150,000 to $200,000, but they couldn't find any buyers. Sales disappeared, support services disappeared, and, within a few years, Chicken Delight disappeared, too. Everybody lost— except the lawyers.

For us, though, expansion through franchising was now real, so, to facilitate meeting with prospects, we bought a desk and a couple of chairs and set up an office in the basement of our Hoboken store. How anyone could have invested money in a Blimpie franchise after seeing that office is beyond me. They did, though, and a few more franchised Blimpie locations opened in northern New Jersey.

Too Busy to Reach a Dream

The next piece of our dream was to open a store in New York City. Once again, operating on momentum and borrowed money, we built our first Manhattan location, our most expensive installation to date, at West Fifty-fifth Street and Eighth Avenue.

As had happened with every Blimpie so far, customers responded, and our New York restaurant began to achieve the highest gross sales of any of our outlets. Peter, Angelo, and I were riding high. At our past jobs, none of us had earned any significant money, and now we were paying ourselves salaries that a year ago would have seemed impossible.

However, trouble was brewing, even as our sales skyrocketed. Behind the scenes was a guy who refused to get caught up in the euphoria of the moment. Vic Mongelli, our accountant, kept trying to express his concern about how the business was being run, but he could get neither our attention nor the basic information he needed.

We were devoting all our attention to what is known in the restaurant business as the *front of the house*—the quality of the menu, the look and feel of the store, the service that employees provided to customers, marketing and promotions, and so on. The *back of the house*—what things cost—was being ignored. There was no time for our accountant. We were too busy.

There's a story I like to tell our franchisees about being busy. It goes like this:

Imagine that you walk into a Blimpie restaurant and you spot the franchisee. He's working really hard—baking bread, slicing meats, taking cash from customers, and bussing tables. At the same time, two employees are standing around idle.

"Excuse me," you say to the operator. "You seem to be very busy, but your employees aren't doing much of anything."

"These employees are not trained," he replies indignantly.

"Oh. Why haven't you taken the time to train them? I'm sure it would make your job easier and you could get a lot more done."

"I don't have time to train them," the franchisee says. "I'm too busy."

Every week, each Blimpie International employee completes a form called a *Progress Report*. It's a way for every staff person to let top management know how things are going with them, what the company can do to help make their jobs more effective, and to let us know about anything fun or interesting in their lives. We used to call them *Activity Reports,* but we changed the name to remind our staff that activity is not good enough. It's progress that counts.

We all must be careful about getting so caught up being busy that we ignore the things that are really important to us. We see it with the executive who spends countless hours behind his desk and doesn't notice that a competitor is taking his sales away, or one who spends so much time working on a career that he doesn't see his kids grow up, or another so focused on the problems of the moment that he loses sight of his dreams.

In our case, we were so busy paying attention to the promotional side of our business that we failed to realize that even though we were selling a lot of sandwiches, we weren't making any money. And, because so much money had been borrowed, it was becoming harder to pay our bills. Nevertheless, we continued expanding and we set up company headquarters in an office building on Journal Square in Jersey City.

To Solve a Problem, You Gotta Know You Have One

One day, reality hit.

The three of us were sitting around the conference table in our newly furnished offices. A receptionist sat out front. Suddenly, the conference-room door burst open and there stood a man about twice the size of any of us. "My name is Irving Watson, and you owe me $10,000!" he said. My eyes focused first on his disheveled flannel shirt, then his mud-stained overalls, and finally his work boots, which were covered with manure and were leaving white turkey dung on our new chocolate-brown, shag, wall-to-wall carpet. "I want my money," the man demanded, pounding his fist on the table. "And I want it now!"

Even in those days when the consuming public was more interested in eating beef than turkey, Blimpie stores sold a lot of those birds and, oh yeah, of course, our turkey supplier was Watson's Farm in South Jersey. "It's nice to meet you, Irving," said Angelo. "Have a seat."

We survived that day at the office, but it had become quite apparent that if we didn't pay Watson's and the IRS and the State of New Jersey and all the suppliers that had extended credit to our stores, we couldn't stay in business without taking some radical steps. Lack of proper planning, poor execution of our concept, and plain old bad financial management had gotten us into a terrible mess. To get out, there was only one thing to do: Sell the company stores as franchises and use the proceeds to reduce debt.

Leaving ourselves without company-store operations didn't sit well with Angelo. He enjoyed running the restaurants. Peter and I preferred, and saw the greatest opportunity, in the franchise end of things. So we struck a deal. Angelo would take the New York store and certain liabilities in exchange for his stock in the parent organization. He would go on to start a company that would supply many Blimpie locations. Peter and I also arranged to buy back the 15 percent of net profits from Vartan.

Buyers were quickly found for the remaining three locations, and people like Irving Watson were paid off. That left Peter and me with a new challenge—running a franchise organization with practically no cash flow.

Never Give Up. Never.

Nineteen sixty-seven was one of the worst years of my life. The euphoria stemming from the creation of Blimpie coupled with our early expansion was over. Undercapitalization and poor management had prompted a financial crisis the likes of which I had never experienced.

My bank account had been depleted, my cars sold, my insurance policies cashed in. Life was not good. My daily challenge was to figure out how I was going to feed my family. Then it happened. My partner and I, in a borrowed car, approached the Holland Tunnel heading into New York. The toll was 50 cents. I was behind the wheel as we pulled up to the toll plaza. As I reached for the money, I realized that my pockets were empty. "Give me

50 cents," I said to my partner. "I don't have any money," was his reply.

"This is the last straw," I thought. I must be crazy. I can't live like this or expect my family to live like this any longer."

Simply put, I was ready to give up and head back to Wall Street. A few days later, I was lunching on a ham, salami, and cheese Blimpie at one of our stores. After all, it was the only place I could afford to eat. Suddenly, I realized that my eyes couldn't stop focusing on our customers. Some were sitting at tables, really enjoying their sandwiches. Others stood in line, anxiously waiting to get their orders filled. Still more were on their way out, satisfied looks on their faces.

I thought: "Conza, is this what you're walking away from? Do you mean to tell me that these people are loving Blimpie subs every day, and you can't figure out how to make money? This product is great and the concept works. You've been a dummy with the way you've managed it. Are you about to become a bigger one by walking away from it? Where will your life go then, dummy?!"

That's when I realized that although I had created something, although I had had what Andy Warhol called my fifteen minutes of fame, I hadn't proved that I could make my creation last. Anyone can start something and achieve temporary success. But the

---

**The ones who truly make it don't give up.
That doesn't mean you should continue with
an obviously losing proposition. But nobody
reaches his dreams without persistence.**

---

ones who truly make it don't give up. That doesn't mean you should continue with an obviously losing proposition or that you should throw good money after bad. But nobody reaches his dreams without persistence. If I gave up, everything I had worked for would have been for nothing. Did I really want to go back to Wall Street? I had an opportunity here that I might never have again. No. No, I couldn't give up.

I see it all the time with franchisees, company employees, and relatives and friends. People bring themselves to accomplish something, then they don't persist. Think of the salesperson who wins the award for the most closings in a year but fades into oblivion, or the franchisee who achieves the highest sales volume, then starts to run a poor operation, or the actor who gets rave reviews for some performances but goes on vacation and misses the opportunity for the next job. These folks all could have achieved greatness had they only exercised persistence.

People who persist always find a way. I found a way. The reason we were having such terrible financial problems was that we had almost no cash flow. We were still making franchise sales, but the initial franchise fees, plus the 6 percent continuing fee from a small number of operating stores, just wasn't producing enough revenue. We desperately needed to enhance cash flow. Here's how we did it.

For every franchise that was awarded, a store had to be built. Our company had always recommended reliable contractors to our new franchisees. These builders received a cash down payment before work ever began. We needed to get our hands on that cash. So, our company went into the construction business. Every time a franchise came along, not only did we have the fee to look forward to, we also had the cash flow generated from the work. As time went by, enough cash and profits came in to keep our organization operating until the ongoing royalties generated sufficient revenues.

The plan could not have come about except as a result of persistence. Had I given up, my life would have been entirely different. Since that time I have always known this for sure: Never give up. Never.

Think Like an Entrepreneur

Even if you don't plan to go into business for yourself, thinking like an entrepreneur can be very helpful as your pursue any of your goals.

For his fiftieth anniversary at the Erie Railroad, my grandfather received a gold pin. To thank my dad for twenty-five years of service, the New York Stock Exchange gave him a Hamilton watch. When he retired after forty-five years, they gave him a framed certificate.

How many young people do you know today that you would expect to be employed by the same place for twenty-five, forty-five, or fifty years? No, today people rarely spend their careers at one company. (The average for people under forty is sixteen months!) Even if they intend to, who can count on a secure job nowadays? Businesses are always downsizing, rightsizing, merging, acquiring, or simply bringing in new people to replace the old.

From the employer's perspective, despite great efforts to keep staffers, some leave anyway. At Blimpie International, we have 401(k) plans, bonuses, medical plans, stock options, you name it. It's never good enough, because employees think more and more like entrepreneurs and that may mean that they perceive a better opportunity elsewhere.

So, just as an entrepreneur must constantly stay competitive, you must, individually, stay competitive.

If your goal is to be a successful artist, writer, doctor, engineer, technical professional—something that won't require the efforts of a lot of people—then your entrepreneurial thinking will not require you to develop leadership skills. But if you plan to follow a management career path, you must be able to pick the right people, people who are receptive to your vision, who are able to

---

Whatever I learned about business, I taught myself. The process never ends. The day you stop learning is the day you stop growing.

---

carry it out, and who have the motivation to follow it. As Teddy Roosevelt once said, "The best leader is one who has sense enough to pick good men to do what he wants done, and the self-restraint to keep from meddling with them while they do it."

Thinking like an entrepreneur means establishing a career strategy. For example, suppose you are Hispanic. You may observe that, more and more, the Latino consumer is becoming a major demographic force in American society. That means that there are many ways for an ambitious Latino to help corporations identify key consumer insights that can be turned into winning new products, packages, promotions, and so on. You can see how that sort of strategy can help you target your education and experience in that direction.

Entrepreneurs create their own destinies for profit and for pleasure. You have control over your career, your personal life, and the business in which you are involved. More than anything, entrepreneurial thinking means that, when a dream takes hold of you, you pursue it. How incredibly sad it is to see someone let a dream go and have to think for the rest of their life what might have been.

Also be careful not to create a trap with an overhead structure so daunting that you keep yourself stuck somewhere.

Let's say you get a job with a good company and begin to work yourself up the ladder. You work hard, make the right moves, and get promoted to a better position with a higher salary. In the meantime, you get married, have a couple of kids, buy a house with a big mortgage, join a country club, and buy a car or two, as well as all the other material possessions that enable you to lead the good life and keep up with the Joneses. Now an opportunity comes along, perhaps to go into business or to take a lesser-paying job with a much more lucrative future. Can you do it? Will you and your family take the necessary steps and accept the necessary risk? Will you devote the time, give up your golf weekends, pass on a few vacations? It's important to think about these things.

Thinking like an entrepreneur means that you never stop learning. You go to seminars, take classes, read books, and constantly engage in self-teaching. Whatever I learned about business, I taught myself. The process never ends. The day you stop learning is the day you stop growing.

CHAPTER 2

DOING THE THREE-STEP: MY FATHER'S PLAN FOR HOW TO GET AHEAD

> If you don't know where you're going, you might end up somewhere else.
>
> **—Yogi Berra**

I learned a lot from my father. Like most people who achieve success at something, Dad started out with a dream—that of owning his own home. He was tired of having his family cramped in a small apartment, fed up with watching Mom struggle to perform basic household chores with poor facilities, sick of paying rent when he could be investing in real estate, and desperate to get his family out of the city and into the country.

Right after World War II, Mom and Dad and several relatives each purchased a piece of land in a town called Oakland. Today, it's considered the heart of the New Jersey suburbs but, back then, it was out in the country. Dad's goal was to put a house on that land but, after almost ten years, the land still was home only to some squirrels, raccoons, and deer.

Nick Conza was a man of a few words but, at an early age, I learned that when he spoke, you'd better listen, because something important was being said. One Sunday during our traditional afternoon pasta dinner, Dad said, "We should have our own home." My Uncle Sunny, who often joined us for dinner and who constantly ignored my father's criticism—"Sunny, you have no ambition"—chimed in: "Do you know how expensive it is to build a house these days? You can't afford it."

"You'll see," was all my father said. Dad had made a decision. He was going to Oakland.

So, Mom and Dad began planning how they could accomplish their objective. Although he probably didn't know it at the time, he was on Step 1 of the three-step plan that gets things done, whether in life or in business:

1. Decide where you want to go.

2. Figure out how to get there.

3. Get there.

Mom and Dad knew that they didn't have many options. They had little money in the bank, and no big inheritances coming up. If they had any hope of owning a home, they knew there was only one way to get there: They would have to build it.

But, how do you build a home? Dad was a white-collar guy. Sure, he may have painted a few walls and added a closet or two to his apartment, but build a house? That was like going into the construction business, as well as needing money to pay for materials and hiring bulldozer men and plumbers and electricians. No matter. Dad had decided on his goal and, by gosh, he was going to get there. He just had to figure out how.

When Mom and Dad bought the land in Oakland, my Uncle Pat and Aunt Rose bought a piece of property right next door. They wanted a home just as badly as he did, but they didn't have any money, either. Dad came up with an idea and proposed a deal to my uncle: "We can do this if we do it together," he said. "I'll help you build your house if you help me build mine." Uncle Pat agreed and they began searching for a company from which they could buy a predesigned, precut home.

Money was still a problem, so they each set out to accumulate funds by taking on extra work. At times, my father worked three jobs, sometimes putting in late hours on Wall Street, other times doing part-time jobs in unrelated fields. How he managed to find the time to do all these things, I'll never know. He also began to study. He read every construction book he could get his hands on, and sought knowledge and advice from the staff at local lumberyards and building-supply stores.

All that was left was for him to actually do it. That meant his working on the house only on weekends and during vacations, because he could not afford to give up his regular jobs. Neither could Uncle Pat. So, they began construction, first on Uncle Pat's house. To save on labor costs, family and friends were recruited to help. Fortunately, that was easier than might be expected. Spending the day in the country was very appealing to city folk. And Mom and Dad always believed in ending the day with a little wine, a big bowl of pasta, and a good time. Incredibly, over three years, both houses were built.

Dad died in 1990 at age eighty-three, but that house is still Mom's home and still a monument to his accomplishment. In the true sense of the word, Dad was not an entrepreneur, but the three-step plan that got him to achieve his dream is the very plan that we all can follow.

Step 1: Decide Where You Want to Go

You must have goals. That's one corner that cannot be cut.

Imagine driving in your car, spotting a policeman, asking him for directions, and, when he asks where you want to go, you say, "I don't know." Sound silly? Of course, but that's exactly what you are doing if you don't have goals.

Just saying, "I'd love to go on vacation," will get you nowhere. If you live in New York City, for example, only after you decide that you want to go to, say, Miami, can you move forward. You can book a flight on Continental Airlines, you can go to Penn Station and get on an Amtrak train, you can get in your car and head

---

Start by asking yourself these questions: What is it that I'm looking for? What will make me happy? Will I recognize it when I get there?

---

down I-95, you can even take out your road bike and start pedaling. However, until you decide on Miami, you won't even be able to think about how you'll get there, and, until you figure out how to get there, you can never enjoy the Florida sunshine.

If someone were to ask you right now, "Where do you want to go with your life?" would you have an answer? If you don't, then it's time to start making some decisions.

"A mind is a terrible thing to make up," was the slogan Jay Leno suggested for New York's former governor, Mario Cuomo, when Cuomo vacillated about running for president. Sometimes the decision to do nothing is wise, but you can't spend your life doing nothing. Start by asking yourself these questions: What is it that I'm looking for? What will make me happy? Will I recognize it when I get there?

I've always liked the way Burt Shryock, a Blimpie subfranchisor for the Tampa Bay area, said it: "If you always do what you always did, you always get what you always got." Burt, with his wife, Judy, and son, Chris, has developed more than sixty Blimpie locations in his area. After various business successes in Dallas, Burt realized that he needed to do something else. He knew that

> **Once you know where you're going, you can figure out the best way to get there. You know what knowledge you already have and you know places to go for more information.**

he enjoyed being in business, so he made the easiest decision first: He would start another business. It was a decision a lot harder to implement than to make in the first place, but he began the search to find a business and came upon several articles in the business press about Blimpie. He remembered seeing Blimpie stores in Dallas and soon learned that the Dallas area had already been awarded to a developer, but Burt knew where he wanted to go. He wanted to be a Blimpie International area developer.

He got Judy and Chris to agree to relocate for a new opportunity, then inquired about the Tampa Bay area. Before long, Burt and his family were in Tampa, with the goal of one hundred Blimpie locations in their territory. "The sooner we ask ourselves what goals we should make, what timetable is feasible, what work habits produce the desired results, the faster success starts appearing in our careers," Burt has said.

The beauty of the three-step outline is that so much follows from the first decision. Once you know where you're going, you can figure out the best way to get there. You know what knowledge you already have and you know places to go for more information. Suppose, for instance, that I decided to start another franchise organization, in, say, office supplies. Food and office supplies are very different, but I would already understand a lot of what I'd need to go through. I'd also know that I needed to learn about office supplies. So, I would make sure I read everything I could on the subject, I would attend conferences, and I would learn from people already in the business. In short, I would know what I wanted to get done so I could find the way to do it.

Although you don't want to rely on intuition for all your decision making, you can't completely avoid it, particularly in certain situations. Should I have a baby? Should I change careers? Will a move to Europe for five years bring me greater opportunity? Even in these cases, you should explore the possibilities, and discuss the issues with family, friends, and others who can be sounding boards. Then, take some time to seriously contemplate your decision. The important thing is to be totally honest with yourself. Listen to others, but make your own choices based on strategy, on rationality, and on a systematic decision-making process. As my Mom would say, "Think for yourself." Then use your intuition.

Remember also that decision making can get emotional and can require courage. That means fear because, without fear, there is no courage. Let's face it, if you are contemplating some meaningful changes in your life, there will be some uncertainty that will cause some turns in your stomach. I always remember from my experience with Wall Street that the market can go up on either good news or bad news, but bring uncertainty into the picture and the averages will head south for sure.

Pete Conforto is a living example in our chain of courage. Pete gave up his position as president of a large corporation and relocated himself, his wife, and their two kids, from Charlotte, North Carolina, to Phoenix, Arizona, to become the Blimpie developer for Maricopa County. Pete knew there were no Blimpie locations in Phoenix, so, regardless of the help he would receive from Blimpie International, he also knew that he would be responsible for his own success. Was he scared? You bet, but he took that fear and channeled it well. "It's all about commitment," says Pete. "I didn't have a choice. I had a family to consider. I committed myself to achieving success." Peter Conforto used courage to accomplish his goals. He has developed more than seventy locations in Phoenix.

Explore your interests, your passions, your fears, and your aspirations. Think about what you really are looking for out of life.

Let it all settle in, then make a decision. If you decide to fish, fine. If you decide to cut bait, also fine. But if you don't make a decision, you'll never have fish for dinner.

Discipline: An Important Ingredient

St. Peter's Prep in Jersey City, where I attended high school, is run by Jesuit priests—widely known to be disciplinarians. One of them, Father Murray, even had the title Prefect of Discipline. When he was around, fear ran through the veins of students. If he spotted you with, say, hair that was too long, or clothing that was not up to the school's standards, or if he caught you clowning around or talking in a place where silence was supposed to be

---

Explore your interests, your passions, your fears, and your aspirations. Think about what you really are looking for out of life.

---

maintained, he'd grab you by the ear, read you the riot act, then send you to Jug, the dreaded place where you'd spend hours after school writing some senseless thoughts on paper.

I got my first dose of Father Murray, albeit a positive dose, when I was a freshman. It happened in the seniors' private lunchroom. One day, at the beginning of the school year, a wild food fight erupted among the seniors. It went on and on, while the underclassmen looked on in disbelief. Enter Father Murray. He was so livid that he removed the seniors from their lunchroom for the entire semester, and, to rub salt into the wound, replaced them with freshmen.

I learned not to mess with Father Murray because, if you did, punishment would await you. However, discipline at St. Peters wasn't just about punishment. It was about hard work, organizing yourself, and following a plan that would lead you to become a better person and accomplish your goals in life.

Somehow, the word *discipline* has come to be perceived as a negative thing, as if exercising discipline meant a loss of freedom. The way I see it, failure to exercise discipline would likely mean a failure to reach goals, and a failure to reach goals would surely bring on a loss of freedom.

Here's a real-life example: New Orleans used to be one of my favorite cities. I loved New Orleans so much that for a few years I kept an apartment on Dauphine Street in the French Quarter. One of the big reasons I was attracted there, of course, was all the wonderful restaurants. At least I thought they were wonderful until I decided to exercise some discipline and cut down on fatty foods.

On a business trip in the mid-1990s, I ended up in one of the French Quarter's famous restaurants. After being seated and searching the menu, I began to ask the waitress a bunch of questions.

"Is there cream in this dish?"

"Yes," she replied.

"Is there butter in this one?"

"Uh-huh."

"Does this have any cheese in it?"

"Oh yeah, it sure does."

Finally, with her hands on her hips and a sarcastic tone in her voice, the waitress looked me in the eye and said, "Honey, you are in Nawlins, you know."

Yes, I knew that, but I had decided that the discipline of eating better would give me the freedom of a longer, healthier life. Using discipline in your planning process will take you a step closer to achieving your goals.

Good Intentions, Uncommon Agendas

Goals don't exist in a vacuum. How many people enter into relationships with the best of intentions, only to discover later on that either they and their partner have different goals or that they have different agendas for reaching those goals?

Maybe they married in hopes of a wonderful life together but never went through the three-step process before tying the knot. So, later they learn that his idea of a wonderful life was to have her stay at home and raise three kids while hers was to pursue a career outside the home.

It's something I observe in my business all the time. Franchisees form partnerships but neglect to discuss their personal goals. The person who plans to operate five stores, for instance, is going to have a real problem with her partner after she realizes that her partner is just looking for something to do and has no such ambitions.

The three-step process led us to initial successes with Blimpie but, as the years went by, a lack of common agendas began to take a toll on our growth.

In 1968, about four years after the birth of Blimpie, a young lawyer named David Siegel approached us on behalf of a group called the Real Great Society. This group, a bunch of guys from Spanish Harlem, had been granted a loan from a New York bank to establish a business. David negotiated their franchise and we set up shop on East 96ᵗʰ Street and Second Avenue. No one in the group was willing to commit to the effort required to run the business, so they quickly got into financial trouble. To rescue the store and the bank loan, we found another franchisee to take over their store. The Real Great Society was gone but, because David was a young lawyer in need of work and we needed some legal assistance but couldn't afford it, David, Peter DeCarlo, and I struck a deal under which David would perform legal work for the company and eventually become a shareholder in our corporation.

By the mid-1970s, it was becoming increasingly clear that Peter's philosophy about the future development of our chain was looking less and less like mine and David's. David and I felt that we should focus on national expansion, while Peter thought we should concentrate on regional development. David and I were determined to keep a tight rein on the company's finances while Peter was a big spender. Our goals were no longer aligned. Our agendas were in conflict. All this was working against the growth of our organization.

Peter and I recognized that we were operating at cross-purposes, so we began to discuss splitting up. Both of us remained passionate about our brand and neither of us had money. So, that meant that one of us buying out the other was not possible: We divided up the country. One day, Peter and I went to a restaurant in Jersey City, listed every state in the country on a sheet of paper, and agreed who would get what. It was like playing Monopoly.

"You can take those five states if I get to keep New York City."

"I'd rather have this part of the country, so why don't you take that part?"

We actually did it, probably because Peter and I had such a strong relationship going all the way back to our teenage years. The deal was completed on a friendly basis and, afterwards, we continued to work in harmony, using common logos, design, food ingredients, franchise documents, and so forth. Many years later, David and I—we had stayed together—negotiated a deal to market all of Peter's company's territories with the exception of several states along the East Coast.

The lack of a common agenda leading to the split hurt the chain's growth but, with separate companies, incentives were renewed. With a new team, David and I pushed expansion in various places across the United States and, in 1983, with about 200 operating locations, we completed a small initial public offering for our company that raised about $500,000.

Loss of Focus

To most Wall Street firms and companies going public, a half-million dollars was a puny sum, but it was not only the largest check either of us had ever seen, it was the answer to the nagging financial problems that had plagued us ever since we set up shop in Hoboken. Finally, we were beginning to look like and feel like a real company.

In retrospect, we should have invested all the money in the expansion of the Blimpie chain across America. Instead, we decided to use our knowledge of the New York restaurant scene and diversify into full-service bar-restaurants.

In September 1984, the USA Border Cafe, a Southwestern-style restaurant, opened on East Seventy-ninth Street in Manhattan. Business was slow at first but, when the turnaround occurred, it was like a rocketship going off. Sales and earnings soared.

It seemed like a winning concept, so we did what we always did at Blimpie. We opened some more, developing two additional Border Cafes and acquiring two other restaurants called Amsterdam's.

While the first Border was extremely successful, the others faltered. Our organizational structure lacked the depth and strength to manage our system, and working capital was not sufficient to sustain the operating losses we were incurring. Worse yet, the time, effort, and money needed for Manhattan restaurants halted any chance of expanding the Blimpie chain.

In early 1988, aware of our loss of focus and what it meant for Blimpie, David and I and our two senior vice presidents, Chuck Leaness and Pat Pompeo, began plotting to get our company back on track. "Look," I said to the group, "we can make this happen, we just have to decide to make it happen." It turned out to be a welcome discussion, and they said, "Yeah, let's do it." We started by setting three goals. First, we would have one thousand Blimpie locations by 1995 (at the time, we had about 275). Second, we would increase our earnings by 30 percent per year (in 1987, we had lost 8 cents a share). And third, the price of our stock would grow by $1 per share per year (it was 15 cents a share at the time).

We had decided where we wanted to go. We were now ready to move to Step 2.

Step 2: Figure Out How to Get There

Certain things became obvious. Chief among them was a complete focus on the Blimpie chain, which meant divesting the company of the full-service restaurants.

Our goal of one thousand stores meant that we needed to become a national chain, and I recalled something that Dave Thomas of Wendy's had said. Thomas is really good at expressing very important things in very simple ways. Thomas said, "Once you decide to become a national chain, you gotta hurry up." Hurrying up required money. It also required establishing a presence in many places simultaneously.

Our plan was to turn to a concept we had used sparingly in the past: subfranchising. No, that's not the franchising of sub sandwiches. *Subfranchisors* are entrepreneurs who get awarded territorial rights, for a fee, based on population of the area. They then have both the right and the obligation to develop the territory by *subfranchising* to store operators. While subfranchisors are legally neither the company's agents nor partners, they act in concert with the company to build the brand in their area. Every time a subfranchisor would be put into place, much-needed capital would come into the company, as store development commenced in a new area.

If we could execute this plan, our goals would be met. To get to our goals, we needed the right people. This became apparent as we began to tackle Step 3.

Step 3: Get There

This is the piece of the three-step process where you really have to be determined. As Napoleon once said, "If you set out to take Vienna, take Vienna." You can establish your goals, do business plans, work out strategies, develop systems, and so forth, but at some point you have to execute. You simply have to go out and do it. You have to put the flight plan down and get the plane into the air. You have to make things happen. Or, to quote Yogi Berra again, "You can't think and hit at the same time."

To get things moving while we were getting rid of the Border and Amsterdam's restaurants, I flew to Atlanta to meet with our key employees. During our meeting, which lasted all day and into the night, we made a project list detailing everything that had to be changed, improved, and deleted. The list was called "101 Small Improvements," and it specified a slew of changes—a new store design, bread-baking ovens in every store, the relocation of our accounting department to Atlanta, new formats for company newsletters, the creation of a national franchisee advisory council and a subfranchise advisory council, a new franchise sales initiative, a mission statement, a marketing strategy, an annual convention. The list went on and on.

After the list was completed and assignments were given out, I knew it was time to begin recruiting some really good people to help us get the job done. It often seems that when corporations

---

**You can't teach someone to have passion.
The secret is to hire passionate people and
make sure you don't take the passion away
from them.**

---

think about hiring the best people, they think of the most expensive people. We couldn't afford the most expensive people, but we could afford the most passionate people.

You can't teach someone to have passion. The secret is to hire passionate people and make sure you don't take the passion away from them. Passion is an incredible thing. It's amazing—absolutely amazing—what can be accomplished with passion.

I don't mean to imply that the people we hired didn't have talent, but talent represents only potential. It bears no relationship to the will, the desire, or the determination to achieve success.

One of the incredibly passionate people we brought on at Blimpie International at this time was Bob Sitkoff. In fact, Bob was so motivated, so enthusiastic about what he was asked to do, that he was able to completely overcome his inexperience. Here's what happened.

Some of the projects on our "101 Small Improvements" list related to the financial side of the business. Our accounting department, part of our New York office at the time, was a mess.

Information was constantly inaccurate and constantly late, and the people in the department couldn't seem to get out of their own way, never mind provide us with insight about running the company. Something had to change. I decided to start by replacing the controller and began a search for a new executive. That's when I heard about Sitkoff. Bob had been a Blimpie franchisee and area developer in Orlando, but he and his wife, Frederika, longed to return to their hometown of Atlanta, so they sold their development rights. To keep busy while he looked for the right opportunity, Bob had been doing some part-time work for us in our Atlanta office, providing our operations staff with statistical and analytical information about franchisee performance. Aware that we were in the market for a new controller, one of our Atlanta executives approached me and suggested I meet with Bob.

From his performance as a Blimpie operator in Orlando, I recognized that Bob had passion. He was a very motivated kind of guy. After doing a little more research on his background, I called

> **If all it took to be successful was talent, there'd be a lot more success stories in this world. If you're looking for talent, check out the restaurants and bars of New York City, where you'll find aspiring actors and other performers waiting for their big break. So many of them are unaware that their talent is no substitute for hard work.**

Bob and made an appointment to meet him in Atlanta. During our meeting, my gut told me that this was the person—his lack of experience notwithstanding—who should be in charge of our company's financial department.

"Bob, our accounting department is in a shambles," I said. "I'm going to have to hire a new controller in New York, someone who can get things organized. However, I have another idea. I know you're not a CPA, but if you tell me you can take over the department and position it to help lead this company into the future, I'll move the whole thing here to Atlanta and put you in charge." Bob's response: "I can do it." It was all I needed to hear. Not one person was relocated from New York. All new people were brought on board.

Bob Sitkoff ran the company's financial department for seven years, rising from controller to financial vice president to chief financial officer before he was given the opportunity to be president of Maui Tacos International, Inc., one of the company's new brands. He succeeded because of his incredible, heartfelt determination. That was far more important than his intelligence or talent.

If all it took to be successful was talent, there'd be a lot more success stories in this world. If you're looking for talent, for example, check out the restaurants and bars of New York City, where you'll find aspiring actors and other performers. As they wait for their big break to come along, so many of these bartenders and servicepeople are unaware that their talent is no substitute for the hard work, commitment, or persistence needed to succeed in the entertainment business.

My good friend of twenty-five years, Jay Thomas, is one of the most talented people I know. Years of observing Jay taught me that it was not his talent that propelled him to stardom on television, in the movies, and on radio. It was his drive, his enthusiasm, his dedication to his work, his determination to succeed, his unfailing desire—every day of his life—to reach his goals that led him to achieve success.

Keeping It Simple

My biggest challenge in creating the rebirth of Blimpie International was to get people to believe that we could reach our goals, that we could become one of the industry's largest chains and make a lot of money for our staff and shareholders.

For starters, *I* had to change, withdrawing from management so I could put myself into a position of leadership. I had to create a vision for the future and set an example for people to follow. Increasing demands would be made on my time, which meant that I had to build people, people who could make the decisions that I used to make. This is a particularly difficult transition for an entrepreneur.

We chose simple goals, and that's important, because the simpler you make your goals, the easier they are for everyone else to understand. They still had to be exciting, challenging goals. Dull goals will be left on a shelf like a boring novel, but powerful ones will set people on fire. "To get to one thousand stores" was a goal that left no one confused, but I had to make sure that our staff and our franchisees believed in my commitment toward accomplishing it.

So, for my part, I announced to the chain my personal goal of visiting one hundred fifty of our locations in one year. This was something I knew our staff and franchisees would understand and appreciate, because it would let people feel that they were a key element in our growth. They would also know that if I took the time and made the effort to travel all over the country to visit with stores and talk to operators, I must be serious about my commitment.

My vision of one thousand stores was communicated through *Tony's Take,* a weekly publication I write; *No Bologna News,* the company's monthly newsletter; and one-on-one group meetings. I knew I had to buy people's hearts. Heads are all well and good, but buying a heart will gain you loyalty, enthusiasm, and determination.

It was incredible. By 1995, we had accomplished more than any of us had ever imagined. We passed the one thousand store mark and had expanded into Alaska and Hawaii. We had begun national advertising, and our sandwiches were being served on Delta and Hawaiian Airlines. *Nation's Restaurant News* listed us as the fastest-growing chain in the restaurant business. *The Wall Street Journal,* CNN, CNBC, *Success,* and *Entrepreneur* magazines were just some of the media that recognized us as a leader in our field. And for two years in a row, *Forbes* magazine gave us high rankings—Number twenty-four and Number thirty-five—on its list of the 200 Best Small Companies in America. To top it off, sales and earnings were at record levels and our stock price was soaring. With considerable pride, we looked back knowing that it all began because we took the three steps to success.

We Need to Set Goals

A few years ago, Blimpie International decided to learn more about the habits of successful Blimpie operators. One of these operators was a guy named Frank Ingram. Frank had been with Blimpie almost since its inception, and he has had a string of successful franchises. Frank told me a story I'll never forget.

One of his best customers was a postal worker who came in for lunch every day, five days a week, week after week. One day, as he was ordering his sandwich, he said, "Frank, I have great news. I'm retiring." "That's wonderful," said Frank. "Let me buy you lunch."

Well, Frank was happy for the guy, but when the following week came and went, he began to think about this lost customer. "Let's see," he thought, "He spent about four dollars a day, that's twenty dollars a week, that's one thousand dollars a year. I just lost one thousand dollars in sales! Worse yet, this can't be the only customer retiring, relocating, or dying. I need to set a goal of replacing these customers." Frank set up a plan that called for him to do

---

Make a full-hearted commitment and your belief in yourself will be automatic. And, once you believe in yourself, you will fulfill your commitment.

---

something every day to promote his business. "Now, I never let an opportunity to attract a customer go by," says Frank, "Everywhere I go, I give someone a coupon for some kind of offer."

Frank realized that if he hoped to increase his business, he had to change his behavior. It wasn't that he just had to work harder, because that wouldn't have solved the problem. Frank had to do something that he had not been doing before. He had to get out from behind the counter, leave his store, and begin drumming up new business. By setting a goal, organizing a schedule, and having the discipline to follow his schedule and execute his plan of attack, Frank was able to accomplish his short-term goal of building his store's business, while taking an important step toward his long-term goal of becoming a successful multi-unit operator.

So often, folks who would never dream of renovating their apartment without a plan go through life without a plan. I read about a study of college business school graduates who had been out of school for ten years. The study was conducted to determine how they were progressing toward their goals. Amazingly, 83 percent reported they were working hard but had no goals. Another 14 percent had goals but they were not written goals. Nonetheless, this group was earning, on average, three times more than the group with no goals. Only 3 percent had written goals, and guess what? They were earning a whopping ten times what those with no goals were earning.

No question, we need to set goals. To begin, simply put down in words what you would like to accomplish, who is involved with you and what their goals are, and where you want to be in one year, two years, five years. If there are partners in the business, have each partner do the same thing. You may be in for some surprises. We once had some franchisees write a business plan and one discovered that, while he expected to have several stores operating in five years, his partner didn't even plan to stay in the business that long.

Here are some pointers:

- Be specific. "I want to make a lot of money" is not specific. "I want to become a restaurant franchise operator" or "I want to be chief financial officer of a major corporation" are.

- Be realistic. What knowledge will you need? Will you be able to come up with the necessary investment capital? How do you feel about long hours? About relocating? Are you really challenged by the idea of your goal or are you just looking for something to do?

- Be aware of your behavior. It's so easy to be busy but not take care of the things that really matter, not work toward fulfilling your dreams.

- Be willing to take a chance. Mom used to say, "Nothing ventured, nothing gained." Yes, going after your goals may mean taking risks. When I decided to go into business, I knew it was very risky. I had no money and no security, but I told myself that, if all else failed, I could always go back to Wall Street. When it comes time to make a decision about going after a goal, don't expect to have all the answers. Otherwise you'll do nothing. Zig Zigler, the motivational speaker, says, "If you wait to leave home until all the lights are green, you'll never leave home."

- Eliminate the word *try*. How many Goodyear tires would you buy if the company's slogan was, "We are going to try to make a tire that doesn't blow out at 60 m.p.h."? You buy Goodyear tires because the company knows its tires will hold up at any speed. Muhammad Ali used to call the round in which he was going to knock out his opponent. He didn't say, "I'm going to try to knock him out." He said, "I'm going to whoop him in the third round," and he did. He said, "I'm the greatest," and he was. Trying does not get the job done.

- Commit yourself. Make a full-hearted commitment and your belief in yourself will be automatic. And, once you believe in yourself, you will fulfill your commitment. Babe Ruth once pointed to center field and hit a home run on the next pitch. Ruth made a commitment, then fulfilled it. Until Blimpie International established its goals, the company had never had a public relations agency. Immediately after hiring an agency, it

---

Expect nothing. Expectations are how you believe other people should behave and how the world should act. Instead, set goals and achieve them.

---

got me a newspaper interview. During that interview, the reporter asked me how many stores we planned to open in the next year. I answered, "Seventy-five," even though we had never before opened more than twenty-five or thirty in a single year. The next day I read in the paper, "Tony Conza, Blimpie International CEO, says the chain plans to open seventy-five stores next year." "My God," I thought, "Did I really say that? Well, I can't change the story. I guess the commitment is made. Besides, I really did think we could accomplish that goal. We're just going to have to open seventy-five stores." And we did.

- Take action. Even if you set goals and figure out how you'll reach them, at some point you have to take action. The story goes that a man suffered a severe financial setback, saw his business fail, and couldn't land on his feet. In utter despair, he turned to God. "Please, God," he prayed, "you've got to help me. Please let me win the lottery. No response. So he prayed again. "Please, God, you've got to do something. The only way I'll get back on my feet is if I win the lottery. Make me win." After a few days, the man thought that God wasn't hearing him. After a while, he was beyond desperation. With the his last breath of hope, he turned to God. "I beg of you, dear God," he said. "All I need is to win the lottery." After a moment of silence, a voice came back to him saying, "Give me a break. At least buy a ticket!" Remember, doing the plan is not the objective, reaching your goal is.

- Expect nothing. Expectations are how you believe other people should behave and how the world should act. Instead, set goals and achieve them. You end up achieving success in life because of planning and doing, not because something is owed to you.

• • •

Sometimes I look back at all the obstacles I had to face and wonder how I kept going. But I know that whenever I got bogged down I always focused on my goals and relied on my will to carry me through.

"I'm not sure what I want to do" is a terrible way to live. "What benefits will accrue to me if I do?" and "Where will I be if I don't?" are much better realities to contemplate.

People tend to look at successful folks and imagine that it's all so complicated. Sure, you need education, training, and, for some businesses, specialized knowledge, but whether you are Ted Turner or the guy who runs the local Blimpie store, you have to take the three simple steps to achieve success.

CHAPTER 3

GET THE PASSION: LOVE WHATEVER YOU DO

I don't want people who want to dance,
I want people who need to dance . . .

—George Balanchine
Ballet Master and Choreographer,
New York City Ballet

People often ask me the reason for my success. My answer always requires just one word: *Passion*. I've seen passion at work in Blimpie people and in non-Blimpie people, in business and in life. I've seen it in myself, and I've seen it vanish. Passion is everything. Just because you can play the notes on a piano doesn't make you a great musician. And just making a sale doesn't make you a great salesperson. Passionate people are always raising the bar; they're always challenging themselves, because they have a burning desire to keep improving on what they do. They don't set up roadblocks. They don't accept, "I can't accomplish my goal."

I once experienced a crisis with my own passion, and I credit a 1988 trip to an exotic, faraway place, one urged on me by my cousin Geri Sicola, for helping me through it. Geri lived in Tanzania, where she was the regional director for Catholic Relief Services, a global charitable organization. Time and again, she assured me that, if I wanted to visit Africa, I would be safe in her hands. Most Americans might initially feel adventurous about the prospect of making such a trip. However, the thought of visas, inoculations, malaria pills, and tales of the friend's wife who contracted some terrible disease from a tsetse fly would prevent most Americans from getting any further. During one of her trips home, Geri noticed how captivated I was by her stories about her ten years in Africa, and said, "Tony, you really should come to visit me. I'll meet you in Nairobi, and we can spend a few days in Kenya. Then, you can stay with me in Dar es Salaam and I'll plan a safari for us."

Geri had offered me her hospitality before. My answer had always been the same: I was too busy building my business and had neither the time nor the motivation to take such a trip. Now, I was at a point in my life that made things feel different. Personally I was very comfortable. I had a beautiful home in the country, an apartment in the city, cars, clothes, and the money to support

---

People often ask me the reason for my success. My answer always requires just one word: *Passion*.

---

them all. Nonetheless, I was troubled. Our Border Cafe foray was a disaster, our company had lost money the year before, and competition was a growing concern. Besides all that, I was restless, bored, and feeling unfulfilled. My entrepreneurial fire had been snuffed out, and I didn't understand why. I scheduled a three-week vacation to Kenya and Tanzania.

In Dar es Salaam, I felt like I'd left civilization behind. Television and radio were virtually nonexistent, telephones were a joke, and newspapers were hard to come by. In Tanzania, I was finally able to relax and think, which was what I really needed to do. Whether I was on a beautiful beach or on a busy street jammed with people shopping at a nearby market, I knew I was in a different world. It didn't take long before I felt very comfortable in my new surroundings. I spent time walking around the peninsula, sitting under a tree on the beach, and offering a friendly *jambo,* or hello, to the people on the street. And, most important, I began to contemplate the dilemma I had left back home.

The distance I had placed between me and my life back in the States was great. I had escaped the business problems of the day, I had run away from my daily routine, I had left my family and friends behind, but the one thing I could not escape was the feeling I had inside. Something was missing, and I had to figure out what it was.

I kept asking myself how, back in 1964, barely past my teenage years and with no experience, no training, no money—how I was able to create a successful enterprise, yet now, with a chain of a couple of hundred stores and living a nice success story, I felt unfulfilled and concerned about my own future and the future of the company?

I thought about it and I thought about it. Then, finally, it hit me. I had lost the passion. Of course. That was it. I was able to start and build a successful business because I had the passion to make it happen. Now it was gone. No wonder I couldn't make it work. No wonder I had lost faith in the company. No wonder I was seeking excitement elsewhere.

Without passion, how could I be fair to my employees, to my family, to myself? By the time I set foot in the Land Rover to begin a safari with Geri, her Ethiopian roommate, Terunesh, and our guide, Joshua, I had reached a conclusion: I had to get out of this business. I had to let go of Blimpie, the business that I had started, and that I had been devoted to for twenty-four years.

I would soon rethink that decision. A few days later, before us on the Serengeti plains, I saw hundreds of zebras and other wild animals. Whenever we approached, the animals scattered, afraid that they would become our prey. One morning, as we entered the great Ngorongoro crater, we spotted a pack of lions stalking a zebra. Our guide shut off the engine and we sat patiently, watching, while the lions, operating like a team, surrounded the zebra and planned their attack. When the leader made the decision to go for the kill, it was all over for the poor critter.

That's when I thought, "What will I be, a zebra or a lion?" As a zebra, sure, I could try to run away, but where would I go? If I left Blimpie International, unless I was prepared to retire and sit on my butt for the rest of my life, I'd have to do something else. And, unless I got the passion for whatever that something else might be, I would never achieve success there, either. Running away wasn't going to work. On the other hand, if I could regain the passion for Blimpie, where I had so much invested, I could become the lion, the leader, and, with a well-organized team, achieve success at anything I set out to accomplish. Once I made that decision, once I decided to regain the passion for Blimpie and regain the passion for success, everything became possible. The Blimpie business became fun again.

What Is Passion?

"A job is nothing but work," they say in *Mo' Money,* a popular 1992 movie. Unfortunately, a lot of people feel that way, and all of them are without passion. Passionate people love their work. They can't wait to get out of bed in the morning to go do it. Passionate people have fortitude, they have staying power, they get excited. And when they get excited, they realize that they can accomplish whatever they desire.

Did you see Mark McGwire when he hit seventy home runs during the 1998 baseball season to set a new record? This was a guy who was excited. This was a guy with incredible passion. Listen to what he had to say right after he hit his record-breaking home run: "I've never gone through a time where my insides were

> **Passionate people have fortitude, they have staying power, they get excited. And when they get excited, they realize that they can accomplish whatever they desire.**

hurting so bad as I did before I hit my sixty-second—the anticipation, the media crush, and then, finally, doing it. Today, I believe I can accomplish anything I set my mind to. I've yet to tap into what I really, really went through this season—but I've said for the last four or five years that your mind's the strongest thing on your body. It will overtake anything you want to overtake. And now, I really, really realize that this is so true."

That's how passionate people feel and act. Yes, they use their heads, because smarts always play a part, but, more important, they use their hearts, combining head and heart with the force of their will to create an energy so powerful that they have to win.

Passionate people make you feel like they are going to make something good happen. You can see it in their eyes, sense it in the touch of their hands, witness it in how they carry themselves.

In the 1970s, when Blimpie International first started to expand in the Atlanta market, an ex-New Yorker named Joe Alfone became a franchisee and built a store on the south side of the city. The next time I visited Atlanta, I went to see Alfone. I pulled my car into the parking lot and even before I could turn the engine off, Alfone was outside his store to greet me. He grabbed my hand and shook it and made the kind of remark to me that I suspect CEOs rarely hear. "Thank you for giving me the opportunity to be part of Blimpie," he said. I knew that this was a man with passion. Joe Alfone went on to own six stores before he retired in June 1991. He remains one of the most successful operators our chain has ever known.

A few years ago, another Atlanta operator, Vickey Shelton, won the "Franchisee of the Year" award, which is given at our annual convention. As the audience applauded and I held the trophy to present it to her, Vickey approached the front of the room. No sooner had I offered my congratulations than Vickey, as she held my hand, looked at me, and said, "Tony, I love Blimpie." Imagine that? "I love Blimpie!" Is it any wonder that she became the best operator of the year?

Vickey Shelton's statement says so much. It says that she's doing what she loves to do, rather than what she is "supposed" to do. It says that she feels that her own goals are aligned with the company's and that she has a stake in the whole thing. From all of this flows loyalty and pride.

Today, work is more personal than it has ever been. When you meet someone for the first time, chances are that you'll be asked what you do. Like it or not, what you do is who you are. There's a lot of truth there, because we all spend so much time at our work, often more time than we spend doing anything else. Obviously, we should be proud of what we do. Blimpie operators who are proud of their restaurants are inevitably the most successful ones. They love the product, they love the brand, they love their customers, and they love their stores. One such franchisee was John Gonzalez.

Responding to an SOS call from his brother Eddie, who operated a Blimpie in Newark, New Jersey, John quit his bank job to become store manager at Eddie's restaurant. It wasn't an easy move for John, but within days he knew he had done the right thing. "It was my cup of tea," he said, "working with customers every day, the product, the concept; I was in heaven."

After a few years, John accumulated enough capital to open his own store. In an interview in the chain's *No Bologna News,* John said, "My advice to anyone opening a Blimpie is, you got a good thing, don't blow it. I can honestly say I love Blimpie. It's a way of life for me. I also eat a sandwich every day because I love them."

Tragically, at the height of his career, John suffered a stroke that prompted doctors to say that he would never walk again, yet he recovered to the point where he was able to come back to his Blimpie store. "This was as serious an injury as anyone can expect," he said, "but my love for the store gave me strength."

Living without Passion Is Unacceptable

With the certainty that I had regained the passion for Blimpie and with the determination to rebuild our business to be a leader in food service, I returned from Africa and called a meeting with the company's senior executives, Dave Siegel, Pat Pompeo, and Chuck Leaness. A big reason that I felt so confident that Blimpie could be reborn was that I knew that these guys also had passion, but that they had allowed it to fade away, as I had.

David had been with me for twenty years, and together we had survived every crisis known to man. David's biggest asset is his self-inspiration. He is always brimming over with self-motivation. Calling on his background as a lawyer, David has always been passionate about making a deal. If you want to see someone get

> **Passionate people make you feel like they are going to make something good happen. You can see it in their eyes.**

excited, just put a deal on David's desk and ask him to go to work. It won't take long to see that this is a man who truly finds joy in what he does, and that inspires him to make things happen. Tony Bonelli, our subfranchisor for Lincoln, Nebraska, saw it, too, and commented about it in his monthly newsletter to franchisees: "When you talk to David Siegel, it is very obvious that he is a man with passion. You cannot help noticing it. He may not use the word or say it as much as Tony Conza, but his enthusiasm is evident. David is clearly ardent about Blimpie."

Enthusiasm? On most days, you can walk into David's office and view a scene like this: David is pacing the floor in front of his desk. The desk is piled with papers that appear to be on their way to reaching the ceiling. He has a phone under one ear. He's meeting with someone, and that person is in the room. His assistant is waiting for him to complete the document she is typing. He's checking his e-mail. And, somehow, he's making it all work. Sometimes, David can get carried away with his own enthusiasm, like the time he had a guy in his office whom he was anxious for me to meet. When he discovered that I was not behind my desk, he rambled through our offices calling out my name until someone suggested that I might be in the men's room. That didn't stop David. He grabbed this guy, dragged him into the men's room, and proceeded to knock on the stall door. "Tony, I want to introduce you to . . ." Such is David's passion.

Pat Pompeo, who is married to my sister Carol, had spent fifteen years on Wall Street when I convinced him to become a Blimpie person in the mid-1970s. We were so preoccupied with survival that we never took the time to properly train Pat, but he dug right in, making sandwiches, building restaurants, and helping franchisees. He learned the business the hard way and rose through the ranks, eventually becoming executive vice president. Pat is an extremely hard worker with an uncanny ability to maintain focus. I know no one who understands the merits of dedication and focus the way Pat does. He's like the pitcher who comes into a World Series game with bases loaded and two out in the ninth. Or the high-wire walker who uses no net. You need total concentration or else you break your neck. So, even as we misdirected the company's attention to the Border Cafe restaurants in the 1980s, Pat refused to lose his Blimpie focus, which proved essential to us as we approached the rebirth of our concept. Pat's greatest strength could be his ability to engender trust, and it's real, because you've never met anyone more honest and sincere.

Chuck Leaness was working his way through Tulane University when I met him in a fashionable men's clothing store in New Orleans. Chuck sold me a shirt and tie, and we became friends, particularly after he returned to New York as a junior partner in his father's knitwear business. After he joined his father's company, Chuck realized that he had gotten himself involved in something that was on the downswing. So, when I proposed an idea to him, he received it with open arms.

Having split up with Peter DeCarlo not long before, David and I now had our office in Manhattan, around the corner from Chuck's office. "Why don't you help us market our franchise?" I asked Chuck, as I looked to fill Peter's former position.

Soon, Chuck's days became a whirl of knit shirts and socks at Macy's in the mornings and franchise presentations to Blimpie prospects in the afternoons and evenings. Our business grew while the knit-goods business declined and, eventually, Chuck joined us full time, even involving his father in the development of Blimpie's South Florida area.

In the early 1980s, after completing law school at night, Chuck became Charles G. Leaness, Esq. That didn't deter him from getting his hands dirty, particularly when I approached him one day, after realizing that the Border Cafe restaurant was losing money. "Chuck, the Border can take this whole company down if you and I don't stop it," I said. "I need you to go into the restaurant and take charge, and I'll help you." Thanks to Chuck's passion, perseverance, hard work, and great personality, we were able to save the restaurant and make it very profitable.

At our executive meeting that day, I explained to our team that we had an incredible opportunity to make Blimpie one of the best brands in food service, but our journey had to begin in our hearts. I quoted Henry Ford: "If you believe you can do something, or if you believe you can't . . . you're right."

"We can do this," I said, "Do you hear me? We can do this! But we have to get the passion. Sure, we all want to make money, but the desire to make money will not get us the passion. We need to get the passion, then the money will follow."

It was what David, Pat, and Chuck wanted to hear, because they, too, understood that living without passion was unacceptable. We made a pact to make whatever moves were necessary to turn the company around. Immediately thereafter, we set our three main goals—one thousand stores by 1995, earnings increases of 30 percent to 35 percent per year, and appreciation in the value of our stock by one dollar per share per year—and we began to take all the steps necessary to accomplish them. It was like starting over again. In many ways, it was more difficult than starting a new business, because it meant taking something that was not working and giving it new life. It meant going to our staff and our franchise operators and getting them on board. At first, I kept thinking that I was trying to push a Mack truck up a hill by myself. Then, one by one, Blimpie people joined me until the force became so great that an incredible momentum was created.

Teammate, Joe Conza

As it turned out, since he created an equipment and design division for the company, Joe Conza played an essential part in the rebirth of Blimpie International.

My much younger brother grew up with Blimpie happening all around him. I guess my dropping out of college set a bad example for him since he didn't even attempt to go. So, by the time he was eighteen, he was ready to become an entrepreneur as well. At least he thought he was ready.

He had certainly learned how to formulate a deal. Raising the necessary money by putting together a partnership of three neighborhood friends, he acquired an operating Blimpie store on East Eighty-fifth Street and Third Avenue in Manhattan from a group of feuding partners.

I don't know what Joe and his buddies had in mind, but it sure wasn't running a good restaurant. Overspending and poor customer service quickly combined with the group's interest in having a good time, and the restaurant was driven out of business.

My brother was forced to return to his hometown with his tail between his legs and only a high-school diploma in his hand. Joe lost his business, but he didn't lose his ambition. First he worked at a supermarket, then got a job at a department store, and finally he worked at the New York Stock Exchange.

One day, my phone rang. It was Joe. "I'd like to get back into Blimpie," he said.

"You have to be kidding. How can I trust you?" was my predictable response. "Look what you did to that good store on Eighty-fifth Street."

"I'm aware of my mistakes and I'm ready to start doing things right," he said.

"Okay," I said. "Let me see what I can do."

I called Jerry Ruscigno, one of our best franchisees. Jerry was a tough operator, but he was also fair. I gave him the lowdown on Joe, assuring him that if he hired my brother I would not interfere with their relationship. "Send him over," Jerry said.

Joe worked for Jerry Ruscigno for about a year, and did really well. After observing his transformation, I was encouraged to approach him to see if he would move to Louisiana to help us develop that market. My goal was to get some experienced help to a new market, but I had an ulterior motive: I wanted to get my brother away from his friends and out of his environment. You can learn so many positive things from role models, but being stuck in a bad environment can exert a negative influence. If you want to win, spend time with winners. If you spend your time with losers, you'll lose.

Joe learned a lot from Jerry Ruscigno. Jerry was a very passionate guy and a very hard worker. That's the kind of person I wanted my brother to observe and study and be influenced by.

While Joe worked in Louisiana, Blimpie was growing in Atlanta, so, after about a year, I asked my brother to relocate again, which he did. Again, he was able to learn from people who

> **I love being around passionate people. They see challenge every step of the way. They work day and night to succeed. They commit and put their heart into what they do.**

had really good skills. Here's where I began to see Joe Conza's real potential. He was good at learning positive skills without copying the negative.

Well, by now, Joe was experienced in Blimpie and accustomed to relocation. "Let's start up another market," I told him. "Why don't you move to Houston?" "Sure, I'll do it," he said.

Over the years, Joe Conza went from operating company stores to developing the Houston market as a subfranchisor to starting up Blimpie International's equipment and design division, which eventually became BI Concept Systems, a wholly owned subsidiary of the company, of which Joe Conza is president.

My brother and I often laugh about those early days on Eighty-fifth Street, and we both realize how irresponsible his actions were. The best things that can come from failure are the valuable lessons you take away from it. I had already learned these lessons, but they were underscored by this experience: There's a price to be paid for treating people poorly, ignorance about money and finance will destroy you, and, finally, without passion for what you are doing, success will never come. Joe and I share a common passion now, the passion of making Blimpie a global brand.

A Passionate Brand

I'll never forget how my passion for Blimpie landed me in a studio in front of a microphone and camera.

It was just a few days before Christmas 1994 when dawn broke around the Silver Cup Studio, just over the Fifty-ninth Street Bridge in Queens. Entering the set in full wardrobe and makeup, I could feel the excitement among the fifty-plus group of producers, directors, cameramen, set people, advertising agency people, and company staffers who were in the room. I could also feel something else—skepticism. You see, the first of three commercials that we planned to shoot that day required me to sing a love song. It was a song written in the 1970s by Sonny Curtis, and made popular by Leo Sayer entitled, "More Than I Can Say." The song would be sung by me alone, without music, to a Blimpie sandwich. It was meant to be funny, but I still had to be able to carry a tune.

"Will Tony be able to do this?" was the silent question on everyone's mind. Of course, I hadn't told anyone of my days as a teenager, when I sang with The Castiles, an amateur doo-wop group that performed on the stages of Jersey City high schools. So, while they wondered, I was confident that I could sing the song. What I wasn't so sure about was whether I could do it in front of this audience.

With the lights down low, one of the camera people called for quiet. As an eerie silence pervaded the room, the director signaled me to begin an a cappella rendition of "More Than I Can Say." A bright spotlight, along with every eye in the room, was on me as I started to sing. And, lo and behold, I was making it work. I wasn't afraid. I was having a good time.

Upon my completion of the song, the director yelled, "*Cut!*" Immediately, the crowd erupted in thunderous applause and cheers. Richard Kirshenbaum, the senior partner and chief creative officer of Kirshenbaum, Bond & Partners, approached me and said, "Tony, I'm leaving. Now I know you can do this."

Two other commercials were filmed that day. One, entitled "Love Seat," has me sitting on a sofa browsing through a photo album filled with pictures of Blimpie sandwiches. Only one photo isn't a Blimpie sandwich, and I point to it and say, with surprise, "Oh, my Mom!"

"Taste Test," the third spot, has me chomping on a Blimpie sandwich while blindfolded. Then, because I love it so much, I refuse to even taste the competition's sandwich.

The decision to shoot those three commercials was the culmination of a process that had begun several months before. In order to determine how to position the Blimpie brand, we conducted research. Company staff, franchisees, subfranchisors, and, most important, customers, were asked how they felt about Blimpie sandwiches. The response was overwhelming. Blimpie people are zealots. They don't just like their sandwiches, they love them, they're passionate about them. Why? Because we make the best sandwiches. Yet, in our advertising, we knew we couldn't tell consumers that we are the best. The principles of advertising do not change, even as the world of marketing has been enormously influenced by consumers' changing lifestyles, experiences, and moods. Today, people are skeptical. They're cynical about business and the marketing of business. They don't believe what they see and hear. "The best? Sure, everyone says they're the best."

To convince the consumer that *we* made the best sandwich, we decided to use our advertising to express our passion for our sandwiches. With this knowledge, I attended a planning meeting with agency and Blimpie International people and Blimpie franchisees. There, I was confronted with this shocker: "Tony, you need to be in the commercials. You are the founder, and you have incredible passion for your product and your company. To the consumer, founder passion will equal company passion will equal the best sandwich." After looking around the room and getting assurance with nods of approval, I responded, "I'll do whatever it takes."

So, our radio spots, TV commercials, print and in-store promotions don't talk about "real food" or "quality food" or the "best food." Sure, that's our strategy, but when we say, "Blimpie . . . It's a Beautiful Thing," we're passionate and we appeal to the consumer's emotions. "It's a Beautiful Thing" works because it appeals to the heart as well as to the mind.

Of course, Blimpie is still a silly word, so, while we take our sandwiches seriously, we can't quite take ourselves so seriously. Therefore, our strategy is "Passionate about sandwiches, whimsical about life."

After our commercials were edited and introduced, we got a terrific review by Barbara Lippert in *Adweek:* "Ads that spotlight an obsessively dedicated CEO are nothing new," she wrote. "The twist here is the way the spots mix comedy with a highly stylized '90s look. But the real surprise is the natural, affable, Perry Como-like star quality of Blimpie's founder, Big Tony C."

Lippert goes on to discuss how the spots were shot minimally, but bathed in the weird primary colors of early 1960s nightclub modernism, and how the campaign takes advantage of the dawning of cocktail culture, a recent pop trend. She compares me to Tony Bennett and says that Vic Damone couldn't have done it better.

On the "Love Seat" spot, Lippert commented, "Conza somehow manages to make it hilarious and even hip. . . . The tagline, 'It's a Beautiful Thing,' really works here."

Wow. I was shocked but really happy. This could have been embarrassing. A couple of years later, with a bigger budget, two more spots were made. "Goofy, but Conza is a more interesting personality than rival honcho/thespian Dave Thomas of Wendy's," reported *Brandweek*.

The time that you must invest, coupled with the risk you have to take by putting yourself out there, makes personality advertising something that most CEOs are unwilling to undertake. However, I think that the five television spots and fifty-plus radio

---

Often in life, the inclination when you have a choice is to take the safe route, to avoid risk, but you are never going to get to second base if you always stop at first.

---

commercials that I've done have served to express the company passion well, and build the Blimpie brand with consumers. At the same time, I believe that franchisees and company staff realize that the commitment that I have made to our advertising underscores my passion for Blimpie.

Aristotle said, "Criticism is something we can avoid easily by saying nothing, doing nothing, and being nothing." I could easily have played it safe and refused to be in the commercials. The agency simply would have been forced to change the campaign concept, and it would have been business as usual. Instead, as I have done over and over again, in both business and life, I chose to go for it and risk falling on my face.

Often in life, the inclination when you have a choice is to take the safe route, to avoid risk, but you are never going to get to second base if you always stop at first. However, if you do decide to take a chance and put your hard-earned money, or yourself, on the line to achieve something that may not be the safest thing to do, make sure you stack the odds in your favor. The only way to do that is to get the passion for succeeding. Just keep in mind that your risk diminishes in direct proportion to the passion you have.

Pride and Passion

Once, at a Boys & Girls Clubs Congressional Breakfast, I listened to Senator Bob Kerrey speak about golf great Ben Hogan. "Hogan lived by something that his mother told him when he was a kid," said Kerrey "You only have one name, and you must never do anything to tarnish that name."

To uphold our name, we must be proud of ourselves and proud of what we do. Take our franchisees. Collectively, they have one name: Blimpie. They invested in it; they work for it; they probably spend much of their lives with it. They'd better be proud of it.

"They tell me that the reason my restaurant does well is because I have no competition in Newnan, Georgia," said retired Blimpie franchisee Bernie Farrington, "That's nothing but hogwash. Be proud of your business and promote your business like I do and you, too, can expect 20 percent sales increases." Does that sound like passion to you? I'd say so.

Everybody needs to feel a sense of pride in how they spend their life. Of course, work shouldn't be the only thing that drives you in life. But why would you spend half your life doing something you're not proud of? Imagine not being able to tell your grandchildren that what you spent your life doing was good, that you're proud of it. This is your life and the only way to be proud of what you do is to love it.

I love being around passionate people, people who are proud of what they do. . . . They see challenge every step of the way. They work day and night to succeed. They commit and put their heart into what they do. They make you feel good.

Mike Ciccarelli is one of these folks. In his early twenties, Mike became a Blimpie franchisee on the Florida panhandle. With a burning desire to succeed, for himself and to help his family, he aggressively built his business and eventually accumulated enough capital to develop a second store, but his ambitions were greater than that.

Though his capital was limited, Mike wanted to be an area developer. He discovered that a low-investment opportunity to develop Blimpie in the Birmingham and Huntsville, Alabama, markets was available. There was just one problem: Three prior subfranchisors had made a mess of the territory. With the exception of one store that still operated, all others in the area had been

---

Why would you spend half your life doing something you're not proud of? Imagine not being able to tell your grandchildren that what you spent your life doing was good, that you're proud of it.

---

shuttered, which meant that consumers had gotten a bad taste in their mouths, that landlords were not happy, that real-estate brokers did not trust us, and that franchise prospects didn't want to look at our offer. In spite of all this, Ciccarelli took the challenge.

Mike devoted enormous amounts of his time making certain that the one store in the market stayed alive and prospered. He also set his sights on growth. Above all else, he needed to establish trust in himself and to reestablish trust in Blimpie. I always respected Mike and, from the first time I met him, I recognized his passion. I wanted to give him all the help I could. Our staff in Atlanta provided a lot of support, but I made the effort and took a trip to Birmingham to do some newspaper and radio interviews to try to get some positive press for us. I also knew that what Mike was attempting to do was hard, really hard, and I wanted him to know that I cared about him and that I supported him. Mike was a bit down and not feeling so good about himself. I tried to encourage him, talking about my own experience of regaining the passion for success and how passion would lead him to success, too.

Entrepreneurs always find a way. Mike was aware that one of the things that discouraged prospects from coming on board was his youthful appearance. Another was that he seemed to have no support team. Mike stepped up to the challenge. Instead of just meeting prospects in Birmingham, he began picking them up in his car and driving the two-and-a-half hours to Blimpie International headquarters in Atlanta. There, they would be introduced to sales, marketing, operations, public-relations, and other staff people. They would witness the Blimpie Business School where trainees were learning the ins and outs of the sub–sandwich business. They got to see and understand the depth of the support services that the company had to offer. Almost every time, Mike's trip resulted in a franchisee being signed up.

It came as no surprise to me that, before 1999 had ended, the area had seventeen locations. As for Mike, he sold his subfranchise at a handsome profit and accepted an executive position with Blimpie International after putting pride back into his area and back into his life.

Pasión en Santo Domingo

"I am sorry my English is not very good," said the reporter from *Mercado,* a monthly magazine affiliated with *Advertising Age.* "Don't worry." I replied, "My Spanish is even worse." It was the start of an interview arranged by the Blimpie Master Licensee for the Dominican Republic, Luis Rodriguez, and his wife, Maria Vasquez, shortly after my arrival in Santo Domingo.

Mercado used to publish for the trade, but expanded into a consumer magazine. In fact, Luis, Maria, my wife, Yvonne, and I

> **An entrepreneur is not born when an idea precedes the desire to go into business. An entrepreneur is born when the desire to go into business precedes the idea.**

spotted one at La Bricciola, a restaurant where we dined one evening. Steve Forbes was on the cover. The reporter spent an hour with us and was very thorough. "How did you start Blimpie?" "Where did the name come from?" "What is the company's philosophy?" "To what do you attribute your success?"

Then, she asked this question: "Subway recently closed two stores here. What makes you think Blimpie will be successful?" My answer was quick and simple. "There are two reasons," I said. "The first is because we have a superior product. The quality of the ingredients, the nutritional value, and the fact that everything that goes into our sub is real makes Blimpie better. The second reason is Luis Rodriguez. Not only is he dedicated and committed to Blimpie, he will make Blimpie a success here because he's full of passion." The reporter looked a bit confused, "I'm sorry . . . my English . . . passion? Does that mean patience?" Luis chimed in, "*No, no, pasión.*" "*Ah, pasión, si.*" She understood.

Besides Blimpie, Luis and Maria own the franchises in the Dominican Republic for Avis, Domino's, and Dairy Queen. "I guess maybe I was in the right place at the right time. I guess I got lucky," said Luis. *Lucky?* Sure, if luck means that you have the vision to see an opportunity when it presents itself. If you're prepared to accept the opportunity. If you have a dream and if you put your heart into it. If you pursue opportunity with a passion. Do all of those things, as Luis and Maria have done, and you'll get lucky too.

Many people think that becoming an entrepreneur starts with an idea, as in, "I have a good idea, maybe I'll start a business." That's not what happens. An entrepreneur is not born when an idea precedes the desire to go into business. An entrepreneur is born when the desire to go into business precedes the idea.

Luis was barely a teenager growing up in small town in the Dominican Republic when he decided he wanted to be an entrepreneur. He began by buying and selling comic books and trading local currency for U.S. dollars. He graduated college, then went to work for a car-rental company. After discovering that Avis was having serious problems in the Dominican Republic, he found a wealthy investor and convinced him and Avis that he could create a winning business locally for the car company. He paid for his share of the partnership out of the profits.

Having accomplished profitability and growth with Avis, Luis began to pursue Domino's. Letter after letter to CEO Tom Monahan got the reply that Domino's was not offering international franchises. Luis persisted. Finally, his persistence paid off when Domino's changed its policy and advised Luis that he could be a candidate for a Dominican franchise. He won, and today has fourteen Domino's locations. "During the last year, I picked up the Blimpie and Dairy Queen franchises," he says. "My dream is to have a family of successful franchised brands."

"Whenever Luis starts to think, I worry," says Maria. "He's a visionary, and I never know what he is going to come up with next. But I know he is very passionate, so I support him 100 percent."

Luis Rodriguez is one of those people who make you feel good. He loves what he does, he's proud of it, and he's about as passionate as you can get.

A Hero

It's certainly not easy to find a hero nowadays, but, a few years back, I found one in the Chairman and CEO of the Coca-Cola Company, Roberto Goizueta.

Roberto and I met in October 1992, after he invited me to join him and several other food-service CEOs for lunch at a Manhattan restaurant. That's where I became aware of how smart he was and

---

You'll never achieve your greatest successes because you want to make more money. You'll do it out of a love, a desire, and a passion for reaching a dream.

---

what a wonderful sense of style he had. I also got a glimpse of his passion for his business and his customers.

During and after lunch, Roberto made it a point to talk to each one of us about our concerns, our needs, how Coke could help us. His love of the brand also became apparent when he took us into the Fifth Avenue Coca-Cola store, which was new at the time, showed us around, and took photos with us, and also when he talked to me about "good businesses" and "bad businesses."

"The airline business is a bad business," he said, "If you added up all the revenues from all the airlines from the time airplanes started to fly and deducted all the expenses, you'd come out with a loss. On the other hand, the Coca-Cola business is a great business. Year after year, our company makes profits." There was something in the way he talked that made you understand his incredible passion.

Roberto Goizueta grew up in a very wealthy family in Cuba. Educated at Yale, he returned to Cuba and his family's business. Then, Fidel Castro took over the country. With his wife and two suitcases, he fled Cuba, leaving everything behind.

Goizueta secured a job in technical operations at Coke earning only $18,000 a year. There he worked himself up through the ranks until he was elected chairman and CEO. During his sixteen-year term as chairman, he earned $1.4 billion, an average of $87 million a year.

Because Coca-Cola has been the Blimpie beverage of choice since 1964, and because Roberto also served on the Board of Governors of the Boys & Girls Clubs of America, of which I am also a member, I got to spend some time with him and got to know him better. I am also very friendly with Clyde Tuggle, who was Goizueta's assistant. Clyde worked harder than anyone I know just keeping pace with his sixty-seven-year-old boss until cancer took

---

Companies that are passionate about their products make the best products. People who are passionate about what they do, do it best.

Roberto's life in 1997. On a number of occasions, my wife, Yvonne, and I tried to get Clyde and his wife, Phyllis, to visit with us for a weekend, only to have the trips cancelled at the last minute because Roberto always had some deal to close or some customer to visit and Clyde had to be with him.

Why did the Coca-Cola chairman continue to work so hard? Obviously, it had nothing to do with money, because he had so much and earned so much. Additionally, he wasn't a spender. He lived a very modest life with modest possessions. So, if not for money, then for what?

Simply put, Roberto Goizueta enjoyed building on his success. He passionately pursued success. During his tenure as chairman, Goizueta built the value of Coca-Cola from $4 billion to $180 billion, a staggering 3,500 percent increase. That made him one of the greatest value creators of all time. Under him, Coke penetrated every market in every country in the world.

Roberto did this because he loved his job, he loved his company, and he loved his brand. Once in his early years at Coke, he was approached by a competitor who offered to double his salary. "I love Coca-Cola," he said, "I would never leave here, even if I had to work for free." That's incredible passion, the passion that drove this man every day toward his dreams.

Passion doesn't come from money. It's the other way around. You'll never achieve your greatest successes because you want to make more money. You'll do it out of a love, a desire, and a passion for reaching a dream.

Though Roberto is gone, the Coca-Cola Company lives on.

Doug Ivestor became the next chairman and was succeeded in late 1999 by Doug Daft. Of course, Daft and company are interested in making money. But, to them, it's about so much more. It's about building relationships, because, when you build relationships, the profits will follow. It's about focus and about following the company mission established years ago: "To have Coca-Cola within arm's reach of desire of every person in the world!" And it's about love and passion, love and passion for the brand.

The Number One Reason for Success

Companies that are passionate about their products make the best products. People who are passionate about what they do, do it best. Doesn't it make sense that if you are going to do something, you should put your heart into it? I don't care if it's driving a taxi, creating a sculpture, throwing passes on a football field, or making Blimpie sandwiches. If you're going to do it, love it and pursue it with a passion. Not only will you produce something far superior, you'll create more excitement and have more fun doing it.

Often people don't recognize that they can be really passionate. In fact, most people probably have at least one thing in their life that they are passionate about. The trick is to harness that passion and keep applying it to achieve success at the things you truly want to achieve success at.

Nick Conza had many passions, and hot peppers were at the top of the list. Fresh, fried, dried, crushed, marinated, vinegared—my father searched them out and had them at almost every meal. One of the burners on Mom's stove was devoted to a pan that was always ready to cook up some peppers. Not satisfied with the inconsistent quality of store-bought peppers, Dad started to grow them in his garden. As expected, he grew the best—if, that is, you could stand the heat. To Dad, the best peppers meant not only how they tasted, but how hot they were.

The news about Dad's passion for hot peppers spread, provoking constant challenges from family and friends. There was always someone who figured they could eat more peppers or a hotter pepper than Dad, but it was always a sucker's bet. No one could beat my father at this game.

After he retired from the New York Stock Exchange, Dad took a part-time job as a bookkeeper in the Blimpie office. It didn't take long for our employees to become aware of Dad's love of hot peppers.

Finding a pepper that Dad considered hot became a challenge. It was like getting Juan Valdez to give the nod on a good coffee bean. Well, one of our employees started dating a woman from Trinidad, a country known for its very hot peppers. But were they? To find out, he brought a jar of Trinidad peppers into the office for Dad to try. My father ordered a sandwich and, when

---

If you are truly serious about achieving your goals, get the passion. Get the passion, and nothing will stop you.

---

it arrived, the entire staff gathered around him. He spooned a heaping mound onto the sandwich, pressed the two pieces of bread together and took a bite. Everyone got quiet. A tense silence prevailed. Finally, my father looked up and spoke, "It's hot!" Everyone cheered. There was no question: Trinidad peppers *are* hot.

Dad's love for his peppers created an inspiration in others. The spirit and exuberance generated by his enthusiasm not only brought him pleasure and enjoyment, it spilled over to those around him. That's what passion does. It builds excitement. It makes life fun. It's contagious. It's a breeding ground for success.

Practice Passion

Start with self-examination. You're probably passionate about something. Maybe it's a sport or a hobby. Maybe you're really passionate about your spouse or child. Suppose you feel, "I love my son so much, I would do anything for him." Well, how about if you felt the same way about your job? Isn't it reasonable to assume that if you did, you'd be so much more successful at it? If you were a salesperson, for example, you might mentally convince someone to buy something and make the sale. However, if you were emotional about it, that emotion would show and not only would you make the sale, you'd keep your customer coming back.

Our most successful store operators are a lot like our least successful ones. They make the same sandwiches; they have the same store décor; they use the same advertising; they charge the same prices. What they do differently is they put their emotions, their heart, into what they do. And it pays off, big time. Our most successful operators consistently report sales that are double or triple the sales of the least successful operators, not because they are more talented but because they operate with a lot of heart. People with passion have an aura around them, and it's contagious. You can't help but feel the excitement.

If you are truly serious about achieving your goals, get the passion. Get the passion, and nothing will stop you.

CHAPTER 4

THERE'S NO MAGIC LANTERN: YOU NEED TO CREATE YOUR OWN OPPORTUNITIES

> Luck happens when preparation
> meets opportunity.
>
> —**Oprah Winfrey**

O pportunity comes along every day. The problem is that it's often brilliantly disguised as a crisis, a roadblock, or an impossible situation. I've learned that the better prepared you are, the greater your confidence will be, and the more opportunity you will see. I've learned that what we think is luck often is not. Rather, it's taking responsibility and seizing the day. It's figuring out when the glass is half full, not half empty.

Don't think I was born knowing all this. There have been times when opportunity came my way but I wasn't ready for it. One big one came in 1998, after Blimpie International scored some important breakthroughs, most notably the opening our first Blimpie outlets in major-league baseball parks—four at Tropicana Field in Tampa Bay and four in Bank One Ballpark in Phoenix.

Not long after the first Diamondbacks game ever, when Yvonne and I were seated above the third-base dugout, quite an honor in itself, I was invited to throw out the first ball at a Devil Rays' game with the Detroit Tigers. I didn't have time to practice throwing baseballs, but I wasn't worried. I had played baseball constantly when I was growing up, and I had a pretty good arm. Never mind how many years had gone by since then, or that, only two years earlier, I had separated my right shoulder in a biking accident—the pain from which had never truly subsided.

I arrived at the park in my khakis and white pullover collar shirt that displayed a discreet Blimpie logo. I appeared ready for my challenge. I was ushered onto the playing field and introduced to several Devil Rays players, including Bobby Smith, who would catch my pitch. "Would you prefer to do this from the grass or do

---

Opportunity comes along every day. The problem is that it's often brilliantly disguised as a crisis, a roadblock, or an impossible situation.

---

you want to throw from the pitcher's mound?" I was asked. "Why, the mound, of course," I responded. Gee, I thought, I may never get this opportunity again. How could they even think that I wouldn't go all the way?

"We'll be ready in about sixty seconds," I was told. Suddenly, I felt the pressure. I looked around. The stands were packed. The Devil Rays were a brand-new team. Baseball fans in Tampa Bay had been waiting a long time for a major-league club, and they were turning out in droves, probably thirty-five thousand of them that night. Then, there were the Blimpie franchisees from the area who were seated in a section of the stadium, and the Devil Rays and Tigers players in their respective dugouts. Perhaps most intimidating were the gigantic matrix screen ready to zero in on my every move and the television cameras that would broadcast all this into homes across America. I'd been in pressure situations before, but never anything like this. I'd given speeches in front of hundreds, even a thousand, and I had appeared on national television many times, but never, ever was it anything like this. I should have been prepared for this moment, I thought.

Then, the public-address system blared: "Tony Conza, the chairman, CEO, and founder of Blimpie International, will now throw out the first ball." It was like God speaking. All eyes were on me as I stepped up to the mound and watched the catcher pound his fist into his mitt, which soon became my target. I couldn't think. I was unable to focus. I should have been prepared.

I choked. I threw the ball into the dirt.

Of course, nothing bad happened because I had failed to throw a strike. No game was lost. It didn't cost anyone any money. No one around me was any worse off as a result. And I still have a beautiful photo that shows me throwing a pitch at Tropicana Field. I would have been a lot prouder, though, had I been able to tell you that I threw a strike. More than that, I would have been a lot prouder if I had remembered what I learned a long time ago: Always be prepared for opportunity.

There's No Magic Lantern

I was a very shy kid. I excelled in school, had creative abilities, and was good at sports, but I was so quiet and shy that my talents were often a secret. Audition for a school play? Unthinkable. Try out for the basketball team? Nah, I was sure I'd get rejected anyway. Debate team? Are you kidding? I could never outtalk that group.

One day, a friend told me about a new Little League team that was being formed. It was an opportunity for me, and my friend urged me to come along. So, glove in hand, I got to the city park and saw a large group of boys standing around, each one looking for a turn at bat and the chance to field a few ground balls. One by one, they stepped up to the plate to hit and scampered onto the field to be hit to.

I could tell that I was better at baseball than most of them. Yet, it didn't matter, because I was too shy to make myself known. I just stood in the background, as if somehow, magically, someone was going to whisk me onto the field and sign me up. I kept letting others get ahead of me. I kept ignoring this opportunity.

Soon, enough kids were selected and the team had been formed—without me. My friend was recruited and I went home, depressed and angry. Why didn't those losers let me get out there and show them what I could do?

Wait a minute. Wasn't *I* the loser? Despite my talent, I wasn't prepared to make that team. I should have tried out for things at school. I should have practiced exercising initiative. I should have had what my Mom used to call "a little more oomph." I should have been prepared for my opportunity.

Maybe you saw the Disney film *Aladdin,* but, even if you didn't, you probably know the story: A young boy, Aladdin, comes upon a magic lantern, rubs it, and a genie appears and grants the boy any wish he desires.

Instead of preparing for opportunity, many people seem to be on a neverending quest to find the magic lantern. Rather than setting goals, rather than getting the passion for something and preparing for opportunity, many people sit back, waiting for the genie to arrive. Yes, lightning does strike occasionally. Someone wins the lottery, and someone sitting behind a reception desk gets discovered and made into a movie star. For the rest of us, I assure you that there are no magic lanterns out there.

Tony Conza, CEO

As I grew older, I worked on putting more oomph into my life. That didn't mean that I wasn't a valuable behind-the-scenes guy. Being in business with Peter DeCarlo, the consummate salesman, made it seem only natural for him to be the front man and for me to work behind the scenes. Peter gave the presentations, made the speeches, and wrote the newsletters. I watched the money, paid the bills, did the bookkeeping, reviewed all the agreements, and handled the other administrative tasks. Those were important things for me, my future, and the company.

When Peter and I decided to split up, it was just David and me. I became the chairman and CEO, and David became the executive vice president. Now, I was in a position to take advantage of the opportunities that the future would have to offer. I'd like to tell you about how I developed skills that prepared me for these opportunities. I hope you can use my experiences to figure out approaches to your challenges that would work for you.

Probably the most valuable thing I did was to take a Dale Carnegie course to learn about public speaking. Everyone, particularly people who fear public speaking, needs to take this course or another like it. I learned how to structure a speech but, even more important, I learned that to be a public speaker you need to simply do it.

I also figured out early on that I need to be learning—constantly. Had I been able to leave the business for a few years, I might have completed my undergraduate college career, maybe gone for a master's degree in business administration. Without that luxury, I knew I needed to learn my business skills by teaching myself.

Probably the most obvious way to self-teach is to read. Almost any kind of reading is worthwhile, but reading that directly helps you accomplish your goals will make the best use of your time. In other words, while I might find a novel about foreign intrigue interesting and, while I may be able to pick up some writing skills by reading it, I would definitely learn a lot more that I could apply to business by reading, say, a book written by Lee Iacocca.

I always look for books to read about franchising, the restaurant industry, leadership skills, finance, sales, public relations, marketing, human resources, the law, and so forth. What I most love to read is the motivational book—books about dreams, visions, hopes, and passion. I don't think you can ever learn enough about those subjects because, without constantly being aware of them and practicing them, you limit what you will accomplish.

I also value reading about current events. Every day I read the *Wall Street Journal, USA Today,* and, generally, the *New York Times* or the local paper of whatever city I'm in that day. You might also find me flipping through business magazines like *Forbes, Fortune,* and *Business Week;* city magazines like *New York, Atlanta,* and *Los Angeles;* and financial and industry magazines, newsletters, and trade publications.

How do I find the time to get through all these? By mastering the art of flipping, skipping, and clipping. Rarely do I let any of the publications on my list pile up. When they arrive, I either read relevant articles immediately or skim them until I see something that interests me. Then, I cut out the article and stuff it into a folder so that I can read it as soon as I have a chance. And, to be certain that's it's soon, I always have something with me so that I can take advantage of any down time. For example, I may arrive at a restaurant earlier than my lunch companion. Instead of staring at the menu for fifteen minutes, I'll peruse several articles. The same goes for any time I'm on a plane, in an airport, on the subway, or in a taxi. You'd be surprised how much time you pick up this way.

And, I constantly take notes, whether related to my reading or just ideas that come into my head.

The trick is to not waste time on worthless stuff.

There are other ways to self-teach: Attend trade shows, seminars, and conventions. I believe that if I can pick up just one good idea every time I attend one of these events, one good idea that will help me build my business, advance my goals, or enhance my abilities, then the time was well spent.

Every year, Blimpie International holds a major convention for franchisees, subfranchisors, and staffers. A lot of time and money is invested in these conferences, so that we can not only entertain and motivate franchisees but also provide them with valuable knowledge and insight to help them with their businesses. I find that the atmosphere provided by our annual convention invariably helps me learn as well, while sparking ideas to help me and our company grow.

Courses that teach special skills can also be important. I already mentioned public-speaking courses as an example. Depending on what your likes and ambitions are, or what specific skills may be helpful to you in doing your job or reaching your goals, countless courses are available.

Make a Commitment

In the late 1980s, around the time Blimpie International was undergoing a rebirth and I was undergoing something of my own rebirth by regaining my passion, I got a call from Steve Simon, president of S&S Public Relations of Chicago. I had no idea who Simon was, but he got right to the point:

"Subway has been our client for four years, and they just fired us," Simon said of our chief competitor. "I can do for you what I did for them. Let me fly to New York tomorrow to meet with you." Blimpie never had a public-relations agency, but we did have a good story to tell. Besides, I was aware of all the press that Subway had received over the prior few years. "I'll meet you tomorrow," I told Simon.

After striking a deal with S&S, Simon assigned an aggressive young woman named Sherri Fishman to my account. "Blimpie's growth story is a good one," Sherri told me. "There's no question that America would be receptive to it. But how much press we get depends on you—on the commitment you are willing to make."

As essential as a game plan might be, commitment is the crucial element. Sherri could have sent out mountains of press releases, called every reporter in the country, and had every photographer in New York City take my picture but, unless I was prepared to conduct the telephone interviews, fly to emerging and developing Blimpie markets, meet with the press, shake the necessary hands, and involve myself in store and chainwide promotions, there would be no public relations.

I made the commitment. As Famous Amos said when he gave a keynote address at one of Blimpie's annual conventions, "Trying don't get the job done."

In the years since we hired S&S and the other public-relations agencies that followed, Blimpie International has received an enormous amount of press. It happened and continues to happen because of a major commitment on my part and the part of countless Blimpie people.

You can see commitment—or the lack of it—everywhere. I used to belong to a fancy New York health club. Occasionally, while at the club, I'd observe new members. They'd join up and plunk down a significant payment for the privilege of membership, which bought them the use of excellent facilities—workout equipment, free weights, running track, swimming pool, and so on—to get into good shape.

Then, I watched them. Some of them would visit the club constantly, use all the facilities, and get themselves into perfect condition. Others would occasionally visit and keep themselves somewhat fit. Then, there was the rest. Despite spending so much hard-earned money on membership fees, they'd never show up. They were never prepared to make the commitment. They could have paid twice the amount, ten times the amount. They never would have gotten into shape because they never used the facilities. They didn't make the commitment.

The franchise business is much like this. It's not an annuity. Regardless of how much a prospect pays to get a license to be a franchisee, no matter how beautiful the sign over his front door might be, despite all the programs the company can offer and all the support he may get from the brand and the parent organization, success will never come without a whole-hearted commitment by the operator.

Mike Murray was a police officer in Lincoln, Nebraska, when he and his wife, Sandi, decided to become Blimpie franchisees. "I witnessed a lot of crime," said Mike, "but the biggest crime of all was that you couldn't get a great sub in Lincoln."

Mike attended the Blimpie Business School in Atlanta, read all the company manuals, and participated in all the required on-the-job training as his store was being built. His commitment to success was such that Mike went much further. First, he trained constantly with other franchisees. Next, every day for two weeks before opening, he saturated the surrounding area with two-for-one coupons. Then, he wrapped his store with grand-opening banners. Finally, he conducted a weekend-long giveaway, backed up with advertising on two radio stations. The result: The ninth-largest opening week in Blimpie International history. Mike's advice to new franchisees: "Listen to the company's advice. Don't cut your training short. Learn everything you can. Promote your business. Commit yourself to excellence."

Pat Conlin, Blimpie International's subfranchisor for Long Island, demonstrates the value of commitment when he tells this story about a location in his area:

"A franchisee entered our system and built one of the best-looking stores in the chain, in Farmingdale. However, after opening, he neglected to spend much time working the business, instead putting it in the hands of a manager and some teenagers. There was no couponing, no specials, no proper attending to customer needs, and late openings and early closings. Sales barely reached $4,000 per week. Fortunately, the business was sold to George Sarkis, a former men's retail clothier. Though Sarkis had no food-industry experience, he immediately exercised some good common sense by scrubbing the store from top to bottom, hanging up promotional banners, and passing out coupons in the neighborhood. He went on to order some additional equipment so he could handle more business and he changed the staff to a group that was more motivated. Unlike the previous franchisee, who rarely worked the store, George comes in every morning at 7:30, often joined by his wife."

Sarkis had set, and exceeded, his weekly goals so that, after a few months, his sales were more than 50 percent higher than

---

If you're not committed to your business or job, then you are merely going through the motions. And while you may fool others, . . . you can't fool yourself.

---

when he took over the store. "It's not a miracle," says Conlin, "it's just hard work, caring management, and marketing. Sarkis made the commitment. The first operator did not."

The commitments made by Mike Murray and George Sarkis prepared them for opportunity. When you visit a quick-service food establishment, or any business for that matter, you can tell whether the owner and staff are committed. What does the place look like? How does the staff treat you? What's the mood feel like? Do the employees know what they're doing? You are going to give your business to the organization that you know will result in a positive experience for you.

If you're not committed to your business or to your job, then you are merely going through the motions. And while you may fool others, at least temporarily, you can't fool yourself. You are the one who has to look into the mirror when you get home at night. Sooner or later, you are going to realize that your lack of commitment is compromising your future.

Pick Your Priorities

Blimpie once operated on the premise that the only way to expand the chain was by opening traditional restaurants, that is, establishing locations and planning on customers coming in. Then, one day, we got together with a convenience store and said, "What if we were to put a Blimpie right here, inside your store." From that day forward, we established hundreds of outlets in convenience stores, on college campuses, in industrial sites, in hospitals, on golf courses, in bowling alleys, and so forth. What we have been doing is bringing our brand to consumers instead of simply expecting consumers to come to us.

The fact is, today's consumers want and demand convenience. Why? Because they are so pressed for time. You know the feeling, the daily struggle to find more time. Every other resource can be replaced. Your car wears out, you trade it in for a new one. A hurricane destroys your store, but insurance lets you build a new one. A gift from Macy's arrives in the mail broken and Macy's sends you a replacement. Once time is gone, however, it's gone for good.

Sometimes, I think digital clocks were invented as a way of reminding us how precious time is. Look at a digital clock and watch a minute tick away. That's a minute you will never, ever have again, a minute that, we all hope, was put to good use. Work, family, hobbies, entertainment, relaxation, learning, living—they all take time. If we have any hope of doing all the things we want to do while at the same time pursuing our goals and meeting our responsibilities, we must properly manage our time.

Establishing goals is the most important piece. Begin with long-term goals, then break them down into yearly, monthly, even weekly and daily priorities.

When we set our long-term goal of building a national chain, I knew that we had to get as many Blimpie people committed as possible. So, I established a personal goal for the year—I would decide to visit, say, Phoenix for three days and make my way to see a dozen franchisees. I couldn't devote myself solely to visiting stores, so I would also establish other priorities. I always keep handy a list of the things that I plan to take care of, and I'm always thinking about what I can do during the day. If I'm on a plane, I can write an article for our newsletter or work on a strategic plan. When I'm riding a stationary bike, I find that I can catch up on a lot of reading. During an exercise run or while I'm using a car service, I can practice a speech that I plan to give.

Mail can be a real time waster. Get rid of useless mail—fast. You can often recognize junk mail just by looking at the envelope. If you do, throw it away without even opening it. If you're lucky enough to have a secretary, have your secretary screen your mail. I find it very helpful to have my mail forwarded to me when I travel. I find nothing more disconcerting than returning to my office and finding stacks and stacks of mail awaiting me.

Didn't they tell us that e-mail was going to make our life easier? Yeah, sure. Make sure everyone knows that they don't *have* to send you a copy of every communication that gets sent out.

These sorts of tricks can help us set priorities for using our time, but setting goals is still extremely important. We must continually examine how we spend our time to be certain that our goals are being met. A Blimpie franchisee's first goal has to be customer experience. That means that if a food distributor is at the back door trying to deliver roast beef while a busload of customers are at the front door, the customers come first.

Some of my own goals are obvious. I need to continue to be the cheerleader for our brand, so I never stop visiting franchisees, subfranchisors, and master licensees around the world. It's clear to me that, if I stopped doing that, the effect on the company would be negative, but it's also clear that it would be a mistake to spend too much time on those activities because I would inevitably compromise my other duties.

With respect to time, we must create a balance in our lives by taking care of our families and by seeking out hobbies and diversions, particularly choosing forms of escape. It's impossible to ski down a mountain and plan a business strategy at the same time.

Unless you set priorities, strike a balance, and make the best use of your time for yourself, you will never have a positive effect on those around you, which means that neither you nor they will be properly preparing for the future.

My final point about using time wisely: Regardless of how busy you are and how many priorities you have set for yourself, it is absolutely essential to make time to reflect and contemplate, to think things through. Often, the person who most needs to do this is the one who is so used to getting things done.

Without taking time out for contemplation, it can be deceptively easy to expend a lot of effort maintaining the status quo or going in the wrong direction. You may be increasing your production or making more money but, without taking a hard look at what you're doing, you may find out sometime in the future that you should have been doing something differently. A bit more thinking and planning will most likely increase your effectiveness and output. It is time well spent.

Learn from Experience

Almost worse than starting the Blimpie business with no money was starting it with no experience and no training. We did everything by trial and error. It seemed as though we never did anything right until we first did it wrong, but we recognized opportunity and we pursued that opportunity. Then, as time went by, we used our experience to create policies, procedures, and a method of operation.

We tried to build the Blimpie franchise system so that others could become operators without making the same mistakes that we had. It was a nice idea, trying to use our own experience plus what we learned from others, but sometimes it seemed that franchisees were intent on making the same mistakes over and over again. Stores are closed, relationships are destroyed, emotions run out of control, and substantial money is lost, all for the same reason—attempting to do more of what didn't work in the first place, doing what we *thought* should work instead of doing what actually *did* work.

So much grief could be avoided if Blimpie people realized that they didn't suddenly become wise when they entered the Blimpie system, but only after they have learned from the experiences of others so that they don't have to make the same mistakes that somebody else already has. The Blimpie system was created from successful strategies. Franchisees who follow the system accomplish quickly what could otherwise take years to figure out.

As kids, we were all taught that experience is the best teacher. However, there's more to that profound statement: "Experience is the best teacher. But if you want to save time, money, and agony, make that experience someone else's experience."

Valerie Bieschel opened British Columbia's first Blimpie outlet in fall 1997. To counteract the slow sales that could be expected for a chain that was new to the region, she mimicked the promotions used by her partner, Ken Jones, a franchisee in Phoenix. Phoenix, however, with almost seventy operating locations, was a well-established Blimpie market. Offers like "Buy a Blimpie sandwich and get a second one for 99 cents" worked well in Arizona, but did little to tempt the consumer in British Columbia.

Enter David Kaiser, who had experience with that very kind of situation. Not long before, David devised a plan that saved a Blimpie in Huddersfield, England, one of first locations in the United Kingdom. He traveled to Kelowna, British Columbia, to present the Huddersfield Plan to Valerie. She listened, as David laid out a marketing plan that included an assortment of techniques involving coupons, direct mail, newspaper advertising, banners, and a sub-of-the-month promotion.

Then, she went to work. This time, she wasn't using a trial-and-error approach. Instead, she was following the advice of someone who had already experienced her exact situation. After a few months, Valerie had boosted her sales by 40 percent and, after a year, her sales had doubled. By applying someone else's experience, Valerie has created a winner.

Play by the Rules

When we built the Blimpie system, we also created a brand. That brand had to be protected, so we established some rules for all Blimpie people. Sometimes, the rules may seem inconvenient, frustrating, stressful, even expensive, but they need to be respected.

Sound familiar? There's really nothing new about following rules. We attend a college whose policies seem outdated, but we want that degree. Or we're involved in a relationship where we feel we are giving more than the other person, but we don't want to break up. Or we try to get something done in our community only to find local zoning regulations to contend with, but we like living there. We play by the rules.

One of my favorite stories about following rules involves Christian Herter, a former governor of Massachusetts, who was running hard for reelection—so hard that he arrived at a church barbecue one afternoon without having eaten lunch. He was famished. As he moved down the serving line, the woman serving chicken put a piece on his plate and turned to the next person in line.

"Excuse me," Herter said, "Can I have another piece of chicken?"

"Sorry," said the woman, "I'm only supposed to give one piece of chicken to each person. Those are the rules."

"But, I'm starved," Herter said.

"Sorry, only one to a person," said the woman.

Now the governor was a modest man, but he was also very hungry, so he said, "Lady, do you know who I am?" he said. "I am the Governor of Massachusetts."

"Do you know who I am?" the woman answered. "I am the lady in charge of the chicken. Now move along, mister."

Blimpie has some rules, too. Everyone entering the Blimpie system joins a co-op association composed of other Blimpie franchisees in the region. These co-ops have a big benefit: Franchisees can pool their advertising dollars, and also have a forum for exchanging information and getting operating advice. Because these co-ops are permitted to use advertising money that would otherwise be earmarked for national advertising, Blimpie International and our National Franchisee Advisory Council established rules with which the co-ops must comply. For example, the co-ops must engage an independent agency, submit marketing plans for approval, attain certain levels of gross rating points in their advertising, report marketing results, and so on.

It may sound like a pain, but it works, and our own marketing research proved it. The groups that complied with the rules reported a 15 percent growth rate in their sales volumes, while the groups that did not comply showed a 4 percent decline. Did this occur simply because some groups signed some papers and reported some figures while others did not? I don't think so. I think it's an indication that people who focused their energy in a positive direction instead of a negative one had better results.

When you fight the rules, you're wasting time and energy. You can complain, you can get angry, you can say it's not fair, you can say, "Nobody can make me do that," but in the end, you lose. On the other hand, the more time and energy you spend trying to reach your goals and dreams, the sooner you benefit.

Why does a brand like Blimpie need to have so many rules? I'll explain with an example: Suppose you traveled to Hawaii for a convention and spotted a Blimpie restaurant. You were familiar with the chain from back home, so you head to this Hawaii Blimpie to satisfy your craving for a turkey sandwich, your favorite. You've had a Blimpie turkey sub many times, so you know exactly how that turkey sandwich should taste. When you order that sandwich, you are confident that the sandwich will meet your expectations. If it didn't, wouldn't that shake your trust in Blimpie? It might mean that the next time you saw a Blimpie store in another unfamiliar city, you may just decide to pass that Blimpie by and head for the nearest competitor, because you couldn't be confident that your expectations would be met.

Honolulu is a long way from Charleston or Colorado Springs or Chattanooga or Panama City but, when the Blimpie brand is displayed at any of those locations, consumers must know that they can trust that brand. They have to trust that every Blimpie location will deliver the same experience. Without that trust, we have nothing.

We have rules to help us build and maintain trust in the brand—rules about the look, smell, feel, and taste of the brand. And, yes, in our advertising, even the sound of the brand. They're not Blimpie International's rules; they're the brand's rules. They are there to protect the brand and to protect the investment of every Blimpie person.

Throw Out the Book of Excuses

When we owned our Border Cafe restaurants, we used to joke about an imaginary *Book of Excuses*. Any time sales were down, we'd refer to our book: Weather conditions were poor. The Jets game was on television. It was Ash Wednesday. The kids just started school. Everyone headed out to the Hamptons. The not-so-funny joke, of course, is that if you want to come up with an excuse for anything that is not going your way, you can always do so.

Back in the early 1990s, I remember driving through South Carolina with a tired and frustrated Paul Waters. Paul, our subfranchisor for South Carolina, had managed to get a few stores in his area open, but they weren't setting any records. Franchise prospects also were not plentiful, and Paul's bank account couldn't exactly support a big advertising budget.

While spending time with Paul, I noticed that he had certain qualities that I was sure would eventually lead him to success. First, he was determined. Paul wasn't used to failure and, damn it, he wasn't going to fail at this. And he was a great people person. He cared about his franchisees and their stores. I didn't take his word for this. I learned it by visiting his stores and talking with franchisees. Finally, Paul never blamed anyone but himself for problems or lack of performance. He could have come up with excuses. We've certainly heard them all before: "The economy's bad here." "The company isn't giving me enough support." "We need more national advertising." "My area's different." Instead, Paul kept focusing on the positive, learning from every mistake and pushing forward with his eye on the future, not the past. Today, with more than fifty operating stores in his territory, Paul Waters has become a proven leader in developing an area.

Unlike Paul Waters, however, too many people in America today are unwilling to take responsibility for their own problems or failures. You know the type. Whenever something goes wrong for them, the first thing they do is look to blame someone else—and today, of course, there are all too many lawyers greedy enough to accommodate them.

I have always believed that if two sides have a problem, they should talk it out and resolve it. I remember learning about one situation that looked like it would turn into litigation. A franchisee, convinced that she could improve the sales of a store that wasn't doing well, bought the business. However, the franchisee who sold her the store neglected to inform her that a new Blimpie would be opening several blocks away in a convenience store. The seller and Blimpie International had agreed on the development in the convenience store, because the alternative would have been to have a competitor open in the same location. When the buyer realized that increasing sales in that location would be much harder than she had imagined, after a few months she began to accuse the seller, and Blimpie International, of creating the potential for her failure, because another store might capture sales that should have been hers. I investigated all the facts and contacted her myself. "Listen," I said, "If you are willing to talk about a solution here, I'll fly down to Tampa to meet with you." I did. She and I talked for a long time. She asked me to take a walk to the c-store to see how close it was. "Look, the selling franchise should have made you aware of the pending location, and I can understand how you feel. The store is a little close," I said. "I don't believe a c-store location will compete with you, but obviously you don't seem happy with this business. We think you have a desirable store here. Why don't we arrange a sale of the business so you can recapture your investment and go on to something else?" She agreed, and within about a week, we had a deal. Everyone left happy.

If only all conflicts could be worked out so peacefully, we'd all save a lot of money and aggravation. Regardless of who is at fault—and often no one is at fault—there are rarely any winners in litigation except the lawyers. As far as I'm concerned, litigation means you've already lost. Too often, litigation results when people feel they have to blame the next person to justify their own lack of responsibility or lack of commitment.

I've gotten a lot of satisfaction because of what I've accomplished in life. I work hard and I take responsibility for my actions and decisions. Obviously, I'm not always right and people often try to put the screws to me. I accept that, and do my best to rise above it. I pity those who can't solve their own problems and have to get a lawyer to try to do it for them.

You don't win in business or in life by dealing with negatives. And I can't think of anything more negative than a lawsuit. With a negative attitude, you may win a battle, but you'll lose the war.

I know someone who had an accident in the early '70s while working for the government. It had no long-term effect on this person's ability to work or enjoy life, but he took his lawyer's advice, which was, "Don't go back to work, because you will no

---

Remember that if you are never failing, you are never taking any risks. When you feel failure coming on, don't take out the *Book of Excuses*.

---

longer be able to collect compensation." In twenty-five years, the person has never returned to work of any kind, instead choosing to collect a monthly check from the government. Can you imagine spending your life like that? What does this person have to be proud of, to look forward to?

Blimpie International was involved in an arbitration a couple of years ago. After failing to meet a development quota, a subfranchisor who had been awarded the rights to develop a territory in the Midwest hired a lawyer and started an action against us, claiming that we misled him. For three years, this guy sat back doing nothing while lawyers battled until the arbitration ruling was handed down. Blimpie International was found to have done nothing wrong. Did we win? Well, even though we were found not to be liable, it still cost us time, travel expenses, and $120,000 in legal fees. As for this individual, it sure would have made a lot more sense for him to chalk up his losses, admit to his own failure, and focus those three years of his life on the positive. I think he would have been a lot happier today if he had left his *Book of Excuses* on the shelf.

Just because you have gotten yourself in a situation that appears to be failing, don't automatically start thinking that you are being victimized. Before you look at the next guy, examine everything that you have done. Keep conflicts focused on issues rather than on personalities. Where would the world be if every time we had a problem or disagreement, we punched someone in the nose or started a lawsuit or launched a missile?

Remember that if you are never failing, you are never taking any risks. When you feel failure coming on, don't take out the *Book of Excuses*. Instead, go back to basics, to your fundamentals, to the things that got you to achieve success in the first place.

Alienating people will always come back to haunt you. Don't look to take out your problems on others. The sooner you focus on the positive, the sooner you'll feel better about yourself and the sooner you'll prepare yourself for opportunity.

Dress to Win

Whether we like it or not, people make judgments about places or people based on what they look like. When I arrived at a restaurant on Manhattan's Upper East Side, for example, the first thing that caught my eye was the discreet signage. Once inside, I noticed the lofty ceilings. Pompeiian columns and murals surrounded by walls made to look like worn leather. There were handsome bowls and giant plates. A nice wine list. With the care that was taken to design and build a place as sophisticated as this, the food must be great, I thought. I couldn't wait to get to the menu.

Customers who walk into a restaurant may not be conscious of it, but they are receiving a message about the establishment based on its appearance. A restaurant that is well decorated, has a sense of style, and is cared for will tell the customer, "This is a special place."

The same applies to the way we dress. The clothes we wear and the care we put into how we dress don't make us the person we are, but they *do* send a message. The way we fix our hair, the shine on our shoes, the way our outfit is put together—they don't need to show that we have money or that we're some kind of hot-shot. They simply need to exude professionalism. There's no need to spend lots of money on designer clothes, especially when it has become so easy to look neat, crisp, and quite fashionable with clothing from places like the Gap and Banana Republic.

In our early years, one guy who worked for us wore the same set of clothes every day. One day, another employee approached me to say, "Tony, you have to do something about Ed. He never changes his clothes. Not only does he look bad, his body odor is disturbing everyone around him." Ugh. It was one of the most difficult things I ever had to do—tell this guy that he had a real problem of body odor. After discussing it with him in a way that I hoped was the best way possible, I offered to help him get a few new suits, shirts, and ties. After Ed got some new clothes and began paying attention to his appearance, he realized that it made him feel better. Incidentally, those around him felt better, too.

Just think about what was happening. This guy was going out to visit franchisees and suppliers and instead of people saying, "Here comes our Blimpie operations person," they were saying, "Here comes that guy with the bad odor."

This is an extreme example, but there's an important point to this story: Before you even open your mouth, you are constantly sending messages to the people you meet based on your grooming, clothing, and even your handshake. The messages you send may not be true, but perception can become reality.

The last thing we need is to miss an opportunity because of a message that our appearance is sending.

Play with People Who Are Better than You

My friend Tony DeGregorio is the president and chief creative officer in New York for Publicis Bloom, one of the world's leading advertising agencies. He recalls a time years ago when he enrolled in an art class in which he was expected to sketch nude models. "When the first model dropped her cloak in front of me, I felt a bit uneasy," Tony said. "Nevertheless, I began to sketch her, slowly, carefully, methodically. Then I looked over at the person next to me. It was an accomplished artist who was using rapid, sweeping motions that put the model's image on paper beautifully and quickly. It was very intimidating," Tony said. It was also the foundation of an important lesson.

Tony recounted how he watched closely, and how he soon began copying the artist's moves. "Then, after several classes, I

> ## I'm always looking to surround myself with people who are better than I am at doing something. . . . I'm going to be pushed harder.

found myself not just imitating him, but viewing him as competition." The experience garnered by observing and learning from an expert coupled with Tony's competitive spirit drove him to the top of his class.

I'm always looking to surround myself with people who are better than I am at doing something. If it's going for a run, I'm going to be pushed harder by the person who is a faster runner. If it's playing a game of tennis, I'm going to learn more from someone who's a better tennis player. If you consider my comments about dressing important, find someone who dresses well and observe that person. My friend and business associate Chuck Leaness has always taken pride in dressing with a sense of style. Calling on the knowledge he gained from years in and around the fashion industry, Chuck is always pushing the style meter. So, because I enjoy dressing up, I always keep an eye on Chuck, looking for a clue that may help me with my style.

My partner David Siegel knows more about the legal side of our business than I could ever hope to know. He's also a smart businessman and a good thinker, which means that we can exchange ideas and keep each other on our toes.

Joe Morgan, the president of our Blimpie Group, is much younger than I, so he brings a new way of thinking to the company that gives me the opportunity to see things the way a younger generation would.

My philosophy about bringing the right people into the company is that I'm always striving to get myself into a position where everything I have to do is being taken care of by people who can do it better than I. Every time I succeed, I can take on new duties. This ongoing process enables the entire staff to continually elevate itself and it opens the door to more and more opportunity for everyone.

Look at the Big Picture

There's a lot of talk in today's marketplace about convenience—about bringing your products closer to the consumer. I guess we've come full circle because, when I was a little kid in the 1940s, just about every business came to you. I'm probably forgetting some, but I can remember laundry, dry cleaning, washing fluid, knife sales, knife sharpening, produce, cake, beer and wine, ice cream, seltzer, newspapers, milk, pots and pans, cosmetics, and bread all being delivered right to our home—or at least to the curb outside our door. On the other hand, unlike today, I don't believe you could get a restaurant to deliver your food back then.

I recall Bob, the beer-and-wine man who was incredibly skinny, lugging two cases of quart-size beer bottles at a time over his shoulders, but the delivery person I remember best was Jimmy the bread man. Twice a week, Jimmy would climb two flights of stairs to bring fresh Italian bread up to Mom. Unless, that is, he spotted me first. "Anthony," he would call out to me, interrupting my playing, "take these to your mother." Then, I was stuck with the two flights to climb. Of course, I got wise to Jimmy, so, when I spotted his truck, I'd run off and hide until he made the delivery.

Once, he got wise to me. After he made the drop-off, he spotted me hiding and said, "I know what you're doing, Anthony." It must have been a bad day for him because he seemed so aggravated that he jumped in his truck, and abruptly pulled away, causing a loaf of bread to fall out of the truck. When the loaf struck the pavement, a chunk broke off and rolled away from the main piece, which ended up under a car. I remember watching from the steps of my house as several birds pounced on the small piece. One bird got his beak on it. As he tugged and tried to fly away with it, another stopped him, then another and another. Soon, this group of birds began a ferocious battle over this tiny clump of bread, all of them unaware that the major part of this loaf, a feast for all of them, was only a few feet away.

I sometimes think about that little incident, because it reminds me of the way many people act. Instead of using their vision, they focus on the trivial, get greedy over the small things, battle over the insignificant, and overlook the big picture.

David Siegel and I have been business partners since 1968. How were we able to stay together for such a long time? By always focusing on the big picture. During the period when our company wasn't producing a lot of revenue, David began to take advantage of his law degree and started serving private clients so he could supplement his income. My first reaction was that he was betraying me and the company. Instead of attacking David and creating a rift in our partnership, I gave the situation a lot of thought and came to a different conclusion. David needed to make more money but the company couldn't afford to pay him more. While I didn't like his taking time away from Blimpie, I knew that I owned twice as much stock in the company as he did so, when the time came to cash in, I'd be well compensated. I knew that David really loved our business and that, as soon as there was enough for him to do and enough revenue being generated, he'd drop his private clients—and that's exactly what happened.

Often, partnerships fall apart because people choose the wrong partner in the first place. Partnerships also go bad because the individuals involved lose sight of the big picture and focus on issues that, in the long term, are meaningless.

Joe Conza, Pat Pompeo, and Chuck Leaness have been with us for a very long time—long enough so that there has been ample opportunity for one or all of us to undo our partnership. Who is

> **Success does not come without problems, challenges, and annoyances. Successful people overlook the small things, realizing that it's the big, long-term goal that is really important.**

spending too much money? Who is not working hard enough? Who is being too stubborn? Who has poor business habits? Who is too conservative? Who is too liberal? Who doesn't understand the concept? Who is handling people poorly? Who is focusing on the wrong issues? Who is making more than the next guy?

Yes, too easily could we have attacked each other on a variety of issues, such that our partnership would have come unglued. But we didn't. Sure, we disagreed, we argued, we told each other off. However, none of us ever lost sight of what we were out to accomplish. None of us ever forgot that we had a vision of building Blimpie into an international powerhouse. All of us always remembered that our complaint of the moment, while seeming important at the time, was in fact meaningless in terms of our much larger long-term vision.

Success does not come without problems, challenges, and annoyances. Successful people minimize pettiness and overlook the small things, realizing that it's the big, long-term goal that is really important. By looking at the big picture, I assume that there's plenty out there for everyone. Success is not a limited commodity. In fact, one of the things I enjoy about achieving success is being able to share it with others. I'm very happy to see those around me—partners, staff, family, friends—doing well. If they do well, it can only be good for me.

Unfortunately, some people look at the success of others and, perhaps because of jealousy or their own insecurities, don't like it. "Why is that person doing better than me?" "Why should she profit because of my hard work?" "Why should I help him grow to another position?"

The division of the trademark that Peter DeCarlo, David, and I undertook in the 1970s created a situation whereby one company's growth could substantially affect that of the others to the degree that we let it. Around 1990, when Blimpie International was awarding development rights and growing our chain across

---

What have I learned about opportunity? I've learned that it doesn't come without obligations, and the first obligation of opportunity is that we must prepare for it.

---

the country, I met with Peter and his partner Nick to explore Blimpie's getting the rights to develop the territories for which their company, Blimpie Associates, had the trademark rights. We struck a deal whereby Blimpie Associates receives a portion of the revenue that Blimpie International generates in certain of their trademark-owned areas. Is it fair that we do all the work and they get a piece of the action? Would they have ever developed their areas had we not done it for them? Have their stores benefited from our marketing and advertising?

All I know is that had we not kept our eye on the big picture, had we instead focused on "Who's making what?" and "Why should we do that and give them the benefit?," we'd have a much smaller chain.

The Obligation of Opportunity

Every franchisee who enters our system must attend Blimpie International's training school in Atlanta. Often, when I'm at our Atlanta office, I will stop by the school to meet the trainees and say a few words to them.

When I look into the eyes of our newest franchisees, I see my reflection. I recall my enthusiasm, my excitement as I prepared to start my own business. I also see opportunity. For each of these newcomers, there has never been a greater time for opportunity.

But what have I learned about opportunity? I've learned that it doesn't come without obligations, and the first obligation of opportunity is that we must prepare for it. We must keep our eyes open for it, seize it when we see it, hold it, and mold our future from it. Finally, we must believe in it, commit to it, and pursue it with a passion—as though our lives depended on it. You know why? Because, in many ways, they do.

CHAPTER 5

FAILURE IS AN OPPORTUNITY: TAKE A FRESH LOOK

*The play was a great success
but the audience was a failure.*

—Oscar Wilde

Did you ever see a painting called The Dream? It's a very large, colorful painting by Henri Rousseau and it sits in the Museum of Modern Art in New York. The painting depicts a jungle scene and with a quick glance at this masterpiece, you immediately spot some animals lingering among the trees and bushes. You move on, satisfied that you have seen the painting. If you return for a longer look, you begin to understand that the artist has tricked you. More animals are cleverly hidden throughout. There's one. There's another. The painting is not what you thought it was. With a fresh look, you realize that what is plainly there, in full view, was, moments before, invisible to you.

The lesson can be applied to the business world, too. In Taco Bell's early days, the company saw itself as being in the Mexican food business. Their customers, they figured, were people who occasionally wanted a change of pace. However, by positioning itself as it did, Taco Bell was competing against all other Mexican restaurants, many of which were just too good to compete with.

Taco Bell took a fresh look. The company realized that it really should position itself against the McDonald's and Burger Kings and other fast-food chains. By doing that, it could charge much less and take customers away from these other chains, something they were unable to do with the other Mexican restaurants.

Fritz Perls, the founder of Gestalt therapy, once said that there is only one correct reaction, and that is a reaction to the situation. Situations change constantly but most people are not prepared to change with them. They see things according to preconceived notions. They do not see what is really happening. They fail to take the time for a fresh look at things. I recently visited a franchisee who has been in business for years. As I looked around at the shabby condition of his unit, he remarked that he used to do a lot more business. He could not understand why he had not been able to really increase sales inasmuch as he "still runs a good store and serves a good product."

This franchisee is a good operator but he was reacting to something in the past, not to the situation of the moment. When he first opened his unit, people loved it. They came in droves and were very turned on by what they saw and felt—the new Blimpie experience. Years later, his unit has grown old and tired looking. It is still clean and well-run, which is why he is still doing as well as he is, but it has lost its glitter. It needs a change. If he would take a fresh look, he would probably renovate his store and probably give his sales a significant boost.

I see this story repeat itself over and over. I see good operators failing to take an objective view of their unit. "When was the last time you walked into your store pretending that you were a customer?" I ask. "When was the last time you took a fresh look at your store? When was the last time you asked yourself, "Does my store need change?" If you've neglected to do all of these things recently, you are not dealing with the situation. You are dealing with what has already happened. You are living in the past!

The Lure of the Restaurant Business

Why does everyone want to be in the restaurant business? Michael Jordan, Joe Namath, Claudia Schiffer, Regis Philbin, Robert DeNiro, Paul Sorvino—the list of celebrities alone goes on and on. In fact, in the 1970s, so many famous people were associating themselves with restaurant franchise systems that the Federal Trade Commission saw a need to include an entire section on celebrity tie-ins with the standard disclosure document given to every franchise prospect.

Yes, the lure of the restaurant business is obviously very compelling, not just for the celebrated, but for the everyday person as well. Of course, smart celebrities, aware of the difficulties and pitfalls of the food business, hook up with the right people. Robert DeNiro, for example, partnered with Drew Nieporent, who is not only one of the best chefs around but is also a very savvy businessman. DeNiro's name and financial backing helped Nieporent create one of the most popular restaurants in New York, Tribeca Grill, while building a reputation for himself.

Unless you are truly prepared to meet the very difficult challenges of the restaurant business, stay out of it. I learned that lesson. Note that I'm making a distinction between the full-service, tablecloth, bar–restaurant business, and the quick-service restaurant business.

In retrospect, I can say with all certainty that, after completing our small public stock offering in 1983, we should have invested

---

If you are trying to get to the top floor, but you place your ladder against the wrong building, the higher you climb, the bigger the problem you create for yourself.

---

every penny in the Blimpie chain. However, one of those little red devils with a pitchfork in his hand must have been sitting on my shoulder saying, "Go ahead, Tony, open a real restaurant."

A combination of factors led us down this crooked path. Ironically, it had to do with our presence in two cities, New York and Houston. If you live in Manhattan, you will almost certainly spend a lot of time in restaurants. From the consumer's perspective, it's all so glamorous. How wonderful it is to be the creator, the owner of an establishment that people are clamoring to get into. There you are, meeting and greeting for all to see. How important you feel. Then, at the end of the night, there are all those receipts that are tallied up after people have paid their checks. We knew many of the city's restaurant owners. We had a lot of Blimpie locations in the city, so we were savvy about good locations and we were in touch with all the good real-estate brokers. Didn't it make sense that we should not only be in quick service but also own some "real" restaurants?

As for Houston, because my brother, Joe Conza, had relocated there, a pretty good Blimpie store growth pattern had emerged, encouraging me to make regular visits. During one visit, Joe said, "Tony, you have to try this special drink." It was a frozen margarita, a drink they make at Ninfa's, a local Mexican restaurant. It was terrific. It tasted great, went down easy, and contained enough tequila to make you feel really good.

I had never had a frozen margarita before, and I certainly wasn't aware of any being served in New York City. On the way home, I kept thinking about that margarita and how New York also lacked a good contemporary Mexican-Southwestern restaurant. Oh, sure, there were the old standards, like El Charro in the Village, but I knew of nothing like the tequila-sipping, frozen margarita-drinking places that were proliferating in Houston.

So, I started researching food indigenous to the American Southwest. I flew to New Mexico and Arizona, bought every Mexican and Tex-Mex cookbook I could get my hands on, and, when I was satisfied that I had a winning concept, went to the other folks at Blimpie International and convinced them that we should

> **A negative attitude becomes a mental wheelchair, and it shows itself in many everyday phrases: "That's just how I am." "I can't do that." "The boss will never go for it."**

diversify by opening a Southwestern restaurant. David was skeptical, but agreed to support the idea. Pat felt that whatever we did, he should not redirect his focus from Blimpie. Chuck, who enjoyed the restaurant scene as much as I, loved the idea.

After recruiting an experienced restaurant manager named Tony Miele and refining the menu, we began to seek out a location. We came across an Italian restaurant that had closed on East Seventy-ninth Street and Second Avenue. The place was for sale by a guy who, having developed a successful pizzeria in Brooklyn, decided that he could operate a fine establishment in Manhattan. No wonder he didn't make it.

In late 1984, The Border Cafe opened. It got off to a slow start. The drinks were great, the food was very good, the staff was trained, the decor was pleasant. Only one thing was missing—customers. I can remember going into the Border on a Saturday night and sitting at the bar. I was alone. A few tables were occupied, but there was no one else at the bar. I couldn't take it. I went for a walk and started thinking. Unless we made something happen, this business was going to fail.

That Monday, I went into Chuck Leaness's office and said, "Chuck, The Border is failing. We're losing a lot of money and nothing is going to change unless you and I make it change. We need to take charge of the restaurant, work there, do whatever we have to in order to turn it around."

Chuck and I kept Tony Miele in place, but we fired a few of the other key people and put ourselves on the Border's staffing schedule. While working in the kitchen and in the front of the house, we began to implement all kinds of promotions: half-price margaritas from four to seven, guest bartender nights, tequila parties, tie-ins with Southwestern artists, and so forth. Most important, we used our personalities to win customers. Soon, we had a crowded bar and patrons were waiting for tables. The Border Cafe became a place to be and to be seen. Sales were soaring. Profits were booming.

If you are trying to get to the top floor, but you place your ladder against the wrong building, the higher you climb, the bigger the problem you create for yourself. That, in essence, was what happened to us. Encouraged by the success of the Seventy-ninth Street location, we sought to expand the Mexican concept by selecting two more locations, one on West 100th Street and Broadway, another in Woodstock, New York. In addition, attempting to grow and gain management expertise at the same time, we negotiated a deal to acquire two more restaurants, both of them a rotisserie concept called Amsterdam's. Now we were solidly in the bar–restaurant business. We even changed the name of our company to Astor Restaurant Group, named after Astor Place, the street where our office was located.

It soon became obvious that the ladder was taking us somewhere we didn't want to be. Three of the five restaurants were losing money and the experienced group from Amsterdam's, well, we just couldn't see eye to eye with them. Cash was flowing out of these places faster than the margaritas.

During this time, as our crisis became more acute, I stumbled across a financial publication that listed the four most important reasons businesses fail. They are:

- Negative attitudes

- Ignorance about money and profits

- Failure to set goals

- Procrastination

I couldn't believe it; we were committing every one of those sins.

Investors Dealer Digest, Harvard Business School, cash flow, price/earnings ratios—when most people hear terms like these, they shrug their shoulders. "I'm a doctor, I'm terrible at business." "I'm in the arts, business is a foreign concept to me." That's because people think about business as being so complicated when, really, it's just common sense. The principles that apply to achieving success in business are not very different than those that we need to be successful with our everyday lives. The four most important reasons why businesses fail are a perfect example of this. Let's take a look at them.

Negative Attitudes

"I'm not being negative; I'm just being realistic." You've heard that one before, haven't you? Whenever you hear that, rest assured that whatever the speaker says next will be negative. Sure, they think of it as reality, but reality can be different things to different people. Is the glass half full or half empty?

Kevin Downes, my wife's brother, was a burn survivor at age nine. Kevin's story is so remarkable that Yvonne, my wife, is in the process of documenting it. Kevin was caught in a tent that went up in flames. He escaped, but suffered burns over 75 percent of his body. During the first days of his two-year stay in the hospital, Kevin's parents were told that he was going to die. He was given last rites. But Kevin is a fighter. He survived the initial trauma and went on to receive numerous medical treatments and skin grafts. Then, Kevin's parents were told that he would never walk again. Kevin wouldn't hear any of this. He endured operations, medications, and skin grafts, but he refused to allow metal pegs, which would have interfered with his walking, to be implanted in his legs. After two years, he proudly left the hospital, again prepared to meet the new challenges that this life would present to him.

Kevin's teenage years were difficult. His scarred face and body were not readily accepted by other kids. He got through those years, though, and finished school. Then he sought to fulfill a childhood dream—to join the Coast Guard. His application was rejected. Recruitment officials had acted on his medical records, which noted that he couldn't walk. Kevin was furious. He was fed up with people telling him he couldn't do something. He mounted his motorcycle and sped to Coast Guard headquarters where he gave a personal demonstration of his ability to walk, run, and do anything else required. He was accepted and served six years.

Kevin's stay in the hospital and his subsequent outpatient visits gave him the idea to develop a home health-care business in which he eventually involved his entire family. After a few years, the family sold the business at a substantial profit.

Next, Kevin continued his education in Buffalo, pursuing a career in physical therapy. In 1997, he was named National Outstanding Physical Therapist Assistant by the American Physical Therapy Association.

About sixty seconds in a room with Kevin is enough to make you forget about his scars. His positive attitude makes him a joy to be around. You realize that this man never allowed negativism to control his life. And now, he uses his attitude to help others. Yes, he's an excellent therapist, and that means that he's always aiding people with their physical problems, but he never hesitates to use the challenges that he's had to face to confront people who are having trouble dealing with the reality of what has happened to them.

I remember when Kevin encountered a man who had been confined to a wheelchair, but thought that if the man worked at it enough he might be able to walk. So Kevin approached him. "The guy's attitude was bad. He was totally negative. He had given up

---

Successful people don't let themselves get stuck in the mental wheelchair. Successful people understand that the decision to stay in the wheelchair or to get out of it is theirs.

---

on the idea of walking again," said Kevin. "I entered his room and pulled my pants down. 'Look at me. If I can walk, you can walk,' I said." The man had no argument. With Kevin to guide him physically and mentally, he's walking again.

Kevin Downes confronts people in wheelchairs all the time. "I can spend every hour of my day trying to convince someone that they can walk, but they will never leave their wheelchair until they decide that they will," he says.

A negative attitude becomes a mental wheelchair, and it shows itself in many everyday phrases: "That's just how I am." "I can't do that." "What am I supposed to do?" "The boss will never go for it."

Life will always be filled with challenges. We all have them. Successful people don't have any fewer of them than unsuccessful people. The difference is attitude. Successful people don't let themselves get stuck in the mental wheelchair. Successful people understand that the decision to stay in the wheelchair or to get out of it is theirs.

During our Border Cafe fiasco, I was in a mental wheelchair. I was frustrated, unfulfilled, feeling like a failure. I was letting something happen to me instead of accepting that I had a choice.

How many of us, at one time or another, have found ourselves in a "mental wheelchair"? We think about rising from it and walking down the path of success. Yet, instead of mustering every bit

---

How you manage your money will make you or break you. And your first obligation is to understand money.

---

of strength to do it, we wait for someone or something to do it for us—or simply decide that we are incapable of doing it.

The human mind is a powerful thing. I'm hardly the first person to observe that deciding that something is impossible has a devastating effect. I agree with it all: Thinking, progress, and effort all stop; hopes and dreams are abandoned.

Often, people don't make choices because they don't want to take responsibility. If someone is having trouble with every boss she works for, chances are she's doing something that's contributing to the problem. Yet, if you brought the issue up, you'd probably get a response like, "Oh, I'm stuck in this crappy place and instead of helping me, you're asking me questions."

Sometimes, a person can be stuck in a bad marriage but refuse to take responsibility and do something about it. Deep down, he may even hope that he, say, catches his wife cheating so that he can justify a breakup.

Until I went to Africa and had my epiphany about the loss of passion for Blimpie and the loss of passion for success, and until I accepted that whether to be negative or positive was my choice,

I was doomed to fail. Once I made the decision to accept responsibility and regain the passion, and once I realized that it was my attitude that was the problem, everything became possible.

If you think that successful people have positive attitudes just because they have money or a nice house or a fancy car, think again. In all likelihood, they had the right attitude in the first place. Whenever I give a speech, I always talk about passion and positive attitudes because I sincerely believe in their value. One night, after speaking to an alumni group at Fairleigh Dickinson University in New Jersey, a man from the audience approached me. "I'm in charge of many salespeople," he said, "I liked what you said about passion. Can you give me any advice as to how I can motivate my people as I go around the country?"

"Look, I responded, "there are two kinds of people out there, motivated ones and unmotivated ones." Motivated people can have temporary lapses when they lose their motivation, lose their passion. I know it. It happened to me. So, it's really worth spending time and reminding these folks about passion and attitude because they will get it. They'll say to themselves, "Oh, yeah, that's right, I do have a choice here." Regarding unmotivated people, well, that's like trying to get water to run uphill.

We have a choice to be "can" people or "cannot" people. We have a choice to use a challenge to become a better person rather than have it be a destructive force. It's our attitude that makes the difference. Is the glass half full or half empty? It's how we perceive it that matters.

Ignorance about Money and Profits

Right after we opened the first Blimpie, one of my partners got a tip on a horse that was running at Aqueduct Racetrack. I had to bet, I was told, because the horse was guaranteed to win.

I've never liked gambling. I don't like Las Vegas. I don't like Atlantic City. I'm not crazy about horseracing, and certainly have no interest in sports betting. I always figure that I work too hard for my money to put it at risk when the odds are stacked so heavily against me.

Nevertheless, probably because I felt compelled to go along with the crowd, this time I decided to take a chance. Edging up to the $100 window at Aqueduct, I placed $200 on Home Style in the fifth. It was a lot of money for me. It made me feel sick to my stomach. I couldn't believe I was gambling so much money on this "5-to-1 sure shot."

As my partners and I hugged the rail, the gates opened. My heart was pounding so hard that I thought the Blimpie logo would pop off of my shirt. At the halfway mark, Home Style was running fourth. Conza, you're finished, I thought. Do you know how many hours you are going to have to work to replace that $200?

Going into the stretch, I could see that our horse was beginning to come on strong. Now he was third, then second.

"Come on, you son of a bitch!" Angelo was shouting in my ear. It was neck and neck as the two leaders charged the finish line. Now I was screaming at the top of my lungs, "Come on, Home Style!"

Suddenly, it was over. The race had ended in a photo finish. Wait for a decision? What about my heart? I stared at the scoreboard for what seemed like forever until, flash, there it was. Was I reading it correctly? Did it say . . . ? No, it can't be. It is! Home Style won. I'm in the money. A thousand bucks.

I left Aqueduct thinking two things: "God, thank you for giving me this gift," and, "This is the last time I will ever gamble such a significant amount of money on anything."

I know some very intelligent people, people who are good with money, who like to gamble. I know that these folks do it out

> **There are no easy ways to make money. It comes from hard work, intelligent thinking and planning, a spirit of enterprise, and a little luck.**

of enjoyment and they are careful about what they are risking, so I don't have a problem with that. But people who gamble to "make a score" are committing the sin of ignorance about money and profits.

How you manage your money will make you or break you. And your first obligation is to understand money. If I said to you, for example, that you can guarantee every teenager in your household that he or she can become a millionaire, you'd probably think that I was about to give you some get-rich-quick scheme, right? Well, actually, without genius, specialized knowledge, risk, management expertise, or even good timing, achieving millionaire status *can* be guaranteed.

The secret is *compounding*. Here's how it works. Let's say two people, Mary and Bob, each contribute $2,000 a year to a tax-deferred IRA and buy quality bonds or other secure investments that yield 10 percent. Mary begins putting in money at age twenty-six and finishes at sixty-five, making forty contributions or $80,000. Bob also deposits $2,000 a year, but does it for only seven years, a total of $14,000. The trick is that Bob begins his contributions when he is nineteen.

Amazingly (and thanks to Dow Theory Letters, La Jolla, CA 92038, and Market Logic of Ft. Lauderdale, FL 33306 for these calculations), and you can check this out on any interest-rate table, Mary ends up with $893,000, an elevenfold increase. Bob, on the

---

The only way to get things done is to break your tasks into small, manageable pieces, write them down, prioritize, set aside quiet time, get whatever help you can, and then, like Nike, just do it.

---

other hand, earns sixty-seven times his original investment, ending with almost $1 million. (A different yield obviously would produce different results.)

Invest $14,000, end up with a million. Hmmm? Why would anyone not want to do that? Well, for one thing, compounding is boring. It requires patience. And it means you have to resist all those stockbrokers, Wall Street analysts, and financial commentators who try to convince you that you can earn a lot more, faster, in the market. Honestly, how many people do you know who have become millionaires by buying stocks? Oh, sure, if you're smart enough to pick the right stocks and buy them at the right price in a bull market, you'll probably do very well. If you select the wrong ones, or if you pay too much, or if you get caught in a bear market, you may not only miss the opportunity to become a millionaire, you may lose your money. And when that happens, it's tragic. Not only do you lose the money you've worked so hard to earn, you have also set yourself back in the time cycle.

Here's what people don't think about when they risk losing money in the stock market or in any other venture. Let's say you buy $10,000 worth of stocks and they decline 50 percent. The value of your investment is now $5,000. Just to get even, your stocks have to go up 100 percent. So, you lost 50 percent of your money, but you need a 100 percent increase to get it back. Your investment has to double.

Pay attention to the law of compounding. It's the easy way to riches. Most importantly, pay attention to how you budget, invest, and spend your money.

In the early days of Blimpie, the most unpopular person in our organization was Vic Mongelli. Vic was our accountant. We were always too busy for Vic. He'd wait hours, sometimes days, just to get us to even talk about finance. The guy selling Chiclets, even the insurance salesman, would get us to sit down with them before Vic could.

By not spending time understanding the financial side of the business, we were doing ourselves a real disservice. We paid for it dearly. Too late, we became aware of our high costs of operation. While we eventually were able to change suppliers and negotiate better deals to improve our profit picture, our financial situation

---

Does anyone care that you worked until two in the morning? What they care about is what you accomplished.

---

had gotten into such dire straits that it was too late to save ourselves. Had we paid attention to our accountant, we could have acted much more quickly and probably avoided having to sell off our first stores at distress prices. Worse than that, we could have avoided the complete loss of cash flow. Regardless of the fact that our stores were not making money, they were still generating a lot of cash. So, every day, we could expect to have money available to us. After the stores were sold, there was no more cash flow. Six percent of gross sales, our royalty fee, from a total of ten franchised stores was hardly sufficient to pay for company expenses and support the partners and employees as well.

In the 1980s, as we struggled with keeping a franchised chain, several company-operated Blimpie stores, and five bar/restaurants operationally functional, our accounting department found itself totally ill-equipped to maintain the financial side of the business. We had a better hand on things than we did in the early days of our chain but, generally speaking, incompetence reigned, which meant that from a financial perspective, we had lost control. Divestiture of our company-operated units coupled with bringing on a new controller and a new accounting department enabled us to save the day for our organization.

I get to witness a lot of successful entrepreneurs in my business. Some of them are great promoters. Some are great customer-service people. But all the really successful ones are good with money. They pay attention to the financials. They establish a rainy-day fund. They realize that repairs need to be made and equipment needs to be replaced and they begin saving now. They make friends with their banker and use procedures to help maximize their cash flow. They control their overhead. They pay their suppliers on time so, if a cash crunch ever arises, they'll be allowed more leeway.

What really bothers me is seeing operators who would be extremely successful were they not so bad about money. A franchisee came into my office with a heartbreaking story. He had been in the chain for more than twenty-five years. During that time, he has owned and operated an extremely successful store, one of the highest-volume Blimpie stores in the chain. However, for some reason, this guy has never been able to get his finances straight. Somehow, his credit is never good enough to enable him to borrow from a bank, a situation that has constantly driven him to high-rate finance companies. So, his payments are always too high. Regardless, you'd think that after franchising a highly successful business for more than twenty-five years, a business that generates enormous gross sales, that he'd be able to get out from under. No, the reason he was in our office was to ask us to try to help him avoid losing his store to the finance company. It seems that, for reasons I don't understand, his spending was such that he found himself borrowing more and more, and now he just couldn't make the payments. After twenty-five years, this poor guy lost his store because he couldn't control his business, or, apparently, his personal finances.

The messages here are straightforward. First, there are no easy ways to make money. It comes from hard work, intelligent thinking and planning, a spirit of enterprise, and a little luck. You won't find any pot of gold at the racetrack, in Las Vegas, or in a greed-is-good stock-market investment. And, if you do make money, no matter how much, unless you watch it closely and make certain that it truly ends up in your bank, stays within budgets, gets spent wisely, and gets invested so that you don't lose it, you will be wasting opportunity and placing yourself at risk.

Take the time to gain an understanding of money and profits. Then cast a vigilant eye in their direction. The sin of ignorance about money and profits is one you don't want to commit.

Failure to Set Goals

"Kick Saddam Hussein's butt out of Kuwait," was General H. Norman Schwarzkopf's mission set forth by President George Bush. The goal was clear. It was simple. It was easily articulated. It was something that every one of our troops could understand. The clarity of this goal enabled Schwarzkopf to wage Desert Storm so that he could be done and out of there in one hundred days. Think of how different that mission was from the one in Vietnam. To this day, I don't think anyone can clearly say what our goal there was.

Once a clear, simple goal is established, the steps necessary to reach that goal come into focus. One of the three simple goals that we set in 1988 was, "Have one thousand stores open and operating by 1995." No one had a problem understanding that. And, from there, the steps became clear. The first thing I knew was that we needed to become a national chain. That entailed many steps, but two stood out: One, build the system necessary to support a national chain, which required money. Two, begin to develop locations in a lot of different places at the same time.

The franchise method of distribution works so well because it combines the individual entrepreneur with the brand and the experience and support of the parent organization. In 1975, we took the franchise concept one step further and issued our first subfranchised territory. In the Blimpie International system, a subfranchisor is an individual or a group with a license to develop a certain geographic area. The cost of buying such a license depends on the population of the area—ten cents a person. That person buys the right—and, through a minimum development quota, the obligation—to expand business in the territory. Most of the time, this is done by subfranchising to individual store operators. The subfranchisor then protects the brand, enforces operational standards, acts as business consultant to the franchisee, and, of course, gets more Blimpie stores in the ground.

Before 1988, only a dozen subfranchises had been awarded. After we set our one thousand-store goal, we began a program to sell these licenses across the country in earnest. Soon, the ranks of area developers was expanding rapidly, generating much-needed capital for Blimpie International while expanding the chain in one city after another. Because we could now begin to project one hundred stores in Atlanta, twenty-five in Denver, thirty in Dallas, twenty in Grand Rapids, and so forth, our goal of one thousand was looking more and more realistic. Had that goal, however, never been articulated, how would we have known what path to follow?

Another example about our goal-setting relates to advertising. In the early years of Blimpie, we never had the foresight to establish any goals about national advertising. Consequently, none of the franchisees signed up in the 1960s were required to pay a percentage of their gross sales into advertising.

Contrast that with 1994 when, with all of our outlets paying 3 percent of sales for advertising, we decided to raise the fee to

---

Think about what you plan to do, sleep on it. Never make an important decision when you are impatient or when others are pressuring you to make the decision.

---

4 percent. Not wanting to have 750 stores pay 3 percent while number 751 paid 4 percent, we set a goal of having the 4 percent become effective when we reached the one thousand five hundred-store level. All the franchisees signed up during the period that the chain grew from seven hundred fifty to fifteen hundred stores were then prepared for the 4 percent goal. Our ad agency, marketing department, and the entire chain could then plan around the additional advertising dollars that achieving the goal would generate.

Goals are not just for companies. They're for us as individuals, too. And it's important that we always take a fresh look at where we are heading, so we can reassess and determine whether we are taking the steps necessary to accomplish our goals.

Suppose you are about to graduate college and are ready for the job market. The worst thing you could do is blindly send out a résumé to every company that runs a help-wanted ad in the newspaper. Instead, you have to set a personal goal. Determine the type of job you're interested in and the kind of environment you want to work in. If you don't enjoy being in a highly structured organization, then a finance-related job at a banking company is not the right job for you. First, seek out an industry that meets your goal, then specific companies within that industry where you might like to work. Once you reach your goal of a position with the right company for you, it's again time to take a fresh look and set a new goal of where you'd like to go in this organization. Then go for it. Come to work early. Leave later. Give the extra slice. Exhibit energy. Seek solutions. Show you're a team player. Whatever it takes to get you to your destination is what you should be doing.

Procrastination

I have a home in the country, in upstate New York, where it gets mighty cold in the winter. A good way to make the home more comfortable and to save heating costs as well, is to have enough wood on hand to keep the home fires burning all winter. I remember watching through a springtime and a summer as a pile of logs sat near the house waiting to be cut into firewood. Only after I cut

---

The world is full of opportunities. There's always another stock to buy, always another piece of real estate to secure, always another day when you can get married or buy a business. Don't procrastinate, but exercising a little patience before making a major decision is always a good idea.

---

the first log did I realize that my work had just begun. However, I also knew that I had finally done the most difficult part of the task, because the first step represented the commitment to completing the job.

In 1749, the Earl of Chesterfield proclaimed, "Never put off 'til tomorrow what you can do today." The earl was right then, and he'd be right now. Procrastination is the silent killer that wastes time, causes lost opportunities, and creates undue stress.

Unanswered phone calls, a computer screen of e-mails, letters to write, periodicals to read, a meeting to attend, and Joe Provolone who "must talk to you" at your office door.

When this happens to me, I put up my hand like a policeman at a traffic crossing and say to myself, "Stop!" If you stood on one side of the room and I threw five golf balls at you at the same time, chances are you wouldn't catch any of them. But if I threw them one at a time, you'd catch them all. The only way to get things done is to break your tasks into small, manageable pieces, write them down, prioritize, set aside quiet time, get whatever help you can, and then, like Nike, just do it. The only way to cut that pile of wood was to take each log—one at a time—and just do it.

Most of us work hard, but working hard is a given. It's what we get done that counts. Does anyone care that you worked until two in the morning? What they care about is what you accomplished.

Duke Ellington, the famous bandleader, said, "Without deadlines, baby, I wouldn't do nothing." Establish clear goals, set priorities and deadlines, then go out and accomplish your objectives.

Patience Is a Virtue

We must be careful not to procrastinate, but we must not confuse exercising patience with procrastination. I see too many of today's young people in a big hurry—to make more money, get a better job, buy a bigger house, make a quick killing in the market. Most have already figured out what their next step is and they are on the verge of taking it. My advice is always this: Slow down, think about what you plan to do, sleep on it. Never make an important decision when you are impatient or when others are pressuring you to make the decision.

After attending a sales presentation in a franchise organization, a prospect often will be so excited about becoming a franchisee that she will be ready to sign up right then and there. Before the institution of the Uniform Franchise Offering Circular, salespeople, hungry for commissions, would push these folks to execute a franchise agreement. The law now requires franchise companies to give a prospect ten days before they can take a prospect's money. During this cooling-off period, it is reasoned, clearer heads will prevail and someone who would make a decision of a lifetime may, after thinking about it, not act on impulse. Certainly pressure from the salesperson is off.

Entrepreneurs are people who, by definition, want to make things happen, so it's not the easiest thing for them to exercise patience. One instance in which the lack of patience sometimes prevails in our business is with location selection. Once a prospect becomes a franchisee, that prospect wants to get a store open as soon as possible. This becomes an issue when a good location, or perhaps the best location, is not readily available, so the franchisee begins to pressure a subfranchisor into letting him lease what we would consider a secondary location. He begins to justify the spot by exposing his plan for building a successful business there—giving out coupons, establishing a delivery service, running ads in the newspaper, and so on. None of those tactics is a

> **You don't learn just by the good things that happen. You learn by your bad experiences. You don't achieve success by having things go right for you all the time.**

substitute for a quality, high-visibility location—and that may require some patience. It's far better to exercise that patience than to pay dearly for mistakes of poor site selection.

Another place where patience needs to be exercised is the stock market. In the world of instant information, instant gratification, and instant quotations, it's very easy to lose sight of the big picture. And, in the market, the big picture is always whether the bull or the bear is in control.

In 1993, I went to Cigar Aficionado's "Big Smoke" gathering at Manhattan's Marriott Marquis. I never had much of an interest in cigars before that but, while I was there, I got the feeling that something big was happening. This cigar thing is going to boom, I thought. The next day, I did some research to determine what companies would benefit if a cigar boom did occur. I settled on a company named Culbro on the New York Stock Exchange and bought stock at $14 a share.

After about six months, during which time the stock had hardly budged, I got impatient. I thought, I'm going to take my money out of Culbro. I sold the stock at $15. My impatience was a major mistake. The next year, Culbro reported the greatest appreciation of all NYSE stocks, rising to $75 a share.

Patience sometimes means sitting and doing nothing while time passes. That's boring, and the urge is to do something, particularly when people around you are urging you to do. In a bull market, you need to take a substantial position and stick with it while letting time be your friend. In a bear market, you need to be ignoring whether McDonald's opened one hundred new stores in Japan or whether the Federal Reserve is meeting about interest rates.

My wife, brother, and daughter give me a hard time, mimicking my response to a request to make a decision: "What, you want me to answer you now?" They, of course, exaggerate my decision-making process, but there is no question that I like to think things through. I don't mean minor decisions. I'm referring to the kinds of decisions that have long-term consequences. I like to get input from others and have time just to reflect. Maybe my decision will be no different than had I made it instantly, but going through the process gives me the confidence that I did the right thing.

The world is full of opportunities. There's always another stock to buy, always another piece of real estate to secure, always another day when you can get married or buy a business. Don't procrastinate, but exercising a little patience before making a major decision is always a good idea.

Successful Failure

My friend Fran Tarkenton, a National Football League Hall of Fame member and a consultant to Blimpie International, wrote a book entitled *What Losing Taught Me About Winning*. The losses that Fran endured on the gridiron made him not only one of the greatest quarterbacks of all time, but also a very successful entrepreneur as well. Tarkenton says, "True entrepreneurs never expect to fail, but they also have no fear of failing because they don't see failure as terminal. They see it as a natural part of the process of learning and growing and developing their ideas and their businesses. They believe that if you haven't failed, you haven't tried very hard."

You don't learn just by the good things that happen to you. You learn by your bad experiences as well. You don't achieve success by having things go right for you all the time. When you make mistakes, face adversity, face failure; when you take a beating; when you're really hurting; when you feel really bad—that's when you'll find out what you're really made of. Only after you've been in a blinding snowstorm can you truly appreciate a warm, sunny day.

If what you are doing has any value whatsoever, than failing once in a while is inevitable. It's what you do with the failures that matters. Ultimately, success arrives as a result of our being able to handle and learn from the setbacks that are dealt to us.

I've failed many times during my thirty-five years of business, but I've come out stronger every time. Probably the greatest thing I learned about failure is not to let it become debilitating, not let it

---

Probably the greatest thing I learned about failure is not to let it become debilitating, not let it get me down. While failure can beat you up, you don't need to beat yourself up.

---

get me down. While failure can beat you up, you don't need to beat yourself up. If you do, it becomes that much harder to get back on track.

Admitting to failure in our Border Cafe venture was not easy. Having survived the early years of business through what seemed like an incredible series of miracles, it was tempting to keep looking for that miracle to happen again. It was hard to say, "We failed." Once we accepted that failure was an option, we were able to take action, in this case, by divesting ourselves of the restaurants. We closed Woodstock, sold the two Amsterdam's back to the founders, and sold the New York City Border Cafes to two separate groups.

Winning is such a part of the American psyche that it is hard to think of failure as an option. Vince Lombardi, the legendary Green Bay Packers coach, once said, "Winning is everything." In *Apollo 13,* they say, "Failure is not an option." Do you know anyone who goes into a bookstore to find a book on how to close down a business? Does anyone continue to see a team that keeps losing? Who buys stock in a company that comes out and says it is failing?

One of the biggest failures of the 1990s was that of Boston Chicken, later named Boston Market. The company, headed up by Scott Beck, Saad Nadhir, and Mark Stephens, the guys who built

Blockbuster into a national powerhouse, went public with Boston Chicken in 1993, and in 1996 the stock hit a high of $41. But by May 1997, the stock had been smashed to $20 and the decline never stopped. In 1998, the company filed under Chapter 11 of the bankruptcy laws, costing investors about $2 billion.

From the time Boston Chicken started, I was skeptical. I felt that its menu was too ambitious, too large. It invited too much waste. I also thought the rents were too high and that the company was booking income that didn't seem justified. That is, the company would raise funds from the public and lend the money to franchisees who would then use it to pay fees to the company. At one time, franchisees were in debt to Boston Chicken for $1 billion. When franchisees started to fail, the company would buy back the stores.

The only analyst who seemed to recognize what was going on with Boston Chicken was Roger Lipton. I know Roger because he had taken an interest in Blimpie International stock. For years, Roger warned against investing in Boston Chicken. Unlike so many Wall Street analysts who were hyping the stock, Roger saw that the ax would one day fall. He was sure about this, because he had been in the quick-service restaurant business, at one time owning fifteen Arthur Treacher's Fish & Chips outlets.

Roger saw the failure coming, but no one else would hear of it. Boston Chicken even blacklisted him, banning him from meetings. Roger was redeemed when the company could no longer avoid failure. Had the management of this company taken a fresh look and accepted failure as an option much sooner, it could have saved jobs and had the opportunity to turn things around.

Refusal to accept failure can be very costly. In retrospect, it was fortunate for us that we didn't have a big bank account when our restaurants were failing. If we did, or if we were able to keep going back to the public for more money, we may have prolonged the disaster. That would have cost us much more money and, worse, much more time. The loss of time is something that may not get considered in a failure but that can really hurt. How many Blimpie stores did we not open during the time lost? How much of a market share did we give up because we diverted our focus? While we were hanging in there, we were unaware of what other opportunities we were passing up.

Failure should not be denied. It should not be looked at as final. It should be viewed as part of the process of success. We mustn't hide from it, or let it wreck us emotionally. We should learn from it.

During our Border Cafe failure, I did a lot of soul-searching. I wanted to understand what part I played in the problem. I realized that I had failed to accept that we were entering a completely different business and that we were not then capable of doing two things at once. I concluded that there were no synergies between Blimpie and Border and that we did not have the capital necessary to grow both concepts. I learned that to successfully launch a venture like that, we needed a much stronger infrastructure. It didn't matter whether or not Border Cafe and Amsterdam's were good

---

Failure should not be denied. It should not be looked at as final. It should be viewed as part of the process of success.

---

concepts. What mattered was that we couldn't run them. It was like having a great race car, then putting it on the track with an incompetent driver.

We took this experience that came out of failure and applied it years later when we established our New Wave initiative and introduced a family of brands. By implementing New Wave, which I will cover in more detail later, we are calling on our learning without being risk-averse. If failure makes you afraid to take risks, that's no good either. Failure should make you a little more cautious. It should keep you from becoming complacent. It should take your enthusiasm and positive attitude—essential entrepreneurial qualities—and ground them in reality. It should make you avoid the "it won't happen to us" mentality and prepare you for a worst-case scenario.

Although failure is not something to be afraid of and turning a catastrophe into a bounty may be a positive thing to do, the most important thing you can learn from your bad experiences is that you should periodically step back, clear your mind, and take a fresh look at things.

Educated Incapacity

In 1992, when I participated in a program at NYU's Stern School of Business, I sat on a board of directors of a simulated corporation to which a group of students report. Other board members were professional businesspeople. One was Edith Weiner, the woman who was so enchanted with the story of how the name Blimpie was invented.

Edith is a futurist, a partner in a well-known market-research firm and a member of the board of directors of several large corporations and charitable institutions. While in Edith's presence, I had the good fortune to listen to some of her words of wisdom, including something that she referred to as *Educated Incapacity*, which means that when people become so knowledgeable, so experienced, so good at what they do, they become incapable of thinking that there may be another way of doing it.

An example is General Motors. GM built cars that, for years and years, captured a large share of the market. When the Japanese came in with a different approach to building cars, a different way of dealing with employees, a different way of running a company, GM ignored them. GM had a board of directors, stockholders, management, workers, and a union that "knew how to run an automobile company." They couldn't conceive of tossing out all that they knew and building a new organization from scratch. That's Educated Incapacity.

What about IBM? IBM owned the computer market. It owned technology. In 1990, IBM made what was then the largest profit ever for a corporation. IBM's problems, of course, began when a couple of guys named Jobs and Gates came along. IBM was convinced that there was no place in America for personal computers. Microsoft thought differently. IBM was suffering from Educated Incapacity. Later on, as Microsoft grew to a $250 billion company, the folks at IBM were spending their time staving off bankruptcy.

Educated Incapacity can afflict a person, a department, or an entire organization. And when it does—especially in today's fast-paced marketplace—it can be deadly.

Don't Be an Enabler

Drop a frog into a pot of boiling water and the frog will quickly leap out. Place a frog in a pot of cool water and slowly bring the water to a boil, the frog will sit there until it cooks to death.

During the 1980s, New Yorkers were like the second frog. They loved their city because it was a great city, but slowly, the quality of life in New York deteriorated. The system was breaking down and New Yorkers found themselves in a pot that was ready to boil.

The problem was that the mayors and the law-enforcement people had become enablers. Do you know that word? An *enabler* is a term used in alcohol- and drug-treatment programs. An enabler "goes along," or makes excuses for the user. "My dad only drinks once in a while," or, "Son, you've got to stop smoking pot. Haven't I told you a million times?" Yeah, and keep telling him. If you're trying to teach kids how to behave, you tell them to do something once or twice and you explain why. By the third time,

---

> **Failure should make you a little more cautious. It should take your enthusiasm and positive attitude—essential entrepreneurial qualities—and ground them in reality.**

---

either the kid follows your advice or there have to be consequences. If there weren't any consequences, why would the person change his or her habits?

In New York, criminals at all levels were getting away with it. Officials had become enablers: "Well, that's against the law and it's bad, and yes, we know it hurts the community, but . . ." Once you say "but," you're finished. No one pays attention.

In 1992, Rudy Giuliani was elected mayor. After he took a fresh look, he determined that a major change was in order. Giuliani went after the small crimes and the little quality-of-life disturbances. He stopped the panhandlers, the windshield washers, the petty drug dealers, and all the people who were making New York a bad place to live. He stepped up police presence and cleaned up the streets, the parks, the subways. He made examples of those who committed crimes and, before long, the word was out. Don't screw around in New York City, or you will pay. As a result, New York became a clean, safe, enjoyable place to live, which led to New York becoming an economic boomtown.

If you have kids or if you are a businessperson, stop and take a fresh look to see whether you are being an enabler. Make sure you send the message that these are rules, and that if the rules are not followed, there will be a price to pay.

Blimpie International Takes a Fresh Look

In 1991, the theme of our convention in Tampa was "Take A Fresh Look at Blimpie." At that convention, we displayed the new us. Franchisees had the opportunity to get a glimpse at all the changes that we had made since the rebirth of our organization in the late 1980s: the Blimpie Business School, our new training facility, the design department in Houston, the research and development facility in New York, the reengineered store-serving area and store look, the fresh baked bread, the marketing and advertising strategy, and the growth in store development. Franchisees were exposed to all the ideas, opportunities, equipment, innovations, and programs that would help them grow. And it all happened because we stopped and took a fresh look.

Reexamine Your Perceptions

The day after I arrived in Tanzania on my African journey, my cousin Geri sent me to beautiful Bahari Beach on the Indian Ocean with her roommate, Terunesh, a young Ethiopian woman whom Geri had befriended while living there.

On the way to the beach, I asked Terunesh and the driver, named Solimani, to pass by the post office and take a quick tour through town so I could take some photos and send a few post cards. "Now, don't photograph government buildings or military personnel," Geri had warned. I wasn't exactly clear why, but I knew it had something to do with security and, I guess, superstition.

To capture the true flavor of the city, Solimani took us down a very busy street, which bordered a marketplace packed with people. Because we were nowhere near government buildings, I rolled the window down in the back seat of the car and began snapping photos. Almost immediately, a man on a bicycle approached the car and started to scream, "No picture, no picture!" which generated a reaction from the normally mild Terunesh as she began to argue with him in Swahili. With coaxing from Terunesh, Solimani proceeded forward, but got stalled because of traffic. This time, the man defiantly took his bicycle and planted it directly in front of our car. Now, Solimani had nowhere to go. As the argument accelerated to a loud pitch, a truck behind us, frustrated with the delay, began blowing its horn. By now, we were creating a full-fledged commotion. As I kicked my camera under the seat and out of sight, a large crowd converged on the car. "Oh my God," I thought. "They're gonna turn the car upside down and set us on fire!"

After what seemed like an eternity, Solimani, who never displayed a tinge of emotion throughout any of this, eased his way around the bike and proceeded forward, inducing the crowd to back away. At that moment, my whole perception of the Tanzanian people changed. I realized that violence was the last thing on anyone's mind. The crowd was just curious, and the screaming man, well, according to Terunesh, he was just looking for some money. From that moment on, I was able to feel comfortable in these surroundings.

Things aren't always what they seem.

CHAPTER 6

STOP, LOOK, AND LISTEN . . . THEN TALK: HOW TO COMMUNICATE MORE EFFECTIVELY

You ain't learnin' nothing when you're talkin'.

—Lyndon Johnson

It's not easy to get your ideas across when you are shy. I was a quiet kid, and, even though I had started a business, I was a quiet grownup, too. My partner was the front man and I watched the checkbook. (I even earned a nickname, "Steel Eyes," because of the way I would stare when someone asked me to write a check and I said no, knowing that our bank account was empty.)

After Peter DeCarlo and I split up, I was forced into representing the company. I began to accept the role of CEO, but I knew that I had to conquer my shyness. My first real test came after the rebirth of Blimpie International, as our area-developer network unfolded and a lot more subfranchisors entered the system. I knew that we needed to have a convention, and a convention meant that I would have to give a speech. How could we have a convention without the CEO giving a speech?

Some people would prefer ten root canals to standing on a public-speaking podium. I was one of them. It had become increasingly obvious to me, however, that I didn't have a choice. Communication was an essential ingredient to reaching our goals. I was the founder of Blimpie. I was now the chairman of our company. I had to lead. I had to communicate. And it would have to begin with me doing the one thing in the world that I feared the most—giving a speech in front of a large group of people.

The words of Saint Francis of Assisi resonated: "Start by doing what's necessary. Next do what's possible. Soon you'll be doing the impossible." I had already come to believe that after I turned my typical three-mile jog into a ten kilometer, then a half-marathon, then a three-hour, twenty-five-minute, twenty-six-mile marathon. I learned it when I became a pianist in my forties. I learned it when I regained the passion for Blimpie and experienced a rebirth of our business. Now I was about to learn that I could become a public speaker.

Despite the obstacles, people with a fierce determination to succeed at something will often end up doing it better than people with a natural ability. People with no fear of speaking in public often do it without a lot of preparation—and it shows. In 1990, for our first

> **Despite the obstacles, people with a fierce determination to succeed at something will often end up doing it better than people with a natural ability.**

subfranchisor conference, I set out to give a good speech. I thought about the message I wanted to convey. Focusing on my audience, I carefully planned my presentation and my delivery. Then I practiced and practiced, repeating the speech over and over, changing it, tweaking it, rehearsing it, until I was certain that I could do it. It was a success and I've been giving speeches ever since.

If communication sounds like a lot of work, it is. It requires effort because what you say, how you say it, and how often you say it are all important. The more you communicate with people, the better off you will be. Tell people what's going on, tell them how they're doing, tell them about the company, let them know why decisions are being made, and listen to what they have to say.

There was actually one advantage to my being shy: It made me a listener. I found listening a lot easier than talking, but I was able to take my observations and channel them positively and creatively. My listening helped me sort things out so I could learn how to communicate. When you're not talking, you're listening. When you *are* talking, you're *not* listening, and if you're always

Our first store, in Hoboken, New Jersey, which we opened in 1964. This was a proud day for my partners, Angelo Baldessare and Peter DeCarlo, and me, shown here with two local politicians.

BLIMPIES

No.		GIANT	HALF
1.	Pressed Ham - Salami - Cheese	65¢	35¢
2.	Ham - Cappacola - Cheese	75¢	40¢
3.	Prosciuttini - Cappacola - Cheese	85¢	45¢
4.	Super (Combination of # 2 & # 3	95¢	50¢
5.	Bologna - Cheese	60¢	35¢
6.	Pepperoni - Cheese	75¢	40¢
7.	Turkey - (White Meat)	95¢	50¢
8.	Cheese	60¢	35¢
9.	Roast Beef	$1.00	55¢
10.	Corn Beef	95¢	50¢

FRIDAY SPECIALS: Tuna - Egg Salad - Cheeses

AVOID WAITING - PHONE EARLY — OL 9-3610

Our first menu, on the back of a business card, for our first store in Hoboken. I've kept it as a memento all these years, to remind me of how far I've come.

I first realized that "You can do anything if you put your mind to it" came when my father made up his mind that if he wanted to own a house, he'd build it himself. Of course, I helped.

When I was seven years old, I told my parents I wanted to learn to play the piano. Because they couldn't afford to buy me a piano, though, they encouraged me to learn the accordion. It wasn't the same, but I enjoyed it anyway...

...and 35 years later, I resumed my goal. It's never too late to try something new or set new goals for yourself!

I ran my first marathon in New York City in 1981 — and I didn't even start jogging until I was 35 years old. So it took me 3 hours and 36 minutes; I'm still proud to have run it and experienced the thrill of that day!

With one of my fellow Governors of the Boys & Girls Clubs, Colin Powell.

Coca-Cola has been a big part of Blimpie since we opened our first store: it's our beverage of choice. Roberto Goizueta, the late CEO of Coca-Cola, was a good friend, and he knew something about success: during his 16-year tenure at Coca-Cola, he increased the company's stockholder value 3500 percent — from $4 billion to $150 billion!

I'm also proud to have worked with former President Jimmy Carter to build a Boys & Girls Club with the Habitat for Humanity. My wife, Yvonne (third from left) and Roxanne Spillett, President of the Boys and Girls Clubs of America (far left), were also part of our team that day in Plains, Georgia.

On October 4, 1999, the day I received the President's Award, Blimpie International presented a $100,000 donation to the Boys and Girls Clubs of America to support violence prevention. On hand to accept it were (left to right) Peter Haynes, Chairman, Boys & Girls Clubs, Roxanne Spillett, President of the Clubs, and my wife Yvonne is with me to make the donation.

Courtesy of the Boys & Girls Clubs of America.

In 1996, I carried the torch in the Olympics in Manhattan — another achievement I'm really proud of.

I was also honored when Al Gore invited me to participate in a business development in the inner cities discussion with other CEOs at the White House. Also present at this meeting were Robert Rubin and SBA Administrator, Aida Alvarez.

At the 1998 awards ceremony of the Boys & Girls Clubs of America, I presented an award to Ted Turner "for outstanding corporate leadership in the future." Ted has been a major supporter for the Boys & Girls Clubs, and it was an honor for me to present him with this award.

Atlanta mayor Bill Campbell and I announced that Atlanta would be one of the cities in which Blimpie International would launch our Empowerment Zone Development Program.

In 1998, I was invited by the Tampa Bay Devil Rays baseball team to throw out the first ball at the third game of their opening season, and Bobby Smith was my catcher that day. I was thrilled at the prospect; unfortunately, it never occurred to me until that day that I probably should have practiced throwing a few balls before actually going out in front of 35,000 fans! Luckily, all went well — but you can never be too prepared in life!

When my ad agency, Kirshenbaum, Bond and Partners, created a new campaign for Blimpie a few years ago, they realized that I had such a passion for our sandwiches that I should display that passion in our commercials.

This is the view from my Blimpie office in New York City. Sometimes, I look out the window at the fabulous Empire State Building, and I think about how far I've come from our first little store in Hoboken to an international chain of more than 2,100 stores. It's times like these that I realize that success really is a beautiful thing!

talking, you never hear what the other person has to say, you'll never know what's on the other person's mind, and you will never be an effective communicator. Effective communication begins where effective listening leaves off, so the first rule of communication is to shut up and listen.

Tony's Take

In February 1990, Blimpie International engaged a new health-insurance carrier. The changes in coverage and deductibles raised so many questions among staffers that I thought I should respond myself, so I wrote a two-page memo to all employees explaining the company's reasons for changing insurance carriers and why the new policy would benefit both the company and its employees.

Writing the memo got me thinking: Health insurance couldn't be the only employee concern. Probably everything that happens in our company affects or interests our employees. Thus began a weekly letter that's now called *Tony's Take*. I thought it would be a good way to communicate regularly with our staff—to explain why decisions were made, to ask for advice and ideas, to open up my thoughts, and to let everyone in on things.

Tony's Take was difficult, but I took it very seriously. Even though I wrote it and it set forth my thoughts, it also became a compilation of the thoughts, conversations, and ideas of all senior executives. I promised our staff that what I included in *Tony's Take* would help them with their jobs, with better understanding their company, with business, and with life in general. Often, I'd include something just for a laugh or because it was simply interesting reading.

At first, *Tony's Take* was written exclusively for Blimpie International staff members but, in 1995, I decided to send it to our sub-franchisors, too. That was a difficult decision. When you express your opinion, you'll occasionally say something that somebody doesn't like, so expanding the audience meant that I would also be increasing the likelihood of offending somebody.

However, I'm more sure than ever that it's a good idea. In fact, several CEOs from other companies have informed me that they liked my idea so much that they have implemented similar communications in their own organizations.

Progress Reports

Our staff really enjoyed *Tony's Take*. It gave them the opportunity to hear what was on my mind every week. What about what was on *their* minds? I began to wish that I had ten minutes to chat with every company employee every week. I know they're full of ideas and thoughts and I'd love to hear them. Time and geography make that too difficult, so I invented *progress reports.*

Progress reports were not intended to be time sheets—not in any way, shape, or form. I made it clear that my interest was in learning how staff members spent their time and what they were accomplishing. Progress reports also presented an opportunity for staff members to offer suggestions and ideas that would be valuable to us.

Time and time again, the combination of *Tony's Take* and progress reports has proven a very effective method of communication for us. One such time occurred in the summer of 1992.

The more you communicate with people, the better off you will be. Tell people what's going on, tell them how they're doing, tell them about the company, let them know why decisions are being made, and listen to what they have to say.

Blimpie International was much smaller then but, in the space of a couple of weeks, two key employees from our operations department left Blimpie for higher-paying jobs. Just before I left for vacation in early September, I read that week's progress reports and saw a rash of comments regarding the two departures. I knew that our staff thought we were having a real problem keeping employees happy. I also knew that my initial plan of skipping *Tony's Take* because of my vacation that week was a bad idea. So, I wrote one, and it began like this:

> A Top 40 tune repeats the phrase "Please Don't Go" for what seems like 100 times. But I seriously doubt that the vocalist will get his girlfriend back just because he says "Please Don't Go." No, the problem likely goes deeper than that.
>
> The recent departure of Craig and Sean was further followed by a rash of comments from you. Yes, some of you are trying to tell me

that we may have a serious problem here. And I'm listening, so thanks for speaking up.

I hope by now you all realize how important you are to me and to Blimpie International. And if you are not happy, I want to know why. Of course, if this is strictly a money issue for some people, then there may not be a simple solution. Are we underpaying our staff, or maybe certain members of our staff, or are you part of a growing company that can afford only so much, so you must sacrifice [now] to get to the future?

Ben and Jerry, the ice cream entrepreneurs, have received much publicity because of their rule that the highest-paid company person cannot earn more than ten times the lowest-paid. Well, Ben and Jerry may have gotten the p.r., but I can assure you that, as the highest-paid person in Blimpie International, I earn much less than ten times the lowest.

Should we all earn more money? Well, ponder this: If everyone got just a 10% raise, it would cost the company [a lot of money], causing a dent in earnings. Don't forget, stockholders have the right to earn, too.

I have felt that everyone who stays with us and helps us grow is deserving. And we've tried to "piece you in" to profits of the company with a 10% bonus plan, a 401(k), stock options, etc. Unless you haven't been listening, you are aware that no one cares more for our staff than I do. So, if there is a problem here, for sure I want to fix it. It may be that each of you [has] to make a choice: higher current salary with another company (instant gratification) vs. less—or no—future growth. Or perhaps the answer lies in getting more productivity from fewer people. After all, the bottom line on salaries is a dollar amount, which has nothing to do with the number of employees we have. [Fewer] employees performing the same tasks would mean more money to those performing.

In any event, this is a very, very important issue, which must be addressed. I want to get to the bottom of this. "Please Don't Go" until I do.

I concluded the letter with a quote from Fran Tarkenton. "Beware the big play: The 80-yard drive is better than the 80-yard pass."

What may have seemed like an insignificant bit of information that employees included in their progress reports turned out to have a profound effect on the company. A human-resources committee turned into a human-resources department, employee profit-sharing plans and awards were expanded, and I stepped up my efforts to keep people informed by using *Tony's Take* to express our no-secrets, open-book management policy. I stressed the need to understand our financial statements and stock ownership. "Don't underestimate what can happen to our stock if we all

---

Effective communication begins where effective listening leaves off, so the first rule of communication is to shut up and listen.

---

pursue the same objective," I said in the December 1, 1992, issue. How true that proved to be.

As a direct line to me, progress reports gave Blimpie people a way to convey information, seek my advice or help in solving a problem, or just let me know how they are dealing with a situation. And, finally, they also could be used to tell a funny or interesting story.

To this day, I read every progress report every week. What I like most about them is that they give everyone in our company equal time. There are people in every organization who know how to work themselves into the communications system so they can always get their messages heard. And, of course, there are those who like to complain and are often the most vocal. But a progress report combined with *Tony's Take* is like being able to hold a private conversation with each employee. Regardless of how shy a person may be or how distant they feel from the boardroom, they can send a message directly to me.

The National Franchisee Advisory Council

Thanks to Pat Pompeo, who led the charge in the state of Georgia, our Atlanta franchise system had grown rapidly throughout the late 1980s. Growth often exposes problems, however, and in 1990, the Atlanta Blimpie franchisees let us know that they had a problem with Blimpie International. They asked Pat for a forum through which they could let us know what was on their minds. Pat scheduled a meeting and I flew to Georgia to listen. With a lawyer present, the franchisees laid out six issues of concern, most of which we consolidated into the following: training, marketing, purchasing, enforcement of standards, location selection, and franchisee recruitment (including franchisees who desired to open additional stores). They were also looking for guidance, leadership, and planning.

After listening to the franchisees, I decided that they most wanted something they had never mentioned—communication. To me, it was obvious that what they were really saying was, "Hey, Blimpie International, you are not listening to us. You are not hearing what we are crying out, so how can we trust you?" We had to demonstrate to our franchisees that we cared, that we were very concerned about their success, and that we were prepared to address the issues that they had placed before us. I always try to put myself in the shoes of the next person, whether it's the franchisee, the receptionist, or a family member or friend. I want to understand them, so I can address them and make sure they understand me. If they don't understand me, I've wasted my time. "Do you care about me?" is the unspoken question on people's mind. That question has to be addressed.

Pat and I were determined to satisfy franchisees' needs while making certain that they were aware of our sincerity so, in October 1990, we hired a private consultant named Marilyn Benveniste. She had eighteen years' experience in human-resource development, and our agreement called for her to probe the minds of all the Blimpie people in Georgia—both franchisees and company staff—with the goal of improving Blimpie in that state. Six months later, Blimpie International called a meeting at which I gave a speech outlining our response to the issues raised and the actions that we planned to take.

Although the steps we took satisfied the franchisees who raised them, I realized that we needed a permanent method of dealing with concerns of franchisees beyond those in Georgia. After all, there would always be new issues and new franchisees, so we needed a formal way to facilitate communication nationally in our expanding enterprise.

Nowhere is the concept of partnership more important than in franchising. Franchise systems draw their strength from a team approach. Unless there is trust among the players and unless everyone—company staff, franchisees, and subfranchisors—is involved in the decision-making, the team will never truly succeed.

Although Blimpie International may have the right to demand certain things from franchisees, only the franchisees have the power to satisfy those demands. Yes, we may get grudging compliance but, unless they understand what has to be done, understand what the goals of the business are, and understand why it makes sense to go along with the reasoning behind those goals, we may never get a united front and never truly reach success.

Listening to the franchisees of Georgia was enlightening. Franchisees needed a platform and Blimpie International needed to have an ongoing dialogue with them. I set out to establish the Blimpie National Franchisee Advisory Council.

David Holt, a good, successful operator, was a veteran Blimpie franchisee. I felt that he had leadership qualities and that, while he was fair, he would not be perceived as a company man. This council could not be effective if the person leading it was perceived to be a pushover for Blimpie International. Skeptical as David was, he agreed to lead the council.

As expected, earning trust was the biggest challenge and, in the beginning, the lack of trust made things difficult. Nevertheless, we held quarterly meetings of NFAC, sometimes traveling to a city and conducting a town meeting with local franchisees as well. Along with several other senior company executives, I attended NFAC meetings, which went a long way toward building franchisee trust. By 1993, NFAC, along with SFAC, a similar council of subfranchisors, had become significant communication venues for our organization.

"Both of the councils have become important foundations and positively impacted the chain," David Holt was quoted as saying. Lisa Knopf, a Long Island operator and council member, summed up the positive effects of NFAC when she said, "Blimpie International, while stressing the value of growth, places a great heap of money and energy in servicing and supporting new and existing franchisees. Their goal is to make each outlet more profitable, and yes, make more profit for themselves in the process."

Lisa's words brought into focus the result of about one-and-a-half years of communication between Blimpie and NFAC. It's not that our goals had changed during this period, it's that the franchisees now understood that our goals were aligned with theirs.

Life is no different. We all have to interact with other people, whether it's our bosses, our fellow employees, our friends, our employees, or our children. Communication becomes the essential ingredient in making sure these folks help us achieve our goals while we help them achieve theirs.

Success is dependent on communication. A perfect example occurred with Blimpie in the mid-'90s. Blimpie International, believing that a major shift was taking place in retailing, began to place some units in convenience stores—something unheard of before. To really take advantage of this opportunity, Blimpie knew that it had to get the subfranchisors on board with the program. So, in 1993, Blimpie called a special meeting of SFAC to communicate the goal of developing numerous outlets—not only in convenience stores but in a variety of other nontraditional venues as well, such as college campuses, hospitals, bowling alleys, gas stations, truck stops, and so on. By the end of the day, all of us, together, had established a strategic plan that would take advantage of the nontraditional opportunity. We had figured out how we were going to generate this new business, finance and service the program, and convince all subfranchisors that this was a once-in-a-lifetime opportunity for all of us.

The result of that meeting was nothing short of incredible. Over the ensuing years, the Blimpie chain has grown by hundreds of outlets in nontraditional venues. It happened only because we had established a forum in which such matters could be discussed and because, through constant communication, trust had been built and a solid relationship established between the company and our area developers.

Engendering Trust

Without communication, there can be no trust and, without trust, there can be no success. In the franchise business, if you don't have good communication with your operators, you may as well throw away all your brand strategies, all your support systems, and all your hard work.

At home or in the workplace, there must be principles and standards that we have to stick by, but, when there's a problem, effective communication is the best way to solve it. There's a big difference between just talking and communicating. You have to make the connection so you don't cause a breach in trust. Once you get into a discussion with someone about what the rules are, you'll find yourself in the middle of an argument, and then you lose even if you win. Sure, you can force a teenager to clean up her room, or require a franchisee to clean up his store but, unless you get them to believe that it's the right thing to do and to do these tasks willingly, you'll be forcing them to do it every time.

Ed Koch, the former mayor of New York City, used to go around asking the city residents, "How'm I doing?" People really appreciated that question, because it gave them a chance to tell Koch what was on their mind. And often, just giving people the opportunity to express themselves is enough.

I travel the country a lot and, when I do, I always try to meet with local Blimpie store operators. Of course, they want to hear from me what's going on in the company and maybe a little history of the chain, but then I ask them, "So, what's going on with *you?*" Generally, there's at least one person in the group who will voice a concern or lodge a complaint. Now, if it's a legitimate concern, one that needs attention, I'll make sure it gets taken care of. The reason I know that simple communication is generally the answer is because, invariably, franchisees from coast to coast are bothered by the same things, things that have to do with not clearly understanding the goals of the Blimpie brand.

Here's one that I hear all the time: "Tony, the company should spend more time helping us increase our business instead of just opening stores." My response is to urge them look closely at the company's many programs to help franchisees build business. I tell them why it's so important to have a lot of stores in one market: The more stores we have, the more funds go into advertising, and that benefits everyone. And more stores mean greater purchasing power for the chain, which translates into lower prices for store owners.

That's the point where one or two other operators may join in and express the positive aspects of unity and teamwork and how the company cannot benefit unless the franchisees benefit. Because I didn't just go there to have them listen to me, I always walk away from a group like this having established a relationship with them. I listened to them. I gave them the opportunity to express themselves. They knew that what was on their minds was important to me. I had gained their trust. The most important thing to remember here is that it's not necessarily what you have to say that's important; it's what you let the other person say.

Some people are out to win every discussion. You know the type, they never shut up. Instead, they get loud and they attack. These people may appear to win because others just don't want to hear them anymore. But is that winning? Winning is when everyone walks away from a discussion feeling good. People are not interested in your proving that you are right. They want to know that they are being heard and that their opinion counts, too. If everyone walks away from a discussion feeling that they are closer to achieving their goals, *that's* winning.

Keep Your Promises

One of the most important ways of communicating comes into play when you make a promise:"Honey, I have to travel this week, but I'll definitely be home on Thursday so I can see you in the school play." Suppose you make that promise to your daughter. Then, when Thursday arrives, she gets a call from you saying, "I'm sorry, honey, but something came up and I'm going to have to stay in Los Angeles one more day." How many times do you think your daughter will let you do that to her before she loses all trust in you and decides that your promises are worthless? If you build a relationship where a person can rely on your promises, you will have built the trust that you need in order to accomplish your objectives. You want to be able to say, "Bob, if you do this, this will be the result." If he trusts you, he will do it.

Have you ever been promised a delivery and then been stood up? Have you ever been sold something, only to discover that it's not what you expected? You probably would have gotten upset enough that you wanted never to deal with the people involved again.

The introduction of our new advertising materials generated a lot of enthusiasm, and rightly so. Radio and TV spots, print ads, and other collateral material was researched thoroughly and professionally executed. The ads positioned our product well, they got the Blimpie name across, and they even entertained. They also did one more very important thing—they made a promise to the customer.

Anyone who views, listens to, or reads one of our ads will get the clear message that a Blimpie restaurant is clean and attractive, the staff polite, friendly, and well-trained, and the meats and cheeses real, fresh food. The customer will expect those promises to be filled. If they aren't, the customer will be disappointed and perhaps turned off to Blimpie in the future. Our advertising materials have been designed to tell the public that Blimpie is simply better than our competition. We must deliver on that promise.

"A product is a thing, but a brand is a promise," says Jack Stahl, president and CEO of Coca-Cola in North America. At one time, there was no need for a brand. If you needed a pair of shoes, for example, you went to the cobbler and he made them for you. You knew him and you knew what to expect. Then mass production came along. Even when the local cobbler still made the shoes, retail stores sold them. You wouldn't know that they were his shoes unless he put a name on them. In other words, he needed to brand the shoes.

If I placed a box in front of you—no printing, no labels, just a plain box—you wouldn't have a clue as to what was inside it. Take the same box and put a Nike label on it. Suddenly, you not only know what's in the box, but you begin to have feelings about its contents. You can talk about features, colors, benefits, and even offer your own opinion. Now, take the same box, but with a different label, say Timberland. Still shoes, but your expectations change to fit a different brand. And, if the same Nike box had a Goretex sticker on it, once again your expectations would change because Goretex would tell you that the product was waterproof as well.

That's powerful stuff. That's what a brand promise is about. Basically, there are four aspects to a brand name:

- The most obvious is the trademark. Do people see it? Recognize it? Respect it?

- The user. Who used the brand? When we think of McDonald's, our image is that of families. Pepsi suggests the young generation, the MTV crowd. IBM conjures up different people all over the world.

- Usage. Where is the brand used? How does it fit into the consumer's life? A Range Rover goes up steep hills and over rugged terrain. A Dirt Devil quickly cleans up a mess at home.

- Associations. Nike is linked with sports. Delta gets you to Disney World. American Express will handle your charges at the best hotels, restaurants, and stores in the world.

Help People Anticipate Problems

Our experience in franchising has led us to label a common occurrence in a subfranchisor territory, the *twenty-store syndrome.*

Franchisees who have recently come on board are the most pleasant to deal with. They are like kids who have stepped into

Disneyland for the first time. They're excited, they're full of energy, and they have lots of hopes and dreams. Veteran franchisees know the franchise game, and, most important, run profitable stores. In between, though, is potential danger, generally lurking two to three years into a territory's growth, about the time that a subfranchisor has opened fifteen to twenty-five stores.

Rather than wait for the twenty-store syndrome to strike, right from the beginning subfranchisors are warned about committing these mistakes:

- Poor franchisee selection

- Poor subfranchisor communication

- Lack of operational support

- Failure to enforce standards

- Insensitivity to franchisee needs

One or all of these factors either affects the franchisee performance, creates the perception that their performance is being affected, or builds mistrust and gives them an excuse to blame the subfranchisor for poor performance. If a subfranchisor allows the mistakes to occur, the problems will surface two or three years down the line. How the subfranchisor prepares for this potential crisis and how it is encountered when and if it occurs will determine the future of the territory. It could end up simply being a speed bump on the highway to success, or a major roadblock from which the territory may never recover. By making subfranchisors aware of the challenges, we help them avoid the twenty-store syndrome.

Napoleon said, "There are no bad soldiers, only bad officers." Subfranchisors are responsible for the success or failure of their franchisees and for avoiding twenty-store syndrome. The ways that they can do that provide general valuable lessons in communicating with people:

- Begin with the selection process. If you are going to need involvement with others to achieve success for yourself, look for motivated people. You can't motivate someone who is not motivated in the first place. Unmotivated people will be problems and will create problems.

- Be a leader. Provide guidance, get consensus, demonstrate the need for action, keep people excited.

- Keep people informed. The easiest way for someone to shirk responsibility is to claim, "Nobody told me." Without information, people have an excuse. With it, they have none.

- Provide necessary support. Don't just leave people on their own. Help them as much as possible.

- Enforce the rules. Once you let people get away with breaking the rules, you're asking for trouble.

- Be open and up front. Don't hide things. Don't give one person a deal that you're not prepared to give to another. Avoid conflicts of interest. And never lie or promise something that you are not prepared to deliver.

What's Your Twenty-Store Syndrome?

Whatever life paths you choose to follow, you can bet that others have traveled there before. Rather than risk encountering problems that could seriously throw you off track, it would be more prudent to anticipate those problems.

Suppose you just got married and are planning to have two children. Your relationship would benefit if you and your spouse learned all you could about the challenges you'd probably face because of your plan. Kids get sick, they interfere with your quiet time, they keep you up nights, they're demanding, they require a

---

If you are going to need involvement with others to achieve success for yourself, look for motivated people. You can't motivate someone who is not motivated already.

---

lot of financial support, they hinder travel plans, and so on. If both of you know about those things and anticipate the consequences, you'll be fine. However, if you expect your lives to roll merrily along as they had in the past, you'll have a couple of beautiful children under your arms, but you'll also get smacked with your own version of the twenty-store syndrome. You'll be very unhappy.

Watch Your Expectations

There are two kinds of expectations.

The first concerns how you expect other people to behave—even though you have no control, or right to control, their behavior. These expectations will bring you only disappointment or anger because you expect one thing and you get another.

The second kind of expectation is the one that you must make clear to the other person. In other words. You state how you expect the other person to behave and make clear that if that person behaves differently, there will be consequences.

Some examples:

"If you don't open ten locations in your area in the next two years, you will lose your development rights."

"Don't expect a raise until you have met your quota for six months."

"You are going to have to earn the money yourself."

Show Personal Integrity

Don't speak badly about a third party, it only makes *you* look bad. It makes a person realize that he can't trust you because you obviously are prepared to talk behind his back.

Don't deceive people. Don't speak down to them or say things that are undignified.

Apologize

The words "I'm sorry" are magical, yet sometimes we find them so difficult to say. Everybody makes mistakes, which is why people are prepared to forget someone else's. All they want is an apology—not a cover-up. Try to cover up a mistake and you will never be trusted again. Admit to your mistake and you remove the other person's argument.

In the process of turning around Continental Airlines in 1995, Greg Brenneman and Gordon Bethune set out on a "forgiveness campaign." They divided angry customer letters among officers and started making phone calls to apologize and explain how they were fixing the company. They did the same with travel agents and corporate customers. "People were incredibly frustrated and wanted us to know how badly they had been treated. By the end of the call, however, they were usually appreciative that an officer of the company had taken the time to seek them out. People couldn't believe we were coming around to say we were sorry," says Brenneman.

Don't Underestimate What's Important to the Next Person

Never minimize the importance of something to another person just because you don't see it as important yourself. I remember when we were renovating our house in upstate New York, my wife, Yvonne, mentioned several times how we should consider redoing our bathroom. I didn't think it was necessary, so I ignored her while making arrangements to do the driveway, the deck, the

---

The easiest way for someone to shirk responsibility is to claim, "Nobody told me." Without information, people have an excuse. With it, they have none.

---

pool, some painting, and numerous other details around the house. Finally, Yvonne sat me down and said, "Tony, you know we like to have guests at our house, right?" "That's right," I said. "Well, did you ever consider the fact that it's somewhat uncomfortable for a lady to have to go downstairs with a towel wrapped around her so she can use the shower? Don't you think with all the work we're doing around here that renovating the upstairs bathroom and putting in a shower could be a priority, so I can feel a little more comfortable in my home?"

She was absolutely right. How could I have ignored her request? The mistake I made was not realizing how important the bathroom was to her.

Don't Let Things Go Unattended

If you sense a problem with someone, talk about it. After announcing to our chain that Blimpie International would be developing Maui Tacos and Pasta Central, we began to hear rumblings from Blimpie subfranchisors. Why were they not being given the rights to Maui Tacos and Pasta Central? That was the question all over the hallways during our convention. After I was made aware of this, I decided to make a special appearance before the group to explain. I told them that the Maui Tacos brand was acquired and that Blimpie International had several minor partners, so we couldn't just give away the rights. Regarding Pasta Central, I explained that our experience showed that when you give away something for nothing, it most often gets treated like it's worth nothing. But the company was willing to entertain granting rights to any qualified Blimpie subfranchisor under very favorable terms.

Just dealing with the issues resulted in a turnaround in subfranchisor sentiment. Sometimes what you *don't* say can take on more meaning than what you *do* say. If we had ignored subfran-chisor feelings instead of tackling the issues head on, the problem likely would have gotten much worse.

Intentionally or not, we sometimes think that being silent will make the problem go away. The problem is that silence *is* communication. It sends a message, a message like, "You are not important enough for me to waste my time telling you things." Silence also awakens the grapevine. As Winston Churchill once put it, "When the eagles are silent, the parrots begin to jabber."

Make a Gesture

Sometimes the simplest, smallest things can be so important. Maybe it's offering to help an employee who's having a problem with her computer. Or sending a note of praise to a worker for doing a great job. Or telling your son, "You really handled yourself well on the court last night. That was a great shot you made with two seconds left."

For the 1998–99 holiday season, Yvonne and I booked a terraced room at the National Hotel in South Beach, Florida. Yvonne is a writer, and she and I had planned to spend some quiet time writing outdoors on our terrace in the warm Miami Beach climate. Although the room and the hotel were very nice, we soon discovered that the building next door was under construction. That meant that we were going to be tormented by a jackhammer for half the day. I brought the situation to the attention of the desk clerk, who was very sympathetic. She let us know that the hotel manager would call us. Later that day, Claus, the manager, called to apologize and offered to relocate us to another hotel or to provide us with complimentary beach chairs and umbrellas so we could escape the noise. We chose the beach, and there we found quiet and comfort. This simple gesture by the manager ensured that we would remain favorably inclined toward this hotel. In fact, it made us more likely to return because we learned that this was a place that cared about its guests. It was a simple gesture that cost hardly anything, and it kept us as customers.

So often, people are quick to criticize and slow to praise. What do you think happens to a kid when he hears things like these? "You are so stupid." "You'll never amount to anything when you grow up." "All you want to do is play music. You never do anything worthwhile." Children, teens, employees—all people—need positive reinforcement. Don't emphasize the negative. Catch people doing something right and tell them you appreciate it. It does wonders.

Don't Criticize, Condemn, or Complain

Most people dislike criticism. Unfortunately, the higher up the ladder you climb, the more your butt gets exposed, and that invites criticism. So, you must be prepared to deal with it. Critics can also provide valuable feedback if we take it the right way.

In a company, it's common for employees to criticize management. That's okay, if it's meant to be positive feedback. It's important to understand, however, that a variety of factors shapes one's thinking. People interpret events based on what they see, hear, and think—and they weigh new information in much the same way, drawing conclusions based on their own slant or viewpoint. Incorrect information can easily lead to an incorrect conclusion.

If you were in charge, you could easily fall victim to someone else's misinterpretation of information. So, don't do the same thing when you have criticism to offer. The other person may be doing what's necessary to run the organization, and it's sometimes impossible for that person to make everyone happy.

At midnight on New Year's Eve 1998 in Las Vegas, with one explosion, the famous Sands Hotel was demolished. Years of vision, years of development, years of building, and years of fun

---

If you want to give someone feedback, do it as positively as possible and remember that those who need criticism the most are the least likely to accept it.

---

and excitement and making people happy all came down in an instant. That's what some folks are prone to do—easily wreck in a moment what took a long time to create. Don't play that role. Be a builder, not a wrecker. Stop finding fault and start finding solutions.

We need to be careful how we dish out criticism. Eddie Rickenbacker, the World War I pilot who was adrift in the Pacific for twenty-one days, said, "If you have all the fresh water you want to drink and all the food you want to eat, you ought never to complain about anything." Those who sit back, point fingers, and lay blame lose respect and limit their impact. If you want to give someone feedback, do it as positively as possible and remember that those who need criticism the most are the least likely to accept it.

Give Recognition

November 4, 1998, was proclaimed "Blimpie Day" by the city of Sacramento, California, in honor of the opening of the two thousandth Blimpie location, which was in that city. After partaking in the celebration with the mayor's office, I returned to New York to find a voicemail message from Pam Gower, our head of human resources: "Congratulations in achieving the two thousandth store level. It must make you feel really good." I immediately called Pam. "How many stores did our chain have when you started here?" I asked Pam. "About two hundred fifty," she replied. "You started here as a receptionist, worked your way into accounting, then human resources, eventually becoming the head of that department. Yes, it makes me feel great getting to two thousand stores, but you've been here for much of the way, so you should feel great, too." I then requested from her a list of all employees who had been with Blimpie International since store number one thousand opened and I sent each of them a memo saying, "You've been very instrumental in helping us get to two thousand. Congratulations and thank you for all you've done in getting us to reach this milestone."

As a company leader, a boss, a parent, a teacher, it's a great idea to acknowledge good performance and give recognition to those who deserve it.

Use the Right Approach

If you want to get someone to do something for you, try starting your conversation or letter like this: "I need your help." Think about it. If you demand something, the other person's back automatically goes up. But if you ask for their help, who can deny you? Inherently, people are always willing to help.

Involve People

A sign I noticed on the receptionist's desk while I was in the waiting area of a major company, read: "The buck doesn't even slow down here." I guess that was meant to be funny, but it struck me as sad. The first contact with this company is most often, I'm sure, with this person, yet the sign betrays a feeling of, "Oh, me, I'm not important. I'm just a receptionist."

In January 1997, I attended a marketing meeting held by our North Carolina and South Carolina franchisee co-op. At this meeting, operators were presented with a carefully thought-out plan to use billboards promoting an 89¢ BLT special at all stores. Instead of just being hit with a "Here's what we are going to do" mandate, the franchisees had the opportunity to view slides of proposed boards and listen to why the concept made sense to the ad agency and co-op board. The franchisees were then told that they would

---

If you want to get someone to do something for you, try starting your conversation or letter like this: "I need your help." . . . If you ask for their help, who can deny you?

---

be given the opportunity to insert specific directions or instructions on the boards closest to their stores. Now, any number of arguments, pro or con, could have been made about that promotion but, because it was openly presented and discussed and because it involved each franchisee, everyone got 100 percent behind it.

When people feel like they have been involved and they have a stake in the outcome, they begin to think about the project—not just at work, but in the car, in the shower, or in the middle of the night. When people feel they have a stake in the success of something, they commit more and maybe even risk more.

Articulate a Vision

Every year at our annual convention, I have the opportunity to talk about my vision for the future. One of the most important times that I needed to do this was in the summer of 1994 at our convention in Copper Mountain, Colorado. The chain was well beyond the rebirth of the late 1980s, but to really reach our goals we needed to get everyone to work together.

It's easy for people to lose sight of their ultimate goal and, if that happens, they lose sight of how to go about getting there. They may focus so much on the challenges as they see them that they overlook the challenges that are important to others within their group.

Whether it's a family, a sports team, a corporation, or a franchise system, the only way for members of these groups to maximize their own success is if everyone else also achieves success—and that means working together.

Toward that end, in Colorado, I gave this speech:

> Much of the progress we have made in recent years can be attributed to our long-term vision of making Blimpie a worldwide leader in food service.
>
> But what is the source of this vision? Where does it come from? What is the basis on which it is built? To answer these questions, we must ask yet another: Why is Blimpie in business?
>
> We ask that question often, and the answer is always the same. Blimpie is in business to make money for our franchises and for our shareholders.
>
> The way we do this is by getting and keeping more and more customers and by selling them more and more sandwiches. But as we go about doing this at an accelerating pace, we get emotional—some of us out of curiosity, some of us out of hope, some of us out of uncertainty, some of us out of fear.
>
> Why: Because Blimpie is on the way to becoming a major force in food service. Because the world is at our doorstep.
>
> Some of us see things differently because of this. Others cling to the past, *ignoring* the changes that are taking place around them.
>
> Since our chain was reborn a few years ago, and since we embarked on a course of rapid and accelerating expansion, almost every person associated with Blimpie has offered her or his opinion on the future of Blimpie.
>
> The optimists say we must grow—that we must be aggressive—that is what will take us to a much higher level.
>
> The pessimists warn of the perils of growth. Many chains, they say, were ruined by over-expansion.
>
> So what do we do?
>
> What we must do is keep returning to our vision of making Blimpie the best, of making Blimpie a worldwide leader in food service.
>
> But just how do we go about doing that? Some say that our focus should be at the store level—that we must strive to make our restaurants models of quality, service, and cleanliness and that our goal must be total compliance.
>
> Others think we need value-pricing. They insist we need to reduce labor costs and purchase better. They feel we need more research and development and innovations in systems and equipment.

Still others think the answer lies in advertising and promotion, that not only must we conduct ongoing regional advertising programs, but that they should be backed up with good, strong, consistent national brand-building and brand-awareness campaigns.

Finally, there are those who feel that we must open more and more stores and that we must get the Blimpie brand out there wherever we can. These folks feel that market share can truly be gained only by getting as close to the customer as possible through more and more traditional and nontraditional development, not only across the U.S., but all around the world.

The reality, of course, is that everyone is right, that none of these elements—model store operations, value-pricing, national advertising, or growth in Blimpie outlets—can succeed without the others.

That means that we must all share the same vision. That means that we must all work "together," subfranchisors, franchisees, corporate staff, and strategic partners. We must not be blinded to changes in the marketplace. We must not be blinded to each other's needs. We must just keep doing what we have always done: get together, sit down, discuss and work out our challenges and problems, while exploring and finding new and creative ways to build our businesses.

And there's no question, the job of doing this will often fall on the strongest. On any team, the strongest player will always be called upon to lead the weaker ones.

So every time a decision has to be made at any level of Blimpie, let's remember the reason Blimpie is in business. Then, every time, each of us will be taking another step toward making money for our franchises and for our shareholders.

The way we go about fulfilling our vision of making Blimpie the absolute best, of making Blimpie a worldwide leader in food service, will change from time to time as conditions change. What will never change, however, is that we must all share the same vision, that we must all work together.

You see, if we all work together toward our vision, we will all reach our goals. I submit to you that to do anything other than that, Blimpie People, is not an option.

A Good Speech Helps Business . . . and Your Career

Whether you're the head of a committee or the head of a company, sooner or later it will be your turn to stand in front of people and say something meaningful while everybody stares at you. Some people say they would rather die than give a speech. But remember: Of those two choices, dying or speaking, only one ends with people applauding you and you going home.

When giving a speech to a large group, your goal should be to stir up excitement. This is your chance to excel. Don't waste people's time by giving a mediocre performance. Make it worthwhile for everyone. Prepare well in advance. Think out what you have to say, carefully. Run it past someone you can trust to help you and give

---

When people feel they have a stake in the success of something, they commit more and maybe even risk more.

---

you objective advice. Be enthusiastic, use your voice for emphasis, and show energy. This is your opportunity to communicate a message that will stay with everyone long after the meeting is over.

Many of us are called upon from time to time to make speeches. Many of us flop. Why? The reasons are many and here are some:

- Lack of preparation. Just because you are knowledgeable about something doesn't mean that you won't be boring. Speechmaking is a form of show business. That's why people like inspirational speaker Zig Zigler get paid so much. Start preparing your remarks as soon as you can, even though the speech may be weeks or months away. Lack of preparation is the major cause of a bad speech. Why are you giving the speech? What do you hope to accomplish? What message do you expect the listener to walk away with? Remember, a speech should not simply be made to convey information. Those are the ones that really get boring. A speech should be used to persuade, to stir people up, to invoke passion.

- Be brief. It has been said that in every listener there is a yawn waiting to get out. My friend, Jeff Jayson, who produces *Good Morning, America,* says that a video should never be longer than seven or eight minutes because you lose the viewer after that. With speeches, it's about thirty minutes.

- Be sincere. Speak from the heart. Tell people about yourself and how you really feel. Never tell people what you are going to tell them, just tell them.

- Watch out for humor. Humor in speeches can be wonderful— if you're funny. And that's a big "if." If you are not a good storyteller off stage, or if you are not certain that your jokes are going to work, forget them.

- Connect with the audience. Try not to read from a written speech but, if you have to, keep looking up into people's eyes. You want people to feel like you are talking to them and not just reading a prepared speech. See-through prompters are great.

- Speak like you talk. When some people give a speech, they sound like someone else. Remember that it's you up there and it should sound like you. Speak to the audience as you would

---

The greatest problem with communication is thinking that it has been accomplished.

---

speak to a group of friends at dinner. Practicing out loud is a good way to determine whether your speech is interesting and whether you are using words that are better suited for writing.

- Prepare for questions. Don't get caught with a question that you are not prepared to answer. Think about what people will ask you, about what might embarrass you, and have the answers ready. Or simply ask the questions yourself: "One question I'm often asked is . . ." Learning how to give a good speech is hard work, but without that skill, you risk hurting your business and your career.

- Get comfortable. If you're not comfortable, your audience won't be either.

- Be aware of your posture. Stand up straight, chest out, stomach muscles contracted. Don't bend down to reach the microphone or lean over the podium.

- Watch the "uh-huhs." Also watch the "you knows" and the "er-ahs."

The Power of Communication

So, although it may not be easy, we must learn how to express ourselves, overcome any shyness and, through public speaking, get our ideas across. We must become good listeners, letting people express themselves and communicating one on one with all those people in our lives, building trust and gaining loyalty. It's important to make people feel liked, respected, and appreciated. Make that phone call and don't let things fester. Communicate our vision and our strategy and remind everyone why they are working so hard. And just when we think we think we have said enough, we need to say it again, for although the constitution guarantees free speech, it doesn't guarantee free listening. The greatest problem with communication is thinking that it has been accomplished.

CHAPTER 7

HAVE A GOOD TIME: CREATING A LIFE OF ENJOYMENT

*If it makes you happy, then why
the hell are you so sad?*

—Sheryl Crow

Say the word "Blimpie." It's kind of a silly word, isn't it? Just saying it is apt to make you smile, right? I sure think so, and I believe that's one reason why our corporate office has attracted a certain kind of person, one with a sense of humor.

Mom and Dad taught me that work and fun can exist together. Tom Peters, the workplace guru, agrees: "The number-one premise of business is that it need not be boring or dull. It ought to be fun. If it's not fun, you're wasting your time."

The word *fun* scares a lot of executives; it shouldn't. Productive days feel more like play than work to me. The hours I spend accomplishing something fill me with excitement and joy, not boredom and unhappiness. I think it's essential that a workplace foster fun and productivity together. It's what I've tried to build into the Blimpie culture, just as I've seen it work so well in other companies.

Southwest Airlines always comes to mind when I think about blending work and play. Southwest's CEO, Herb Kelleher, has instituted fun as part of the company culture. That doesn't mean that Kelleher's first concern isn't the safety of his passengers. Of course it is, and Southwest won't let its employees mess around where people's lives are at stake. But if you've ever been on a

Southwest flight, you know that these folks have fun, because they make sure *you* have fun.

I don't think it's any accident that Southwest was making money even in the early 1990s, when the rest of the airline industry was losing billions. Southwest works to maintain a culture of fun by recruiting only people who have the right attitude, and it begins with the job interview. Typically, an interviewer might say to a candidate, "Tell us how humor helped you deal with a difficult situation in your life." Or the candidate might be asked, "What's the most embarrassing situation you've been involved with where you used humor to change your perspective?"

The company has been known to have pilot candidates interview in a pair of Southwest shorts—not permitting them to come in a suit and tie. Job candidates who are really uncomfortable simply don't get hired. Face it, unless a flight attendant is a little bit of

---

The hours I spend accomplishing something fill me with excitement and joy. I think it's essential that a workplace foster fun and productivity together.

---

a ham, like Larry Edwards, he's going to have a tough time advising passengers, "In the event of a water landing, please remember: Paddle, kick, kick, paddle, kick, kick all the way back to shore." It's employees like Edwards who have made Southwest Airlines downright entertaining.

Life is too short to go through it without humor.

Her great sense of humor is one reason I fell in love with my wife, Yvonne. Right from the beginning, she made me laugh—sometimes at my own expense. She was an actress when I met her, and when she moved to New York City from a town near Buffalo, she sometimes used her acting ability to get a good laugh, even when it made me look like a fool—like the time we checked into the Harbor Court Hotel on Baltimore's waterfront.

In the elevator on the way up to our room, the bellhop gave us what he thought was some juicy inside information, "If you think you see Bill Cosby while you are here, you are right. He just checked in." We got up the next morning, planning to go to the workout room, but we hadn't had any breakfast. "There's a nice little espresso bar downstairs," Yvonne suggested. "Why don't I pick up a couple of muffins for us." When she returned to the room, she said, "You're not going to believe what I have to tell you. I just ran into Bill Cosby in the elevator. He began to stare at me and then he said, 'I'm doing a new movie and you look perfect for the part. Here's my card, call me. I want you to come to L.A.' "

I bit. After all, Yvonne has screaming red hair and the kind of look that would make someone say, "There she is" if that's what he was looking for.

"You mean, you are considering picking up and going to L.A.? What if you get the part?"

She knew she had me.

"Well, it probably will only be for about six months or so."

"We just got married and you're going to leave me for L.A. and a movie?"

Oh, I was hooked. She went on until she couldn't stand it anymore. Finally, she gave me one of those fish-on-a-hook gestures, and she began laughing. I felt like an idiot and started to get mad, but then I smiled, and soon we were both laughing uncontrollably.

Whether or not you think this story is funny isn't the point. The point is that I found it funny and that I consider it the kind of humor that's really important in life.

More than Practical Jokes

Fun in the workplace can be a lot more than practical jokes. When the fun and the business are woven together tightly, the result can make an important point in an unforgettable way.

For me, a memorable example came at a Blimpie International convention, when I was introduced to the blaring sound of The Doors and their hit song "Light My Fire." While the music played, I shocked the franchisees in the audience by entering the room in a bandana and tie-dyed T-shirt imprinted with the words, "Try a Cherry Garcia Blimpie." I paraded through the room, flashing a peace sign and shaking hands 1960s-style.

As the music quieted down, I told the audience how I had recently seen Ben & Jerry at the Entrepreneur of the Year Awards, where they received first prize.

"I thought Ben & Jerry had the right idea," I said, "So I dressed up like this. What do you think?"

The volume of the music increased again.

"Wait, hold it, stop the music," I said. "Pam, I see your head shaking. Don't you think this is a good idea?"

It was a setup, of course.

Pam Gower, one of our staffers, responded, "No, I don't."

"Why not?"

"Because you are not Ben or Jerry. You are Tony Conza."

"Why does that make a difference?"

I picked another Blimpie employee out of the group.

"Because Ben & Jerry stand for something different than what Tony Conza stands for."

"And what is that?"

"Peace, love, environmentally concerned, socially responsible . . ."

It was all leading up to the point I wanted to make.

"And what does Blimpie stand for?" I asked.

"Freshness."

"Quality."

"Value."

The entire audience was involved now. I continued, "So Blimpie stands for something very different than Ben & Jerry's, or to put it another way, Blimpie's brand image is different from Ben

---

When you are running a company, things aren't always going to go smoothly. Things are going to break down. Troubles are going to erupt. So, if the staff members have a sense of humor, they don't freak out when something goes wrong.

& Jerry's. It's not that we have anything against love, peace, and social responsibility. It's just that it's not what we want to come to consumers' minds when they think of Blimpie. When people think of Blimpie, we want them to think 'fresh, quality, value.' "

My point was getting made.

"I represent Blimpie, so I should look like freshness, quality, and value, because if I don't, what happens?"

"You confuse people," a franchisee shouted.

"Right. And when people get confused, they don't like it, do they?"

"No, and they don't come back," said another operator.

The setup was complete, so I left the audience, walked up to the podium, and removed my T-shirt to expose a Blimpie uniform. Then I gave a speech about the importance of presenting an appropriate, disciplined, consistent brand image.

In a fun, entertaining manner, I had given a lesson about the importance of brand image.

The reason a culture of fun works so well is not just because the CEO is willing to do silly things, but because a sense of humor gets instilled in the hearts of the staff. When you are running a company, things aren't always going to go smoothly. Things are going to break down. Troubles are going to erupt. So, if the staff members have a sense of humor, they don't freak out when something goes wrong. They don't make mountains out of molehills and blow things out of proportion. They are able to deal with things better.

It's a good thing. Just before the 1994 New York City Marathon, Blimpie's sense of humor helped us cope with a minidisaster. As the official sandwich of the marathon, we provided twenty-five thousand sandwiches after the race to participants and we were invited to a pre-event VIP press party at Citibank's Park Avenue headquarters. To raise Blimpie International's profile at the affair, Bobby Schnurr, our vice president of product development, and Fritz Gutting, our senior customer service executive from Hazelwood Farms, the chain's bread supplier, came up with the idea of presenting a gigantic cake inscribed with the Blimpie and New York City Marathon logos. And a gigantic cake it was—eight feet long, sixteen inches high, and four feet wide, filled with chocolate custard and topped with a rich, creamy white icing.

Because of its size, the cake had to be baked at the Hazelwood plant in St. Louis. Fritz, concerned about its safety in travel, arranged to personally accompany it to New York. When he arrived at Citibank, Bobby was there to greet him. Their plan, with the help of a few Blimpie workers, was to move the cake from the truck to a large table in the bank's main floor area.

All went well until the cake and the movers reached the entrance to the room. They knew they would have a problem getting a four-foot-wide cake through a three-foot-wide door.

"Let's see, if we just tilt it just a little bit. NO, just a little bit more. Okay, almost got it. Just a little—wait, watch out, hold it!"

In a flash, the cake let go of the pan and splattered all over the marble entrance of the headquarters of America's largest bank. Bobby and Fritz couldn't believe their eyes. All that planning. All that work. All the recognition and publicity that Blimpie was going to receive. Gone. And the embarrassment! They wanted to cry, but when they called my office, my first reaction was to say, "Did you get it on videotape?" Then all of a sudden, laughter broke out. The thought of this sight was hilarious to comprehend.

Because of our sense of humor, this little mishap turned out not to be a failure, but a fun story that will live with Blimpie people forever.

A Lesson from Home

From the time I was a young boy, I learned about having fun from my parents. They were very hard workers, but they always knew when to take a break, go on vacation, or have a party with close friends. They weren't drinkers, but they knew when it was time to have a cocktail, a beer, or a glass or two of wine. They knew how to have fun and they made fun contagious. Friends and relatives wanted to be around them because they had fun too.

Remember I told you about my Dad building his house in New Jersey? There's no better example. Weekend after weekend, he got relatives and friends to join him, cutting wood, measuring, hammering, screwing, lifting, cementing—all without power tools, because there was no electricity on the property. Why did all these folks willingly offer their time and sweat? Because Mom and Dad made sure they had a good time.

They would arrive early in what was then the country. Mom would go right to her garden, where she grew fresh vegetables. Then, after a few hours, she'd start a fire in the barbecue that my grandfather had built out of the stones from the land. In a short time, a great lunch was ready and Mom would call the men off the job to join her at the table. Dad would send me to fetch some beers that we had set in the cold water of the small brook that ran through our land. Voilà! Suddenly, it was a country picnic. Everyone was having a ball.

After lunch, the men would return to their work while Mom and her sisters cleaned up and began preparing for dinner, when we did it all over again. At the end of the day, they all went home smiling—and Dad had taken another step toward building the home of his dreams.

The point, to quote an old saying, is this: "Nothing is work unless you'd rather be doing something else." I work really hard and that has led some people to ask, "Conza, are you a workaholic?" There's a reason that the word *workaholic* sounds like the word *alcoholic*. Both are addictions. Take a drink or two and you have a good time. Take too many drinks because you need to drink, and that's no fun. If you are working all the time and not enjoying your life, then you are a workaholic.

If you are strictly attuned to making money, if money is your only motivation for working, then I don't think you are going to have fun. And considering how much time you spend at work, you really should enjoy being there. I love what I do and I feel

> **I love what I do and I feel very lucky to be able to say that. When work is fun, it's easier to be successful because you're not always looking to separate the two.**

very lucky to be able to say that. When work is fun, it's easier to be successful because you're not always looking to separate the two. If you always have an eye on the clock in anticipation of five o'clock, or if the only thing you're thinking all week is, "I can't wait until Friday," then your chances for achieving success will be severely limited.

A Fun Company Is a Better Company

"If you do something for fun and create the best possible product, the profit will come," says Richard Branson, the founder of Virgin Atlantic Airways, Virgin Records, and a host of other companies. When people have fun, when they enjoy what they are doing, they perform better and they build camaraderie, all of which result in greater success for the organization.

During my frequent visits to our Atlanta office, I think about our employees there. Life is difficult for many of them. They get up early, make breakfast, get the kids dressed and off to school, then get ready themselves and make the traffic-snarled drive to our offices. When they get there, the last thing they need is to have work be a drag. If their job can be fun, if they enjoy coming to work, if they smile when they accomplish something, then to me that has real value to the company.

What makes work fun? Well certainly incorporating humor into the workplace. Humor is the great icebreaker.

I have known so many people who find going to work depressing. Often, it's because they work for bosses whom they can't stand—bosses who fly off the handle without notice; who make unreasonable demands; who never praise good work; who think no one is as smart as they are. In short, they make your life miserable because they themselves are miserable or because someone or something is making them miserable.

Jack Welch, chairman and CEO of General Electric, once fired five senior executives and made a public announcement about it in front of five hundred managers. The point he was making was

> ## Employees need to know that what they are accomplishing has value to the company, to the customers, and even to society.

that, just because these guys made the numbers, that wasn't good enough, because they made their numbers without taking care of their people.

"You know the kind," says Welch: "Good old Harry always delivers. Yeah, over ten dead bodies and nine carcasses. Harry had to leave us because he couldn't support his people. You want to win, you want to compete, but not against each other. The competition is out there; it isn't in here."

Sam Walton, the founder of Wal-Mart, once said that in a service company, it takes about two weeks for the employees to start treating the customer the same way the employer treats the employee. Employees need to know that what they are accomplishing has value to the company, to the customers, and even to society. When someone in our real-estate department secures a good lease, that person is providing a very valuable service because he may have secured a lifetime of success for a franchise operator. When someone from construction and design comes up with an innovation for dispensing our sandwiches, she may have created a whole new venue for Blimpie International to reach more customers, bringing more profits to the company while creating a new convenience for consumers. When someone from accounting figures out how to provide information to management that will help the company operate more efficiently, he may be enabling us to give better service at a cheaper cost, which, in turn, benefits customers. When the company opens one hundred new restaurants, we are creating more than one thousand new jobs for Americans.

It's up to the company to let these folks know not only that we appreciate their accomplishments but that they are doing a service for consumers and for society in general. Then they will be excited. Then their self-confidence will be boosted. Then they will feel good about what they did. Then they will enjoy what they are doing. Technically, they are all working, but they are proving that work can—and should—be fun. Sure, work can be tough and tiring, but so is riding a bike on a mountain trail. In both cases, however, there's nothing like the feeling of joy you get when you complete what you set out to do.

Celebration Makes People Happy

Over the years, we've found that creating celebrations in our office is a great way to relieve stress and to get people involved. Sometimes, it's small—such as coffee and cake to celebrate an employee's birthday or giving everyone a free lunch to test new menu items. Sometimes, it's big. We've had our share of celebrations at Blimpie International: the five hundredth store opening, the one thousandth, two thousandth, the completion of a $10 million stock offering, our high rankings in two consecutive *Forbes* "best small companies in America" lists, and being named the No. 1 Quick Service Growth Company by *Nation's Restaurant News*. But no celebration was as exciting or preceded with so much anticipation as our Super Bonus celebration.

During the rebirth of Blimpie International in the late '80s, we had implemented an employee bonus program where 10 percent of company profits went to staff members after Blimpie reported year-end earnings. The real excitement came at the end of fiscal year 1992, when I announced to our staff that we had set an earnings target for the fiscal year ending June 30, 1993. "Should we hit that target," I said, "Blimpie International will pay a Super Bonus, or double the 10 percent bonus, to company employees."

Employees got such a kick out of following the company's progress that year. Every time a franchise was awarded, every time an operator reported record sales, every time our quarterly earnings statement was released, people cheered and grew more and more excited. It went right down to the wire, as everyone waited with bated breath for the results to be announced by independent auditors. When the word finally came down that we had done it, that we had reached our goal and that our staff would receive the Super Bonus, there was mayhem in our offices. Some folks

---

There's nothing like the feeling of joy you get when you complete what you set out to do.

---

screamed with delight, some applauded, some even cried. It wasn't just because they would be receiving an extra large paycheck. It was much bigger than that. It was because they knew that a diverse group of people, through hard work, passion, and teamwork, had coalesced and accomplished a goal that they deemed worthwhile, not just in their pockets and not just in their minds, but in their hearts. And they had a whole lot of fun doing it.

Shake Off the Sticky Things

One day, while I was walking down a Manhattan street, I observed a little black dog on a leash being led by his owner. The dog appeared to be enjoying his stroll until he accidentally stepped on some sticky thing. The owner, unaware that his dog had encountered the obstacle, continued to lead the pet forward, even as the dog struggled to free himself, shaking his leg, taking a step forward, shaking his leg, taking another step. Finally, the little animal's efforts succeeded and the sticky thing was left behind. Man and dog moved along as if nothing had ever happened. The incident struck me as being very funny, but it also made me think: We should all be like that little black dog. The sticky things that life will always deliver to us should never stop us from moving forward. The sticky things should never prevent us from enjoying life.

When my Uncle Carlo was ninety-four, I ran into him at a family affair and my curiosity led me to ask him about himself. He was a handsome man, appearing no older than, say seventy-five. "Uncle Carlo, do you smoke?" I inquired. "Oh no, I quit smoking twenty years ago." Okay, I thought, the guy smoked cigarettes until he was seventy-four. "You look great, Uncle Carlo, how do you keep yourself in such good shape? What's your secret?" "I take life easy," he said, "I don't worry about things. Worrying will kill you. Don't let the little things bother you."

Sounds like that little black dog, doesn't it?

It's easy to believe that there is no way to get rid of certain sticky things. They might be related to job, family, society, government, religion, other people, who you are, or who you think you should be. So long as you don't take the steps necessary to remove the things that have a hold on you, they will restrict you, take away your freedom, and stop you from having the fun that you should be having.

Let's look at what some of these sticky things might be and explore some alternatives that may be available. Because, whether or not you realize it, you DO have a choice.

Sticky Thing Number One: The Obligation

I have lots of relatives. Aunts, uncles, cousins, second cousins, friends of cousins—someone was always celebrating something to which I was invited. Because I was expected to be there, I generally obliged and attended. So, often, I would find myself at a birthday party, a Fourth of July barbecue, or a graduation party, even though I had no desire to be there. I was doing what I thought I *should* do rather than what I *wanted* to do. I was letting other people decide what would make me happy.

One year, as Thanksgiving approached, I took a new stand. Instead of joining my parents and relatives for their traditional pasta and turkey dinner as I had always done, I informed my family that I was going to spend it with my friends. "What, you're not coming for Thanksgiving?" Dad couldn't understand. Of course he couldn't. He was seeing it from his perspective. To him, this was an important family holiday, one that he and my relatives really looked forward to. To me, it was more of an obligation than a good time.

The fact was that my enjoyment from being with Mom and Dad happened on Sunday afternoons in Mom's kitchen over fabulous home-cooked dinners surrounded by talk about life. Or when Dad and I lounged on his front porch and discussed the stock market or the latest baseball trade while we sipped a glass of wine. Big holiday bashes where I was forced to deal with screaming babies, distant relatives I hardly knew, or friends of relatives I had no desire to be with were not for me. I decided that I just wasn't going to do it any more. I had the best parents any person could ever hope to have but, at a certain point in my life I had to live in a way that suited me, that made me happy.

When people have expectations of you, you simply need to change their expectations. You don't have to be mean, indignant, or emotionless. You don't need to overreact and risk tearing down

---

I've always found that the most successful people do things the right way even if they are not tied to a formal agreement.

---

the good parts of the relationship. Continue to show love and respect, but decide how you want to spend your life. If they don't like it, it's their choice, not yours. I promise you though, the most likely result of this will be more quality time with the right people and a more enjoyable life for you.

Business obviously presents some obligations that you have to honor whether you want to or not. To protect the Blimpie brand, for example, we have franchise agreements that obligate the franchisor and franchisee to conduct themselves in a certain way. But I've always found that the most successful people do things the right way even if they are not tied to a formal agreement. David Siegel and I have never had a contract between us, even though we have been together for several decades. While we often disagree about things, our focus on the big picture coupled with our sense of humor has made our relationship stand the test of time.

What's important to remember is that we all have choices. Sure, we have obligations, but if the obligations do not suit us, we can get rid of them. If, in our judgment, they are necessary to accept because they lead us to our goals or to a better life, that's fine. It's when we realize that the obligations are nothing more than a sticky thing that we need to pass them by.

Sticky Thing Number Two: Expectations

If you expect other people to behave in ways that conform only to your wishes, then you have the expectations sticky thing.

I was listening to morning radio when a twenty-something woman called in to complain about a guy she had met a few nights earlier at a bar. Apparently, the two got along really well and the guy took her phone number. A few days later, a Saturday, the guy called from his office. The woman was offended. She didn't think this was right. Why didn't he call from home? She couldn't understand his behavior.

Now, this is a great way to begin a relationship, I thought. She doesn't even know this man and already she has expectations of how he should behave.

For sure, you will be disappointed if you place labels on people and relationships and then have expectations about those that you have labeled. In the mind of that woman, the guy was already her boyfriend, and she obviously had decided how a boyfriend should conduct himself.

Here are some things you can do in order to avoid Sticky Thing Number Two:

- Don't get involved with people who are incompatible with you. The more you have in common with a person, the less likely it is you will have to deal with unsatisfied expectations.

- Realize that every person is an individual, someone who will think and act differently and have different goals, aspirations, and motivations than you.

- Remember the other person's self-interest. Once you start asking the other person to make sacrifices for you, you are looking for trouble.

- Understand that people and circumstances are always changing.

Whether or not you have a contract, it doesn't make sense to keep someone in a relationship that they no longer find beneficial or enjoyable. In the Blimpie system, when we detect that a franchisee is increasingly failing to adhere to operational standards, in addition to taking the necessary remedial steps, we attempt to sell his store and have him leave the chain. If we force an operator to comply with his contract because he is unwilling to do so on his own, we end up with a franchisee who is not happy and, consequently, one who is no good for the system.

The same rule applies to most relationships. What good does it do to force a husband to comply with his marriage vows, or require a business partner to live up to the agreement he signed with you? If the other person is unhappy, you will be unhappy. Then what's the point?

If you don't ask, demand, or expect things from people, you will more likely end up with the genuine love, friendship, understanding, and appreciation that you are seeking. Remember, you can't change other people; you can only change the way you deal with them.

Sticky Thing Number Three: Preconceived Notions

Sticky Thing Number Three happens when you try to fit your happiness into a box created by your preconceived notions. Some examples of this might be:

- A woman who hastily gets married because, "If I don't have a baby soon, it will be too late," then discovers she hooked up with the wrong man.

- A woman who continues to convince herself that she has to be happy because after all, she has a wonderful husband, three kids, and a beautiful home in the suburbs.

- A man who is unhappy in his $100,000-a-year job but won't quit because he finally has the salary, position, and office that he was sure he always wanted.

Todd and Paula Recknagle are among the most successful Blimpie franchisees. In March 1999, at the Fontainebleau Hotel in Miami Beach, they received the coveted Franchisee of the Year Award from the International Franchise Association. If there's one

---

Be careful that your emotions and your logic don't blind you to the consequences of what makes you happy or unhappy. Be honest with yourself.

---

thing that makes a chain founder and chairman very happy and proud, it's having a representative of the organization receive such a prestigious award.

Todd and Paula did not get to that place without a lot of hard work, determination, passion, and courage. Before getting involved with Blimpie, Todd had climbed the corporate ladder, building his annual six-figure salary in the investment banking business. But he was not satisfied. He was searching for more out of life. He wanted to be his own boss. In 1994, he risked everything by quitting his job and becoming a Blimpie franchisee, opening three stores within the first six months. Initially, things didn't go very well and the Recknagles reported a loss of about $100,000 the first year. "Paula and I prayed to God," says Todd. "We asked him to advise us whether we should stay with Blimpie or give it up." The couple gained the inspiration to stay with the chain. Four years later, they had seven locations and had reported an 800 percent growth rate.

Todd Recknagle didn't let the preconceived notion of what he was supposed to be get in the way of achieving happiness. He didn't want to spend the only life he has in a job that didn't excite him. Paula agreed with him.

Be careful that your emotions and your logic don't blind you to the consequences of what makes you happy or unhappy. Be honest with yourself. Think ahead, then create the path that produces the feelings that engender enjoyment in you. And watch out for preconceived notions.

Sticky Thing Number Four: The "Expert"

Don't be bullied by the so-called experts into acting in ways that live up to someone else's beliefs and standards.

How many times have you seen a movie or a play that you really enjoyed and then read a really negative review about the performance. "Hey wait," you want to say, "I liked that movie." Or, "I liked that play." Relax. It's okay.

And how about the experts who warn that red meat will clog your arteries. But wait, protein is good for you. Chicken is a good thing to eat. Except you've got to watch out for salmonella. Don't forget about apples. Then again, there are all those pesticides. A drink or two a day is good for the heart, the experts say. But be careful of your blood pressure. How about the fact that the sun is a good source of Vitamin D, and certainly improves your mental outlook? But please wear a hat, sunglasses, and sunscreen and make sure you cover up.

People are always trying to tell you what you can or cannot do. One year, I made a commitment to myself to run the New York Marathon. My plan was to run consistently, three days on, one off, and to increase my mileage every week as the race drew closer.

About two months before the race, I slammed my right foot into the leg of a sofa. It hurt enough to get me to a doctor who informed me that I had broken my big toe. "Well, fix it, Doc, I'm running a marathon in October," I said. "Your toe is broken," he replied. "Forget about the marathon!"

What a depressing thought. I went home feeling very sorry for myself. But by the next morning, I was reconsidering what the doctor had to say. "This guy is overweight," I thought, "he probably never even ran a block in his life, never mind a marathon.

Don't be bullied by the so-called experts into acting in ways that live up to someone else's beliefs and standards.

Who is he to tell me I can't do this?" So I cut off the side of my running shoe so the toe splint could stick out, went to my health club, got on a stationary bike, and started pedaling.

During the weeks that followed, I rode that bike for hours at a time, occasionally using an ice pack and eventually getting back on the streets. I ran the New York City Marathon in three-and-a-half hours, no thanks to the doctor.

When we first got the idea for Blimpie, I told a friend who owned a successful diner about it. "What? You are going to sell only sandwiches?" was his response. "You will never make money selling only sandwiches."

So much for the experts.

Sticky Thing Number Five: Society's Rules

When he was a teenager, my brother Joe was a classic hippie. In need of a job, he and his long hair applied to the New York Stock Exchange, where my father worked. "The job is yours," he was told, "but you have to get rid of that hair." Well, my brother was a rock musician and playing guitar with his long-haired friends is what made him happy. But he also needed a job. So he bought a short-haired wig, tucked his real hair neatly under it and went to work every day, conforming to the image required by the Exchange. Of course, Joe soon realized that he didn't have to spend his life trying to please people with whom he did not agree.

The concept of society is really a myth. Your life is yours and how you choose to live it is up to you. You can do what you want, whatever makes you happy. Do you want to start a business? Be an artist? Wear jeans to work everyday? Travel the world? Whatever it is, you can do it so long as you can afford it, survive it, or not give up things that are more important to you. It's your choice.

You don't need to own a Mercedes or a big home just to impress your neighbors and friends. You don't have to go to the "right" parties with the "right" people or dress the "right" way just so you can be accepted. Decide what's really important to you and what really makes you happy. The only person you really have to please is yourself.

Sticky Thing Number Six: Past Investments

Wall Streeters joke that when you speculate on a stock and the stock goes down, your speculation becomes an investment.

If you buy a stock and its value declines, the amount of money you invested is almost irrelevant. In other words, the stock is worth what it's worth at the moment, and whether you should keep it depends on what you feel about the future of the stock and how that compares to other possible uses for your money.

This logic applies not just to financial investments but also to investments of your time. At twenty-nine, I had been married for ten years. I had a nine-year-old child. You could certainly say that I had a lot invested in that marriage. However, I didn't see my future happiness coming from that marriage. What did it matter that I had ten years invested? What mattered was the future.

The more time that goes by during which you don't know what you want to do—about your work, your family life, your charitable or social obligations—the harder it gets to figure it out. That's why people keep doing what they've been doing. It's easier.

Spend the time necessary to figure out what is really important to you—what you really want to do. The past is gone. Whatever money you put up, whatever time you expended—it's irrelevant. What's important is how you view your situation now. You must act in a way that will bring you the most profit, the most opportunity, and the most happiness in the future. Recognize your mistakes, take your losses, and get out. Don't perpetuate a problem and make it worse.

Keep yourself focused on the future and avoid Sticky Thing Number Six.

Sticky Thing Number Seven: Just Say No

A Blimpie franchisee from a small Southern town called to invite me to attend the opening of his second location.

"I'm sorry, Bob," I said. "I can't be there."

"But the mayor is going to be here," he said. "It would be good for you to be here."

"Sorry, Bob. I just can't do it."

You don't need a reason to decline a dinner invitation, a family gathering, an all-day work assignment, a trip to Timbuckthree. Life will never be enjoyable if you use up your time in ways that leave nothing for just you. Since I know that my schedule can fill up very quickly, I block out time for myself. Maybe it's to spend a few days in the country, or have lunch with a friend, or to extend a trip so my wife and I can see the sights in a city that I'm visiting for business. This part of my schedule becomes as important as any other, and if someone wants to meet with me during that time, my response is simply, "Sorry, I can't do it."

A Time/CNN poll revealed that 65 percent of people spend their leisure time doing things that they would rather not do. That seems kind of ridiculous, doesn't it? In business, while it's necessary to learn to say no, often there are things you have to do whether you want to or not. But leisure time? I'm not sure what this 65 percent are doing, but if they are not having fun, then why are they doing it?

A good thing to do is take some time out to examine what you are spending your time on. Do you really want to remain friends with certain people knowing that it eats up your time to do so?

You don't have to go to the "right" parties with the "right" people or dress the "right" way just so you can be accepted. Decide what's really important to you and what really makes you happy.

You're probably spending time with them, on the phone or in person, and that's taking away other time. Is it necessary to be involved in all that volunteer work? I must get five to ten requests a week to attend some event or be involved in some charitable function. Obviously, I have to say no to most of them.

Earlier in this book, I discussed clipping and skipping when it comes to reading materials. Information is important, but you have to decide what information it will be. Do you need to sit in front of the TV and watch the news? Remember night after night of the same old Clinton-Monica stuff? What value could you have taken away from all of that? When I went to Africa, I didn't see a *Wall Street Journal* for two-and-a-half weeks. When I got on a flight from Dar es Salaam to Amsterdam, the flight attendant handed me a *Journal*. As I began to read it, I thought, "The news sounds all the same. I didn't miss a thing."

When you are working at a good career, or when you are building an enterprise as I have done, work can become all-consuming. Sometimes, you may even feel guilty if you are not working. All this has a cost. Assuming that you absolutely love the work you are doing, you still must put balance into your life or you will wake up one day and say something like, "Gee, my kid is in college and I never noticed her growing up." You can't put a price tag on those kinds of things. The irony of it all is that if you spend all your time working, you will likely be less productive.

Here are some other things to learn to say "no" about:

- Lending money. I have lent money to about a dozen friends and relatives. The result is always the same. You don't get paid back and you lose the friend or relative. If you want to do something for a friend or relative, give the person a gift.

- Someone whose presence drives you crazy. Recognize your reaction and find a way to either change the way you have to deal with this person, or, better yet, arrange not to deal with him at all.

- Any investment of money, time, or emotion that you are not prepared to lose.

- Any situation that makes you unhappy. Believe me, if you died tomorrow, somehow your relatives would find someone else to lend them money, your friends would find others to do them favors or give advice, your spouse would find another mate, and your favorite nonprofit organization would find someone else to raise money for them. I'm not suggesting that these folks wouldn't miss you. I'm also not saying that you should cut off relationships with everything and everyone you are involved with. But if a relationship is not right for you (and often it's not right for the other person, either, but that person may be afraid to let you know it), if it's making you unhappy, then end it. It's your choice.

Take the time and figure out what you need to start saying "no" to.

Sticky Thing Number Eight: Debt

So often, individuals have their enjoyment of life zapped because of too much debt. I've been very deep in debt and I've been debt-free, and I can tell you that being out of debt is much better.

No one knows better than I that you may have to undertake a sensible risk if you want to achieve success. That risk may involve going into debt. I'm not talking about that. I'm talking about the keeping-up-with-the-Joneses kind of debt. Borrowing to buy a bigger house, a third car, a fifth TV, going out on the town when

---

Spend the time necessary to figure out what is really important to you—what you really want to do. The past is gone. Whatever money you put up, whatever time you expended—it's irrelevant. What's important is how you view your situation now.

---

you can't afford it—you know the story. Debt immobilizes you. It causes family problems. It takes away your freedom. Spending the present to pay off the past is not a good way to ensure a happy life.

A big-spending friend of mine used to say, "If I live like a millionaire, doesn't that make me a millionaire?" Well, he may be right—if you can handle the pressure, sleep nights, and live your life constantly in debt.

Sticky Thing Number Nine: Security

The best thing to remember about Sticky Thing Number Nine is that security comes from what's inside of you, not from a guarantee by someone else.

Is it certain that the corporation you work for will never downsize and lay you off? Can you be guaranteed that the stocks you own will always increase in value? Are you sure the people whom you love will always love you?

Your most valuable asset is you. You must be concerned about yourself and your future because you can't count on anyone else to do so. Most people stop investing in themselves after they leave school. Gain all the wisdom and experience that you can, be vigilant and aware of changes in the marketplace, realize that you can never be too prepared for whatever life has in store for you. Learn to minimize your weaknesses and build on your strengths.

Having a passion for something will help you do this. After my trip to Africa, when I regained my passion for Blimpie and my passion for success, I was able to effectuate an entire rebirth of our organization because I realized that I could accomplish anything that I desired. Getting to feel that way is the best kind of security you can have.

When things are not going well, if you start losing faith in yourself, if you begin to blame others, if you start to make excuses, your self-esteem will decline and your insecurity will rise. Look in the mirror. That person you see cannot lie to you. Are you working hard enough? Are you setting goals? Do you have sound strategies about life? If you are not feeling good about yourself, you will never achieve true success and enjoyment in anything you do.

After running the New York City Marathon in 1981, I continued to train very hard. Confident that I could improve my time in another like event, I registered for the 1983 Orange Bowl Marathon. It was January, but a hot-and-humid Miami January. Despite being well trained for the 26.2-mile run, I, like anyone who knew about long-distance running, was aware that I had to drink a lot of water starting about an hour before the race. However, my driver got lost and I ended up at the event just five minutes before I was to run. There was no time to prepare.

As I ran mile after mile, I downed as many cups of water as I could, but it was too late. At the halfway point, the heat, humidity, and then pouring rain began to take their toll. Every mile from there on got more and more difficult. I was slowing down with each step. Finally, at the twenty-four-mile marker, I stopped for yet another cup of water. This time, I just stood there. I was convinced that I was finished. My confidence in my ability to complete the race was shattered. I was sure that I couldn't go on.

Noticing my semicomatose demeanor, a volunteer who was distributing water beckoned me, "What are you doing? You have to finish. It's only two more miles."

"I can't. I can't move anymore," I said.

Without offering another word, she took a full, cold cup of water and threw it in my face. It shocked me into reality. My legs began to move forward. My blistered feet were again hitting the pavement. Dammit, I was going to make it. At three hours and thirty-three minutes, I crossed the finish line.

Since that time, whenever insecurity begins to creep up on me and I start thinking I can't reach my goal, I pretend that the Orange Bowl woman is there with a cup of cold water in her hands. It helps me regain my belief in achieving success. From

---

Your most valuable asset is you. You must be concerned about yourself and your future because you can't count on anyone else to do so.

---

there on, my actions become automatic. Sticky Thing Number Nine has been shaken off.

Get a Life

Having more fun in life means realizing that you are different from everyone else. Take some time to think about the nine sticky things I have listed. List your own sticky things. Recall the happy moments of your past and the people who brought you enjoyment. You may not be able to repeat the good times or bring the people back, but it's possible that you can use your experiences to create new ones.

Consider your dreams. Many of them may be more possible to reach than you imagine. Try new things. Move away from the treadmill. Experiment. There are absolutely many things that you *could* do with your life. The question you have to answer is which ones do you *want* to do? What are you willing to give up? What sacrifices are you prepared to make?

Sometimes, you may deem it necessary to endure hardships or pain in order to get to a place that's truly enjoyable for you. Renoir had such terrible rheumatism that simply holding a brush in his hand was extremely painful. It didn't stop him from painting, however. "The pain passes," he has been quoted as saying, "but the beauty endures." Every time he went onto a playing field, Joe Namath, the New York Jets' star quarterback, suffered constant pain from all the knee injuries he had endured over the years. Yet he expressed his sentiments this way: "When you win, nothing hurts."

If you don't like the work you do, if you don't like the people you work with, if you like your work and your colleagues but the only thing you ever do with your life is spend time with them, then maybe you should start asking yourself, "If I'm so successful, why aren't I having more fun?"

If you are spending more time organizing your vacation than planning the rest of your life, then it's time to perform a good X-ray on yourself. There are a lot more options available to you than you think. The choice to get a life is yours.

When You're Smiling

In February 1999, Rep. J. C. Watts, Jr. of Oklahoma was quoted in *USA Today:* "In the end, success begins with the fundamentals. You know, a smile can go a long, long way. We Republicans sometimes act as if a smile will break our necks."

It takes twenty-six muscles to smile but sixty-two to frown. Shouldn't we make it easier on ourselves and just smile more? Smiling relaxes us, it relieves stress, it creates a better atmosphere. Remember Ronald Reagan? He always seemed to have a smile on his face. That's why people liked him so much. That's why the country felt so good during his terms as president.

You don't need to walk around all day doing a stand-up comedy routine, but a smile and a little laughter are great for relieving anxiety and getting people to let their defenses down. Whenever I give a speech, do an interview, or make a presentation, I always try to do it with humor. Delivering a meaningful message is the goal and using humor is a great way to break the ice and advance my points.

If you have any doubts about happiness being contagious, try putting a smile on your face and walking down a busy street. You'll quickly learn about that famous song lyric, "When you're smiling, the whole world smiles with you."

On one of my frequent trips through the Lincoln Tunnel, I must have pulled up to the toll booth with a very serious expression on my face. "Smile," said the toll collector. A toll collector telling *me* to smile? I couldn't believe it. But you know what? I couldn't help smiling, and I smiled all through the tunnel just thinking about it. With the thousands of cars, trucks, and buses that journey through the Lincoln Tunnel every day, can you imagine the profound effect that this little bit of shared happiness could have on the entire New York metropolitan area?

Singer Bobby McFerrin puts it this way: "We keep looking at the big social and political problems. But when you're walking down the street and someone simply smiles at you—what a tremendous difference that makes."

Dealing with Tragedy

The front-page headline on the September 16, 1986, issue of the *New York Post* was devastating: 2 SLAIN, 2 SHOT AT BLIMPIE. A berserk ex-employee of the Broadway Blimpie had burst into the restaurant and shot four members of the Ahluwalla family, our franchise operators for the location. "I'm going to shoot you all because you fired me. I'm going to kill you all," the killer was reported to have shouted. Peter Ahluwalla, thirty-eight, and his brother Daljit, thirty-six, were killed, while a twenty-two-year-old nephew and thirty-year-old brother-in-law were wounded.

When you are building a family of thousands of employees and franchisees, tragedies are going to occur. Besides that shooting, our restaurants have been the site of a robbery-murder, a bomb

---

If there always seems to be a roadblock to your happiness, take a fresh look at your life. Don't look for the way to enjoyment. Enjoyment is the way.

---

threat, a car that crashed through a storefront, an explosion, construction and employee accidents, heart attacks, strokes, and cancer deaths. These things happened to ordinary people, strong and seemingly invincible people like you and me. The incidents made me conscious of how fragile life is. They reminded me that life must be enjoyed to the fullest every day.

After he discovered that he had terminal cancer, actor Michael Landon said, "Someone should tell us right at the start that we are dying. Then we would be more inclined to live life to the limit every day." If there always seems to be a roadblock to your happiness, take a fresh look at your life. Don't look for the way to enjoyment. Enjoyment is the way.

What are you doing? Waiting until you get married, having kids, watching the kids get old enough, getting divorced, making more money, losing twenty pounds, retiring, getting a new home, paying off your mortgage, getting a promotion, taking a vacation, dying? Decide that now is the time to have fun. Now is the time to enjoy life.

A few years after we started Blimpie, things went bad. The company was in serious financial distress and I was broke. It began to affect my stomach. Day after day, I was in pain. I found a gastroenterologist and scheduled regular visits. He told me there was no ulcer, but he told me not to consume liquor and many foods and he prescribed one of those milky liquid medicines. Nothing helped. During every visit, however, the doctor told me a story of another patient, a businessman. The guy apparently lived with a stomach problem until he went on vacation. Then suddenly, I was told, he could even eat hot dogs and he'd be perfectly fine.

There's probably something to that, I reasoned. Maybe it's not what you eat, maybe it's what's eating you. Recalling what Dad, Grandpa, and Uncle Carlo had told me, I vowed to stop worrying.

During a visit to a local bookstore, I got a copy of Dale Carnegie's *Stop Worrying and Start Living.* Another book had a picture on its cover. It was a man lying on his back with a pillow under each foot, each leg, each arm, and his head. The caption read: "If you can't relax, try this." I did. It worked.

I even cast aside fears about a threatened lawsuit by a franchisee. It wasn't even a lawsuit, mind you, just a threat. Yet it had kept me awake nights.

Never again did I stay awake worrying about that lawsuit (which never materialized, by the way), nor about any other. Never again did I allow anything about business to affect me physically.

Working too hard is not a threat to your happiness. Neither is working too little. What makes you happy is okay. Can you think of a person who works harder than Federal Reserve Chairman Alan Greenspan? Yet he's a happy guy. "I've been lobbying for more vacation time," his wife, Andrea Mitchell, was quoted as saying in *USA Today.* "But he's having so much fun at work, he doesn't want to go away."

That's Alan Greenspan. On the other hand, I know guys who don't want to work very much and that's what makes them happy. I don't care if you are a CEO, a rabbi, a stay-at-home mom, a toll collector on the New Jersey Turnpike, or a beach bum. If you are happy with your life, that's great. Regardless of our age, our occupation, or whether one or two family members work outside the home, we can be happy, provided we don't act in ways that hurt our relationships, we like what we do and the people we work with, and we bring balance into our lives.

A Happy Person Is a Successful Person

I feel success daily, not in making money but by the people in my life—my friends, my family, my wife, Yvonne. I find success when I visit a well-run Blimpie restaurant with satisfied customers, or

---

You have the opportunity to create a life of enjoyment for yourself. Use your future to accomplish the only really important kind of success for you—your happiness.

---

when one of my employees tells me she has accomplished something great in our organization, or when I find out that I have made a difference in the lives of children served by the Boys & Girls Clubs of America.

I feel success when I realize that I am happy. Not because of the material things in my life, and not because of status, self-indulgence, or because I can go to the best restaurants in the world, but because there are so many things in my life that I am passionate about.

You have the opportunity to create a life of enjoyment for yourself. You have everything. You need to make it happen. Use your future to accomplish the only really important kind of success for you—your happiness.

CHAPTER 8

DOING WELL BY DOING GOOD: SUCCEED BY GIVING BACK

We either build our children or
we build more jails.

—General Colin Powell

Leroy "BJ" Brown never intended to be a hero. He was just an eight-year-old boy, a kid trying to get through the tough environment of Bridgeport, Connecticut, and grow up to be a man. One day, he witnessed a shooting, a drug-related killing but, unlike those around him, he refused to stand idly by.

BJ's courage, leadership, and desire to do the right thing, to protect his family and his community, cost him his life and the life of his mother. Because he agreed to testify against the gunmen, even though no one else would, he and his mom were shot in cold blood in their home in January 1999.

BJ was one of the more than three million members of the Boys & Girls Clubs of America, where he would spend much of his time. His mom knew that the Bridgeport Club was a bright light in BJ's life. She knew he was safe there, surrounded by people who cared about him and were willing to help lead him in a positive direction. It wasn't enough.

This was a sad, frustrating experience for the Boys & Girls Clubs because it is an organization dedicated to children like BJ, kids who face serious obstacles to achieving productive futures, kids who deserve a chance to achieve their full potential as adults, citizens, and leaders. For BJ, the clubs just couldn't be there twenty-four hours a day.

The good news is that while Boys & Girls Clubs cannot save every American child, the organization is doing a great job of saving many of them. In fact, 52 percent of club alumni said that "the club really saved my life," according to a survey by Louis Harris & Associates, one of America's leading public-relations firms.

You may recall Denzel Washington or Gen. Colin Powell talking about their experiences with the Boys & Girls Clubs of America in nationally televised public-service announcements. Such celebrities are generally not the ones who command center stage at any club function. It's always the kids. Kids like Liberty Franklin, the 1998 National Youth of the Year.

Liberty was raised by a single mother in a low-income housing project, where drugs, crime, and violence are everyday realities. Liberty has witnessed her mother's excessive drinking and watched her brothers drift in and out of prison and drug-rehabilitation programs. Despite grim surroundings, Liberty is defying the odds. The teenager is the inspiration for her mother's sobriety. She works three part-time jobs for fifty-two hours a week, to help pay household bills and save for college. The future orthodontist is a 4.0 student and on track to be the first person in her family to graduate high school. Liberty hopes to one day provide free dental care to low-income children—a service she received when growing up. At the Everett, Washington, Boys & Girls Club, Liberty started "Teen Talk," a forum for teenagers to discuss their problems and offer solutions.

At the 1995 Blimpie International convention, Kelly Zimmerman, the first young woman ever to be named the National Youth of the Year by the Boys & Girls Clubs, mesmerized her audience by relating the story of her childhood:

"I grew up in a family severely affected by alcoholism. When my home life became too overwhelming, I knew I could always go to the Boys & Girls Club," she said.

Kelly provided her mother with moral and financial support through two divorces. While her mother juggled two jobs and attended college, Kelly ran errands, baby-sat her younger sisters, and helped them with their homework while working herself.

"Zimmerman was selected National Youth of the Year because of her leadership ability and accomplishments at school, at home, at the Club, and in her community," said Ray Combs, host of the TV game show *Family Feud*. "Her strength of character and determination have enabled her to achieve success despite the many adversities in her life."

These kinds of stories go on and on. Another is that of Michael Jefferson. At age ten, Michael had to dodge bullets and drug deal-

---

If we want to solve the kinds of problems that children will face tomorrow, we must teach them how to believe in themselves today.

---

ers just to make his way to the Salvation Army Community Center in Techwood, Georgia, which became a Boys & Girls Club.

"It was scary just to be out," Michael said in an article in the *Atlanta Journal-Constitution*. "A lot of my friends dropped out of school or ended up in prison on drugs," he said of his neighborhood, one of the most crime infested in Atlanta, where he was raised solely by his grandmother.

"Boys & Girls Clubs provided me with a social and athletic outlet . . . and with positive role models." Today, Michael Jefferson is in his twenties and is the assistant to the executive director of the Salvation Army's five Boys & Girls Clubs in Georgia. "The clubs make a tremendous impact on lives," says Michael. "They teach kids that you can be what you want to be."

Since I have been involved with the Boys & Girls Clubs, I hear constantly about the triumphs of kids like Liberty Franklin, Kelly Zimmerman and Michael Jefferson. The reason is because Boys & Girls Clubs work, because they teach children to be self-confident. If we want to solve the kinds of problems that children will face tomorrow, we must teach them how to believe in themselves today.

"This Is Better than McDonald's!"

It was a kind of strange, fateful occurrence that led me to the Boys & Girls Clubs of America. It was 1991 and we were planning to celebrate and publicize the opening of our four hundredth Blimpie restaurant. The location was Tampa, Florida, and our idea was to invite four hundred children from the local Boys & Girls

Club to our restaurant so we could serve each of them a Blimpie sandwich.

I traveled to Tampa for the event and it was a big time. The press was there and, for the kids, there were clowns, jugglers, acrobats, and games. I soon found myself in the middle of it all, where it became apparent to me that, although the kids were really enjoying all the fun and excitement around them, the happiest moment for each of them came when they had their chance to line up, view the menu, and order the Blimpie sandwich of their choice, then take their place at a table and enjoy it.

The event was a blast for me and apparently a huge success. Then, suddenly and unexpectedly, in the midst of the fun, noise, and laughter, two things happened that gave me a whole new perspective on life.

Glenn Permuy, the director of the Boys & Girls Club of Tampa at the time, approached me. Shaking my hand with his right hand and cupping it with his left, filled with emotion, he looked at me and said, "Tony, I really, really want to thank you. This, I hope you know, will be the most nutritious meal that most of these kids will have all day." I was speechless. Oh sure, I love Blimpie sandwiches. I can eat them for breakfast, lunch, dinner, and under most any other circumstance. But the most nutritious meal? I never quite thought of my subs that way. "Did you say . . ." I wanted confirmation.

As I strolled among the tables, I couldn't stop thinking of Permoy's statement. Then, I began to focus on the kids' faces and on their remarks. I heard comments like, "Wow, this is better than McDonald's!" What an opportunity, I thought. Here's a chance to help children while helping ourselves at the same time. An opportunity to do well by doing good.

When I got back to New York, I contacted the Boys & Girls Clubs of America's headquarters (since relocated to Atlanta) and offered to create an association. Thanks to the efforts of Rick Goings, the chairman and CEO of Tupperware Worldwide, who was then chairing the clubs' marketing committee, the clubs were initiating a program of cause-related marketing. The clubs told us about a proposed violence-prevention program that it wanted to develop but that needed funding. After consulting with our National Franchisee Advisory Council, we agreed to have the

Blimpie chain fund the program, pledging $100,000 to get it started.

Our staff immediately launched a chainwide promotion that raised $25,000. Simultaneously, we conducted research in Tampa, Atlanta, and Jersey City. We conducted focus groups with male and female members of the clubs and asked these youngsters to discuss their perceptions about violence. After all, we couldn't be part of the solution unless we first understood the problem. By applying some of the skills we use in business, we felt we could help the clubs achieve their objectives.

I attended one of the sessions. As I sat, unseen, behind a glass wall, I heard how these children were terrified of the streets but also afraid to be at home. Violence was present at every turn of their lives. I observed as these twelve- to seventeen-year-olds drew pictures of violent situations, and I listened as they let us know that weapons were the preferred method of settling disputes.

"How many of you know a friend or family member who was ever shot?" asked Marissa Thompson, a Blimpie consultant who served as group moderator. Every boy raised his hand. Eight of the nine girls did the same.

"I was stabbed last week," said Ebony, seventeen.

"What happened?" asked Thompson.

"Well, I was playing basketball with this girl, and I threw the ball at her too hard."

"So she stabbed you?"

"Yeah, look, right here in my back."

Next, Angela, a fifteen-year-old from Jersey City, spoke: "This twelve-year-old boy from my neighborhood was taking his four-year-old cousin to prekindergarten. At least, that's where everybody *thought* he was taking her. Then, one day, the little girl went home and told her father that, instead, the boy was taking her to a park and molesting her."

In a matter-of-fact tone, Angela continued: "When the father found out, he got a gun and killed the boy. Now he's in jail."

"There's a fight every day in my school," said Dareen, fourteen. It's so bad, they have a police station on the first floor. You have to bring something to protect yourself."

In mostly poor neighborhoods, where Boys & Girls Clubs are likely to be located, young men and women are killing each other in astounding numbers. While some cry for more police and sterner jail sentences, it's obvious to us that these measures will not stop two emotionally charged individuals from settling their differences with a gun. Someone has to teach these young Americans how to deal with anger, how to resolve a conflict without using a weapon.

"Some kids don't even know anyone with a job," says Jim Cox, director of urban services for the clubs. "There's a sense of help-

---

Like all good relationships, partnerships work best when people care about the other's needs.

---

lessness and hopelessness out there. For some of these youths, the Boys & Girls Club is the only thing they have."

These were tough kids, street-smart kids, yet they were still just that, kids. They simply had been dealt a bad hand in the game of life. They needed love, they needed someone to care, they needed a safe place to go. They needed the Boys & Girls Clubs, and the Boys & Girls Clubs needed partners like Blimpie. Occasional chainwide promotions were not enough, so our marketing department got the mandate to develop a long-term tie-in with the clubs. The result was an idea called "Buy a Drink—Build a Link." To this day, whenever a customer buys a soft drink in most Blimpie locations, a portion of the profits goes to the clubs. This program, as well as other promotions that our company regularly conducts, continues to raise hundreds of thousands of dollars for the clubs. More recently, the program was expanded to include Blimpie's private-label products such as Blimpie Potato Chips and jarred peppers.

Cause-related marketing is a great way for a corporation like Blimpie International to help non-profit organizations like Boys & Girls Clubs of America while taking advantage of the Clubs' brand and reputation to help itself. Cause-related marketing is nothing more than a partnership. Like all good relationships, partnerships work best when people care about the other's needs.

Why Do Good?

Without help, the chances of many of America's youths making it in life are slim. Unless as many of us as possible give our brainpower, our influence, and our financial resources, the lives of so many children will remain hopeless.

It is said that people who volunteer themselves for a good cause live longer. I can't say whether that's true, but here's what is certain: Creating balance in your life—work, family, friends, community—will result in your being a happier person.

Let's not kid ourselves. While giving back may be a fulfilling experience to many, there are just as many who need a better reason than "the bottom of my heart."

Today, business has emerged as such a dominant institution in our society that the public expects community responsibility. Customers expect companies they do business with to be generous with the community. Employees want to work for a company with a policy of giving back. And, according to Hill &

> **It is said that people who volunteer themselves for a good cause live longer. Creating balance in your life—work, family, friends, community—will result in your being a happier person.**

Knowlton, a major public-relations firm, investors make stock-buying decisions based on a company's track record as a good corporate citizen.

Blimpie International's "Buy a Drink—Build a Link" program brings together a philanthropist's plan and a business goal. We are looking to drive more traffic into Blimpie restaurants. More customers mean more drinks sold. That means we are able to draw on the resources of the chain for a good business reason and to benefit our partners, the not-for-profit Boys & Girls Clubs of America. The partnership also gives each of our franchises the opportunity to develop their own local promotions with one or more of the more than 2,300 local Boys & Girls Clubs.

Blimpie is committed to the Boys & Girls Clubs and to violence reduction, and we use this as a way to gain positive press and media coverage for our chain. In short, we intend to continue to do well from doing good. Other corporations do, too, supporting disease research, safety, technology, and many other causes.

More happiness comes from giving happiness to others, so we all need to think about what happiness we can give. While corporations may take aim at improving their businesses through cause-related marketing, the ones that do it successfully must truly develop a corporate soul. Yes, at Blimpie International, we feel that our partnership with the Boys & Girls Clubs of America is good for business, but we also feel this: Violence in America is not someone else's problem. So long as this ominous trend continues, sooner or later, it will affect each of our cities, our neighborhoods, our businesses, our families, and ourselves. *We can't help every child in America, but we can sure help some.*

Of all the organizations that I am involved with, none has gotten the commitment from my mind, my body, and my pocket as much as the Boys & Girls Clubs of America, where I currently have the honor of serving on the National Board of Governors and as chairman of the clubs' marketing committee. In fact, I feel so strongly about the cause of the Boys & Girls Clubs that I have designated any profits that may come from the sale of this book to that organization.

My association with the Boys & Girls Clubs of America has given me the opportunity to meet so many wonderful kids. I've repeatedly heard stories that would break the heart of a man of

---

More happiness comes from giving happiness to others, so we all need to think about what happiness we can give.

---

steel. Over and over, I've listened to tales of struggles that were followed by Olympic-sized triumphs. Then, once in a while, one of these kids will touch me in a very special way. Here's one I'll never forget:

I was planning a business trip to Tulsa when Kevin Turner, the Blimpie International area developer there and a Boys & Girls Club supporter, asked if I'd like to include a stop at the local club on my itinerary. Knowing that local clubs always appreciate a visit from a member of the national board, I said I would. The next day, a call came in from Turner. He let me know that the club director was really excited about my upcoming visit and requested that I give a little talk to the kids while I was there.

The first thought that popped into my mind was, "What will I say? I've given numerous speeches to audiences large and small, but kids? I've never given a speech to kids." My immediate silence must have been deafening, because Turner said, "Tony, if you don't want to do this, its okay." "No, no," I said, "I'll be happy to do it, I just never gave a speech to kids before. I give speeches all the time, just not to kids." Of course, the more I thought about it, the more I realized that kids are just ordinary people and I could speak to them like I would speak to any group.

About one hundred fifty children were gathered in the gym when I started talking about the beginnings of Blimpie. Next, my conversation switched to something we should always talk to our kids about. Children should constantly be reminded that you can accomplish anything in life you desire if you just make up your mind that you are going to do it. Finally, aware that children respond well to questions, I began to ask some: "What would you like to do when you grow up?" "What's your favorite food?" "What kind of sports do you like?" Then, I asked this question: "Why do you come to the Boys & Girls Club?" It was a hot summer day, so some kids responded that they loved the pool. Others commented on how great it was to play basketball or baseball or have a quiet place to do homework. Then, I spotted one little girl who was raising her hand. "Yes, why do you come to the club?" I asked. She looked me in the eye, paused, then said, quietly, "It's better than having nothing to do."

That stopped me in my tracks. At that moment I knew, I knew, that *this* was what the organization was really about. My mom used to say, "An idle mind is the devil's workshop." It's true. After all, aren't so many of the problems of today's youth caused because kids have no place to go and nothing to do? People tend to think that kids get into trouble only at night. That's not true. Without productive and positive things to do, after-school hours can be dangerous. The gangs, the guns, the violence—they are all the things that fill in the vacuum caused by the absence of the positive things in life, the things that, in many ways, Boys & Girls Clubs provide to kids—because "it's better than having nothing to do."

How Far Are You Willing to Go?

Because I've often been willing to spend the time and make the effort, I've been able to capitalize over and over again on Blimpie International's philosophy of doing well by doing good.

There was the time in 1994, when I headed to Fort Meyers, Florida, to enter the Kiss-A-Pig contest sponsored by the Boys &

Girls Club of Lee County. I know it sounds strange, but the winner got to kiss the pig. The idea, of course, was to raise money from folks who wanted to see you pucker up to the pork. The more they gave, the better chance you had of winning. We turned the contest into a public-relations event by having Bacon, a cute oinker, meet me at a Blimpie location in a stretch limo. That led to two radio interviews, a TV appearance, and numerous photos of me holding and kissing Bacon. While I admit to having second thoughts about entering this contest and risking my dignity, I decided that it was to raise money and awareness for a good cause and was a way to gain attention for our chain.

On another occasion, I traveled to Washington, D.C., and testified on the clubs' behalf before Sen. Nancy Kassebaum's Committee on Labor and Human Resources. The hearings, which took place in October 1995, were for the Youth Development Community Block Grant Act, which called for federal assistance for youth development programs.

Later that year, I was present at the opening of the Blimpie Learning Store for the Boys & Girls Clubs, which took place at Atlanta's West End Club. We were able to get company staff and a group of Blimpie franchisees to volunteer to work with sixteen- and seventeen-year old club members to run the store and teach them skills about operating a business. The opening garnered TV coverage by NBC news, a story in the *Atlanta Journal,* and positive press by community organizations. There are always opportunities available whereby you can do something that will raise awareness for yourself or for your business. It's really worth taking the extra steps necessary to make them happen.

Introducing Our New Blimpie, er, Clubs Commercial

Something I've always liked about the Boys & Girls Clubs is that they share my philosophy of taking business seriously but taking life lightly. Because of that, I've been able to have some real fun with the organization.

The clubs' 1995 Annual Convention was exciting. More than 1,300 people attended. My speech was to an audience that was anxiously awaiting the first viewing of the newest TV public-service announcement, featuring actor Denzel Washington. I spoke about our marketing initiatives, gave out some marketing awards and, finally, knowing the audience was focussed on Denzel Washington, said: "It's now time for me to premier our long-awaited public-service announcement. The spokesperson you are about to see is talented, sincere—and incredibly handsome. Let's roll it."

And, on the big screen, there it was, a Blimpie commercial with me in it. The crowd roared.

Immediately afterwards, we showed the real ad, and Denzel Washington gave a short motivating speech. He's a very passionate guy, and he is dedicated to the clubs.

I was glad to be able to add a little fun to the convention, and, of course, I was always happy to get Blimpie awareness.

In Plains View

The first time I met Yvonne, we talked for a long time. During the course of our conversation, she told me there were two things she always wanted to do. The first was to visit Amsterdam. "I can't explain why, but as a child, I always dreamed of being in Amsterdam. I was always fascinated with being in the city and seeing the canals," she said. The second was that she wanted to meet former President Jimmy Carter. "I've always admired Jimmy Carter. I think he's a really good man. I'd love to meet him."

Later that year, we completed a second public offering for Blimpie International stock. Nick Pronk, one of our investment bankers, it turned out, was Dutch. In fact, because he had sold a bunch of our stock to investors in Holland, he called me one day

---

**It's your responsibility to support the causes
that you deem worthwhile.**

---

and said, "Tony, if you can, I'd like you to make a trip to Amsterdam to meet with a group of investors over there and bring them up to date on the outlook for the company." I immediately picked up the phone, called Yvonne, and said, "Guess where we're going?"

In 1999, I found out that Jimmy Carter was building a Boys & Girls Club in Plains, Georgia, and that he needed financing. I had a phone conversation with him and promised to try to raise money for his project. A few months later, I got a call from the clubs' senior vice president, Kurt Aschermann. "A group of us are going to Plains, would you like to join us?" he asked. "You bet," I answered, then called Yvonne and said, "Guess where we're going?"

Most of the people who were supposed to travel to Plains cancelled out. Yvonne and I decided to go anyway, and Roxanne Spillett, the clubs' president, agreed to go with us and drive us there in her car. Before we left, however, I was forewarned by Kurt. "The president is there working. This will not be a social event. If you go, be prepared to work."

I was in Washington just before going to Georgia, and, as a light packer, had only my business suit and a pair of khakis and dress loafers with me. Yvonne was smarter. She wore Timberland boots and a pair of jeans.

When the three of us arrived in Plains, Jimmy Carter was there in his work clothes, electric saw in hand. He stopped to greet us, handed each of us a hammer, then, pointing in the direction of the sky, said, "There's the roof." The roof? I figured maybe we'd be putting up a few two-by-fours, but it never occurred to me that we might be installing a roof! Yvonne is afraid of heights. Roxanne never held a hammer in her hand before. And me—I was in pressed khakis and dress shoes.

Nevertheless, the thirty-ninth president of the United States had pointed the way, so up we went and, for three hours, we nailed shingles into the roof of Jimmy Carter's Boys & Girls Club until the president gave us the signal to join him and his wife for lunch on the work site. After lunch, Roxanne and I presented Carter with a couple of checks for the clubs.

The president gave us the opportunity to partake in a photo shoot with him and, all in all, it was a fun, rewarding and, yes, exhausting experience. And the community is now home to a brand-new Boys & Girls Club.

When I was young, I never volunteered for anything. Later on, I learned that that was a mistake. Volunteering usually makes you have fun while it creates a warm, fuzzy feeling inside of you because you're doing something good.

Saving the Dolphins

Over the years, it has become ever more important for corporations to form relationships with their customers. These relationships must be based on trust because, if consumers don't trust you, they may not buy your products. Corporations that do good, that act decently, will inspire trust.

Blimpie stores sell a lot of tuna—about two million pounds, enough for 11.5 million sandwiches, a year. I was horrified to learn, early in 1990, that our tuna may have been purchased from companies that were using fishing methods that harmed dolphins.

I was awakened to this possibility by a publication from the Earth Island Institute Dolphin Project. Tuna fisherman had unknowingly hired an Earth Island reporter who photographed and recorded what happens on tuna boats. It appeared that as many as one hundred fifty thousand dolphins a year were being slaughtered by tuna fishermen.

A book called *The Green Consumer* (Penguin Books, 1990) describes what happens:

> Yellowfin tuna, for reasons unknown, often gather below herds of dolphin so tuna fleets watch for them. Then, in a practice known as "setting on dolphins," fishermen chase the dolphins with helicopters and speedboats. Exhausted and terrified, the dolphins are then encircled in nets up to a mile long. Trapped, the air-breathing dolphins suffocate and drown. The result: Mixed in with 100 dead dolphins may be a dozen tuna.

Armed with this knowledge, Blimpie International immediately began working on a solution. First, we adopted an environmentally responsible stance: Blimpie International would sell only tuna that is completely dolphin-safe and that carried a dolphin-safe guarantee from our national food distributors. Next, we offered to

---

Children should constantly be reminded that you can accomplish anything in life you desire if you just make up your mind that you are going to do it.

---

help solve the problem by supporting the Dolphin Research Center in Marathon, Florida. Finally, we set out to build public awareness of the issue by contacting newspapers and making TV appearances.

Soon after, NBC news interviewed me and a Starkist representative, and the world's largest tuna brand agreed to sell only tuna that did not harm dolphins.

Today, all tuna sold in Blimpie locations remains dolphin-free, and Starkist has become our tuna supplier.

Of course, having a corporate soul is not always that simple. After all, corporations are in business to make money. Suppose, for example, that serving dolphin-safe tuna meant paying substantially more for the product, enough to, say, double the price of our sandwiches? How would our customers react to that?

We cannot forget that corporations work for shareholders. Although a healthy company can have a positive and seemingly infinite impact on others, a sick company is a drag on the social order of things. It cannot serve customers. It cannot give to philanthropic causes. It cannot contribute anything to society. Roberto Goizueta, the late chairman of Coca-Cola said, "We as a company, take it upon ourselves to do good deeds that directly raise the quality of life in the communities in which we do business. But the real and lasting benefits don't come because we do good deeds, but because we do good work, work focussed on our mission to create value. We must not fail to fulfill this mission. There are far too many people depending on us." Ultimately, a corporation will respond to the wants and needs of its consumers. As consumer and as a good citizen, it's your responsibility to support the causes that you deem worthwhile.

Generosity Can Cut Your Taxes

A well-timed gift to charity can not only support a worthy cause but, at the same time, can slash your taxes.

When you donate tangible personal property that you have owned more than a year and that has increased in value, you can deduct not only the cost of the item, but the full fair market value. Say you invested $10,000 in a stock and the price of the stock has tripled in value to $30,000. If you sell the stock, you end up with a $20,000 gain, which must be reported on your tax return. On the other hand, you get a double tax benefit by simply giving the stock away: First, you avoid tax on the capital gain, and second, you get to write off the fair market value. The same rules apply to real estate, artwork, antiques, used cars, and other personal items. It's Uncle Sam's way of taking the pain out of giving.

Giving Back Brings Back

"When you stop giving, when you stop offering something, it's time to turn out the lights," said George Burns. While I believe wholeheartedly in the concept of doing well by doing good, I've come to understand that the "doing well" part doesn't have to relate to money.

A nonprofit organization that I've enthusiastically supported is the Limón Dance Company. I've always loved dance. I am enthralled with how performers can communicate a story through dance while wonderful music accompanies them. We attend probably two dozen dance performances a year, including those by the New York City Ballet, American Ballet Theatre, and various modern-dance performances at New York's Joyce Theatre. So, when I was approached about joining the board of directors of Limón, I was interested.

José Limón died in 1972, but the modern-classic company that he founded lives on under artistic director Carla Maxwell but, as the company approached its fiftieth anniversary, it was struggling to stay alive. Fortunately, it was now being managed by Executive Director Mark Jones, who is credited with eliminating the company's deficit. When I took a close look at the company, I became

> **There are always opportunities available whereby you can raise awareness for your business. It's really worth taking the extra steps necessary to make them happen.**

aware of how wonderful its repertoire was. Also, I realized that a turnaround process was in place. I liked that. It reminded me of the rebirth of Blimpie International. I felt that I could bring my business experience, not just my financial contributions, to the table, so since 1992, I've been a member of the board and for two years, I served as the company's chairman.

My involvement with Limón, although offering limited exposure to Blimpie International and not particularly bringing me business benefits, has fulfilled my "doing well" requirement by delivering intangible benefits to me. I've garnered an education about dance performances and what goes on behind the scenes. I've learned a little about what life looks like through the eyes of an artist and an arts organization. I've also admired the dedication, sacrifices, and commitment of the dancers, observing them as they endure long hours of practice while sometimes tolerating painful injuries.

Of course, I've also been able to appreciate the choreographic works of a wonderful dance company, and know that my support helps preserve the arts, which contribute so much to the lives of Americans.

EZ Business

In 1998, as we were exploring ways to accelerate the expansion of the Blimpie chain, we reminded ourselves that we had very few stores in inner cities, in locations designated as Empowerment Zones or Enterprise Communities by the U.S. Department of Housing and Urban Development. Our policy of doing well by doing good provided the impetus for us to search for ways to develop our chain in these zones at the same time that we created opportunities for deserving entrepreneurs.

Our company approached a HUD official and asked what we could expect if Blimpie International was to award up to two hundred franchises—with initial franchise fees waived—to qualified

---

Volunteering usually makes you have fun while it creates a warm, fuzzy feeling inside of you because you're doing something good.

---

and deserving entrepreneurs in Empowerment Zones or Enterprise Communities across the United States.

After receiving a favorable response, here's how we proceeded:

Blimpie would promote this opportunity to Empowerment Zones or Enterprise Communities across the United States. Initial fees would be waived to qualified applicants, who would be able to start their own businesses and create jobs for zone residents. Their applications would have to include a business plan, a financial package, and an essay indicating why they believe they should be awarded a Blimpie franchise. Each application would be reviewed by a committee of civic, academic, and business leaders from the local community—people who have committed their time to help us select our franchisees.

After receiving the committee's recommendations, Blimpie International is prepared to make selections. This plan, we feel, will not only help us accelerate the growth of the Blimpie chain, it will do so while creating opportunities for those who live in the communities, understand them, love them, and want to do something for themselves and those communities.

Previous efforts to stimulate economic development in the inner cities have generally been ineffective. They have taken the form of subsidies or special programs or have been directed at fields such as housing or real estate. These efforts have failed to recognize that inner cities, unlike the other parts of the cities, are underserved by local businesses, particularly retail businesses. Establishing a Blimpie restaurant, for example, would:

- Provide an opportunity for an aspiring entrepreneur

- Create jobs

- Build wealth

- Take advantage of the community's own spending power

Inner-city populations are huge and, although incomes of residents are lower, there simply are a lot of people there, making for substantial overall spending power. These are also young and

---

Having started this business with no money myself, I know that just because someone doesn't have money doesn't mean he or she can't create a success. All they need is the opportunity.

---

growing markets. All this provides an opportunity for Blimpie to increase its market penetration while building brand loyalty and brand awareness.

To get our program started, after consultation with HUD, we proposed that Atlanta and Detroit become the cities in which to create the model that could be rolled out to Empowerment Zones across the country.

Although there remains a lot of old thinking among business and government about what is needed to develop the inner cities, I see a new attitude developing, one that makes the public and private sectors partners in economic development. Organizations like HUD and the SBA are absolutely needed to provide capital and the proper environment, but they must combine with the hard work, determination, and passion of individuals and the support of an organization like Blimpie International to create real success stories and real economic development in the communities.

Having started this business with no money myself, I know that just because someone doesn't have money doesn't mean he or she can't create a success. All they need is the opportunity. The Blimpie International philosophy of doing well by doing good cannot be perceived as exploitative. By not charging an initial fee, the only way our company can benefit is by collecting our 6 percent royalty on sales. Everything else stays in the zone—to the benefit of zone residents.

When we first struck up the Empowerment Zone initiative at Blimpie International, I couldn't help noticing two parallels with the Boys & Girls Clubs of America. The first relates to the essence of strategic alliances and the reasons why companies like Blimpie get involved with worthy causes: an opportunity to do well by doing good. The second parallel has to do with helping people

---

We can create new jobs, we can train workers and teach them real-life skills, we can bring millions of new dollars into the local economy, and we can give deserving entrepreneurs an opportunity to own their own Blimpie franchise.

---

realize their dreams. With the Boys & Girls Clubs of America movement, it's kids—helping them meet the challenges of the streets and grow into productive adults. With the Empowerment Zone initiative, it's entrepreneurs—helping them with opportunities so they can get their own businesses and achieve success.

There are a lot of deserving people in the inner cities and it would be great to give each of them a Blimpie sandwich, but that would only feed them for a day. On the other hand, we can create new jobs, we can train workers and teach them real-life skills, we can bring millions of new dollars into the local economy, and we can give deserving entrepreneurs an opportunity to own their own Blimpie franchise. Then, we'll be feeding them for a lifetime.

People Want to Help

"A friend in need is a pest," said comedian Joe E. Lewis. I sincerely believe that most people don't feel that way, that most people want to help yet, often, they don't know how.

If someone is facing bad times and needs help, he may discover that people seem to vanish. So often, it's because they are not sure what to do. They get shy, or they're afraid of embarrassing the other person, so they stop calling, stop communicating. Maybe they want to say, "Hey, I can't afford much, but here's a few bucks."

The same is true when it comes to charitable contributions. That's why charities have a policy of, "If you want, ask." Sometimes, people just need to be asked. Sometimes, also, you need to give them a little incentive. At Blimpie International, we are always inventing ways for employees to make contributions to the Boys & Girls Club. We've had Jeans Day and Slipper Day where by if you wore one of those items to work on that day, you had to

---

When there is a need, most people are willing to help. By no means, have expectations. But if you need something, ask.

---

pay $3 to the club fund. We've also done things like sell our old computers to employees, agreeing to donate all proceeds to the clubs. Before you know it, you end up with $1,000 here and $2,000 there. It all adds up.

One group that never needs a reminder to give is the staff of the Boys & Girls Clubs organization. I'm always amazed at how much these folks ante up. In 1999, 192 employees contributed a total of $120,000, an average of $625 apiece. When there is a need, most people are willing to help. By no means, have expectations. But if you need something, ask.

Feeling Good by Doing Good

All the organizations I am involved with—the Boys & Girls Clubs of America, the Limón Dance Company, the Dean's Council at Harvard University's John F. Kennedy School of Government, the National Italian American Foundation—offer rewards. There's the opportunity to make important business and social contacts, the value of upgrading corporate image, the chance to enhance professional skills, the cachet of being recognized as a community leader, and the prestige of serving on a board filled with CEOs and chairmen of some of America's largest corporations, government leaders, celebrities, and other people of influence and means. The real reward comes, I feel, when you can look in the mirror and say to yourself, "I am advancing a cause that I believe in. I am doing good." That's a very powerful reward indeed.

CHAPTER 9

BUILDING ON THE BEST: SUCCEEDING AFTER SUCCESS

> The greatest challenge a business
> faces is surviving success.
>
> —**Malcolm Forbes**

B uilding on the Best—succeeding after you've already achieved success—is often surprisingly difficult.

That's why we chose Building on the Best as the theme for the 1998 Blimpie International convention in St. Louis, Missouri. There's a pun in those words. The main message was straightforward: Just because you have achieved the best at something doesn't mean that you should stop building. By choosing that title for the biggest company event of the year, we were also recognizing that all over the world, the sandwich that we call the Blimpie Best has traditionally been our most popular menu item.

Why is it so hard to keep going after you've achieved some success? I think there are four important reasons that you should avoid as much as possible.

Avoid Creeping Complacency

In 1995, we completed our second public offering of Blimpie International stock. Included in this multimillion-dollar offering was some personal stock, held by me and the company's other three largest shareholders. All four of us had been with Blimpie for at least twenty years (for me, it was thirty-one). Although we had done very well financially, for much of that time our personal stock had been unmarketable. That meant that, although we always thought that some day it would be worth real money, none of us ever assigned much value to it when we computed our personal financial statements.

Then, in 1995, we were able to cash in. Oh, percentagewise, the stock we sold was a relatively small piece of our ownership, but our proceeds made for the largest checks any of us had ever

---

Complacency leads to passivity, to mental laziness. Instead of a motion picture, you become a still photo. You stop thinking, you stop getting things done.

---

deposited in our lives. You could almost hear the sighs of relief and accomplishment from our group, as if we said, "Whew, we finally arrived. We achieved success."

Amid this euphoria, aided by a tripling in the price of Blimpie International stock, we realized that complacency had a chance of invading us. We reacted. I urged our group to work on a new initiative that we had on the table, something we called "New Wave . . . Toward A New Century." New Wave would lead us toward global development and change us to a company that franchises a family of brands, instead of just one brand.

You never want to be in the position of being *re*active instead of *pro*active. You don't want to take your successes and say, "Let's keep expanding. What can possibly go wrong?" Or think you are so smart for picking the right stock and making a lot of money that you bet the farm on the next one. Success can make you feel so good that you think you can walk on water. That's when you get into trouble.

If you stop exercising, you get fat and flabby. That's the kind of effect complacency has. Complacency leads to passivity, to mental laziness. Instead of a motion picture, you become a still photo. You stop thinking, you stop getting things done, new ideas become a thing of the past, and before you know it, momentum starts to work against you. Complacency will hurt your marriage, your job, your business, your relationship with your kids, your golf game. It will stifle your creative process. It will turn you into a lemming.

Building on the Best demands that you be aware of change, that you open your mind to the future, and that you maintain the passion for success.

Beware of Thinking You Know Too Much

You've heard the old saw that a little knowledge can be a dangerous thing, and I believe that a lot of knowledge can be even worse.

If knowledge and experience are applied to opening your mind to new ideas, yes, that will take you toward continued success. However, if you become so knowledgeable, so experienced, that you close your mind to change, you are merely looking into a rear-view mirror. That can be dangerous.

One of the best partnerships that Blimpie International has had since we opened our first restaurant is our liaison with the Coca-Cola Company. Ironically, though, Coke's knowledge, experience, and efficiency almost destroyed that relationship.

It was in the late 1980s, during the rebirth of Blimpie International, when we were rebuilding, restructuring, and reexamining our relationships with all our suppliers.

Pepsico got wind of the situation and proceeded to aggressively pursue our account. It wanted our business, wanted it badly, and let us know that in no uncertain terms. The temptation to make Pepsi our cola beverage of choice was becoming great.

But Blimpie International has always been a loyal customer. Coca-Cola had served our needs well over the years, and we weren't prepared to discard our relationship so quickly, at least not without giving Coke the opportunity to accommodate the changes that we thought were necessary.

Into the picture came two Coca-Cola executives who reported directly to their company's Atlanta headquarters. Hugh Gordon and Jack Clark took the time to listen. They made it known to us that they cared about our partnership and they assured us that Atlanta's sentiment was equal to theirs.

Negotiations were difficult, and sometimes strained, until one day at the offices of McCann Erickson, the ad agency for Coke. As Hugh Gordon sat beside him, Jack Clark looked me squarely in the eye and said, "Tony, I want you to know this right here and now: Coca-Cola is not going to lose your business." I could tell that this was not an empty promise. The company had finally gotten the picture. Blimpie International was an account it wanted to keep for the future. We worked out our issues pretty quickly, and Blimpie and its franchisees entered into a new long-term agreement with the Coca-Cola Company.

Coca-Cola is one of the most widely recognized and respected brands on the planet, and that's because Coca-Cola is so good at what it does. As a Coca-Cola customer, Blimpie knew that it could always count on Coke to provide the best quality soft drinks at a reasonable price. The product, we were sure, would always be

---

Building on the Best demands that you be aware of change, that you open your mind to the future, and that you maintain the passion for success.

---

delivered on time and dispensed properly through efficient equipment, provided by the company. After all, Coke had a consummate knowledge about its business.

Unfortunately, it was so good at what it was doing that it wasn't really looking for new ways to do it better. The company's own knowledge was acting as a deterrent to succeeding after success, and it was beginning to cost the company market share.

In a small way, I believe that Blimpie helped Coca-Cola understand why it had to change the way they looked at its customers. Blimpie was not simply another syrup account. Rather, it was a business that put the Coca-Cola brand into the mouths of millions of consumers every year. If Coca-Cola wanted to grow, the best thing it could do was help companies like Blimpie grow, which meant having an intimate understanding of, and relationship with, Blimpie International, our management, our franchisees, and our customers. Coca-Cola needed to expand its knowledge to incorporate what inspired, motivated, and interested the Blimpie customers.

I told this Blimpie–Coke story during a speech I gave to Coke executives at their Pan Latin conference in Buenos Aires in the spring of 1997. Soon after, I received a letter from the beverage company's chairman, Roberto Goizueta, in which he said, "Your speech was outstanding because the story it tells is an unbelievably exciting one. I want you to know that I am sharing a copy of your speech with our five Group Presidents, the President of the Minute Maid Company, and with Doug Ivester (chief operating officer at the time) because there are a number of lessons that all of us can derive from reading it."

Today, Coca-Cola has a strong culture based on Building on the Best. This culture has not only helped the company grow and achieve continued success, but it has done the same for its customers as well. Blimpie is now referred to as a strategic partner, and Coca-Cola regularly focuses on marketing programs to enhance the Blimpie consumer experience and franchisee experience. It also works on marketing strategies for our new brand concepts, and Coca-Cola developed an *International Briefing Document* that can be used by Coke distributors around the world to help them optimally service Blimpie restaurants in every country. The Blimpie–Coke partnership, where together, everyone can accomplish more, has proven to be an excellent way to Build on the Best.

Don't Be Afraid to Fail

"Success is 99 percent failure," says Soichiro Honda, founder of Honda Motor Corporation. Babe Ruth came close to proving it, since he struck out 1,330 times in his career.

Yes, failing is okay. Admitting to your mistakes is not a negative thing. Failure should serve as a teacher. When you learn from your mistakes, your experience makes you wiser, stronger, better at what you do. It's when you become so afraid of repeating a failure and you avoid taking any risks that it militates against "Building on the Best."

This almost happened to us in 1998. After completing the acquisition of the trademark and development rights for a small, quick-service chain in Hawaii called Maui Tacos, we were confronted with the challenge of opening the first location on the mainland. Internally, the question of whether Blimpie International should open and operate the restaurant became controversial. Maui Tacos was, after all, a Mexican concept (though with a Hawaiian flair), and a decade earlier we had failed miserably with our Border Cafes, another Mexican concept.

Had we let that failure affect our judgment, we would have avoided a financial risk, but at the same time we would have missed the opportunity to learn as much about the concept as possible, work out the bugs in the system, and take an important step toward moving the chain to the next level of growth.

Instead, we carefully analyzed our failure:

BEFORE	AFTER
Loss of focus. Company incapable of developing two businesses at the same time.	Strategic plan calls for development of a family of brands.
Border Cafes were a different business—table service, full liquor bar, not franchised.	Maui Tacos are quick-service restaurants established to be franchised.
No infrastructure had been built.	Management realignment is a component of our current strategic initiative.
The company had limited finances.	Blimpie International has a strong balance sheet and a strong cash position, with a stock listed on the American Stock Exchange.

Our analysis made it obvious to us that we shouldn't fail to make the correct move now because we feared repeating a mistake in a prior situation.

The most successful people never stop Building on the Best, regardless of their failures. One of these is racing legend Richard Petty. Petty has won seven Daytona 500 races, seven Winston Cup Championships, and two hundred races. He also helped transform stock-car racing from a regional Southeastern sport to a national pastime watched by millions of fans across the United States. The most amazing aspect of Petty's continuing pursuit of success is that it occurs despite his failures—and when you fail in a high-speed race, something really bad usually happens. Petty's failures have resulted in two broken necks, both shoulders broken, numerous broken fingers, both feet broken, and ribs shattered so many times that he can't even count them. Yet, for example, in spite of spinning into one of the worst wrecks of his career at Daytona in 1988, he raced the next weekend. And what makes this legend go on? "Just to be remembered covers everything," he says.

Can you imagine if Mark McGwire started worrying about striking out every time he came up to the plate? Can you imagine if he stopped swinging as hard as he does just because swinging hard increases the risk of missing entirely? What would be his chances of ever being a home-run champion again?

If you start looking to avoid risk so that you can avoid failure, you're dead. Failure is an important ingredient in Building on the Best.

Watch Out for Self-destruction

Throughout this book, I've discussed success, and I have not defined it as making or having money. As an aside, though, I repeat a story told by Jackie Mason in *Laugh Your Calories Away:*

> Very few people know how to be happy. That's why you see so many books telling you how to be happy. The other day I saw a book, *How to Be Happy Without Money.* This book costs $15. It goes to show you—if you've got no money, you can't even find out how to be happy without it.

Making money, of course, is a fundamental responsibility for all of us. But if your view of life is that making money is all that matters, not how you make it or what makes it grow, then I promise you that you will stifle creativity, smother passion, and promote stagnation. Once that happens, all the fun goes away.

Today, young people are making more money faster and sooner than at any time in history. In fact, there are more millionaires in this country under age fifty than ever before. Yet many of these folks seem to self-destruct. After achieving financial success, they get depressed, they take Prozac, they drink too much—and it

---

If you start looking to avoid risk so that you can avoid failure, you're dead. Failure is an important ingredient in Building on the Best.

---

all seems intentionally self-destructive. You read about the Wall Street genius who gets convicted of insider trading, the football star who gets caught with ten grams of cocaine, and the well-known newspaper reporter who fabricates a story. It's as though financial success has become a drug in itself. Self-esteem gets tied to bringing in more and more money, but all to please others, not to please yourself.

Successful people should be mindful of the signs of self-destruction:

- You are so obsessed with making money that you ignore your family, your hobbies, and all the other pleasures of life.

- You know you are good at making money but your self-esteem is faltering.

- The more you see others making money, the more your anxiety level increases.

- You're not having any fun.

- The only time you relax is when you are taking a drug or some kind of medication.

Building on the Best is a goal that all of us should have, but the price of success shouldn't be the loss of your dignity, principles,

---

If your view of life is that making money is all that matters, not how you make it or what makes it grow, then I promise you that you will stifle creativity, smother passion, and promote stagnation.

---

or self-respect. Don't lose sight of the fact that true success means doing meaningful work, reaching your dreams, and enjoying life, *not* just making money.

Building on the Best will never happen for you because you want to make more money. It will happen because of a love, a desire, and a passion for reaching a dream.

You may ask: What if we don't have great aspirations? What if we don't have far-reaching dreams? What if we're happy with what we have, happy with what we do?

Well, then I say your task is *still* "Building on the Best." And that means two things:

- Understanding exactly what it is that you do and the best way to do it.

- Executing it at higher and higher levels.

I don't care whether it's growing a garden or dancing on your toes, slam-dunking a basketball or making a Blimpie sandwich. If you're going to do it, put your heart into it, pursue it with a passion, get it to the point where it becomes an energy force in itself.

I hung up my long-distance running shoes a long time ago, but I still remember the feeling I would get during one of my runs. I'd really have to struggle to get started on my ten-, fifteen-, or eighteen-mile journey but, then, passing the seven- or eight-mile marker, I'd suddenly find myself with a new energy. I'd moved to a new dimension. It was as if my body was traveling the road by itself and I was along for the ride. I was in a moment that should have been complete misery, but I was having a great time.

I've witnessed this same feeling seeing well-operated Blimpie restaurants during, say, a very busy lunch-hour rush. Customers keep coming from what seems like an endless line. But the franchisee and the crew are not bitching and complaining, they're having a ball.

Not only are they executing their skills accurately and swiftly, they are performing as though they were on stage. The customers have become the audience and the crew is putting on a performance for them—and it's not just a performance out of the Blimpie International Operations Manual, it's the spirit and passion of people who are enjoying what they are doing.

And customers love it.

Eight Challenges of Growth

In the Coca-Cola Company's 1996 annual report, Chairman Roberto Goizueta wrote this to his shareholders:

> Even after another rewarding year, the Coca-Cola Company is still unquenchably thirsty—thirsty for more ways to reach more consumers in more places with more of our products. . . .We have worked hard to make that unending craving one of the trademarks that define us as a company, like our contour bottle and our script logo.

Think about it: To the Coca-Cola Company, growth is not just important. It's as important as Coke's trademarks.

Everyone wants to grow, but growth always raises new questions. When do I hire people to do my job so I can do something else? How do I maintain a small-company mentality if my company is getting bigger? At what point must I worry that growth will control me? Will my skills, my product work in the future? How much money do I want? How much power? How much is enough?

The different stages of growth always present new challenges. Let's take a look at some of these.

1. New Paths

A brand is a promise. It's about a collective set of expectations and the delivery of those expectations. The Blimpie brand promise has always meant that the ingredients that are served in Blimpie locations are *real,* not requiring small-print explanations. When our menu says "ham," it's not turkey-based ham. When it says "cheese," it's not a cheese substitute.

There was never a question about this brand promise—until we awarded a franchise in the Middle East. Muslims don't eat pork, yet the Blimpie menu contains many pork items. In fact, the ingredients of the Blimpie Best, our best-selling sandwich world-wide, are ham, salami, prosciuttini, and cappicola, all of which are

---

Don't lose sight of the fact that true success means doing meaningful work, reaching your dreams, and enjoying life, *not* just making money.

---

pork-based. This presented a brand crisis at Blimpie International headquarters. Do we adjust the menu so that our most popular sandwiches are eliminated, or do we go with turkey-based meats, as our competition does? After much debate, it was decided that we needed to accommodate the marketplace and give our customers in the Middle East what they want. Our restaurants in that part of the world serve turkey-based meats.

Another example of accommodating the marketplace had to do with slicing our meats and cheeses in front of the customer. For thirty years, there was no variation on this policy. Then, along came Delta Airlines. In an attempt to upgrade its food offerings, Delta sought an agreement to serve Blimpie sandwiches on many of its flights. It didn't take us long to figure out that the airline was not going to have its flight attendants roll a slicing machine down the center aisle, so we allowed Delta's commissary to slice the meats and make the sandwiches in advance.

2. New Responsibilities

I know an architect who started his own firm years ago because he enjoyed designing buildings. Success led him on a growth path and his company got larger and larger. As the firm grew, he found himself devoting more and more time to administrative duties while foregoing the creative side of the business. This, he found out, was no fun. He missed doing the work that he really wanted to do, so he sold the business and went back to doing what he loved, designing buildings.

Some folks like what they are doing and don't want to take on any more responsibility. Others may want to take certain steps so that they may grow into a position demanding more leadership or vision. I have always chosen the second path.

In the early 1990s, as I looked into the future, I saw that the best I could do, long-term, for the company and for me was to hire someone who could eventually assume the responsibilities of running the Blimpie chain. So, in 1992, we brought Joe Morgan on board. Joe is my son-in-law, and that naturally raised a few eyebrows. Rather than having him report to me right away, and also because he was a young lawyer, we placed him under David Siegel. This worked out well because not only is the legal side of our business essential to the functioning of Blimpie International, it's also a great way to get an overall learning experience about company operations. Since his arrival, through hard work, smarts, drive, and passion, Joe has gained the confidence of the Blimpie International staff and executives so that he now runs the company's day-to-day operations. As a result, I am now in a position to spend more time on executive, strategic, and visionary issues instead of administrative and operations issues.

It all depends on what you want your lifestyle to be and what you enjoy doing the most. You have to establish your own rules, your own goals. Decide how you want to grow. When you wake up five years from now, who do you want to be? What do you want your life to be like?

3. Thinking Too Big

This is an interesting phenomenon, and I've witnessed it. Someone starts a business with a small amount of capital and quickly achieves tremendous growth. Thinking that he has already arrived, he'll start bringing in expensive consultants and high-priced executives while radically expanding his staff. He'll also pick up that Porsche that he had always wanted and start dining regularly at fancy restaurants. All the time, he's moving farther away from the entrepreneurial skills that got him there in the first place.

Obviously, new levels of growth require that you take advantage of the growth. You have to hire the right people and integrate them into your growing organization. But you can't get disillusioned by growth and start acting like you're a Fortune 500 company. Decisions shouldn't be based on whether or not you want to grow; they should answer the question, "How fast?"

Sometimes speed is important. For example, in the mid-1990s, we became aware of a paradigm shift in the convenience-store business. Convenience stores wanted to install quick-service food

---

**Building on the Best will never happen for
you because you want to make more money.
It will happen because of a love, a desire,
and a passion for reaching a dream.**

---

places in their outlets, and we concluded that this was a window of opportunity that wouldn't last very long—that the rush to do this would be over in a few years. So we threw people and money at this situation, enabling us to capture a large part of this opportunity.

On the other hand, while we also see international growth as an opportunity, we visualize it only as long term. For sure, we are making the investment, but we are careful about trying to grow too fast and losing control.

"If you are going to think, you may as well think big," says Donald Trump. Well, this is the way to go for some of us. Just keep in mind that if you experienced extraordinary growth in the short term, don't automatically think that you have arrived. To do so may be a little like playing Russian roulette: The odds of winning may be very good, but you can't play again if you lose.

4. A Step Back

One of my favorite activities back in the 1970s was go to discotheques. It was such a great way to escape from the real world, if even for just a short while. In a crowded disco, you'd find yourself on the dance floor elbow-to-elbow with hundreds of people. Loud music would blare from overhead speakers as smoke billowed out and camouflaged half your body parts. You couldn't see more than about eighteen inches in front of you.

I also remember something else about most discos—that there usually was a place where you could take a step back and stand above the crowd. Now you could see everything. Suddenly, you were focusing on the whole place, not just your eighteen inches.

One of the most valuable things you can do in life, particularly during a period of growth, is to periodically take a step back. Any kind of growth can change your life, and you need to get some perspective on that.

When Blimpie International was a regional company with restaurants only in the Northeast, I didn't need to travel very much. Today, I'm a Continental Airlines Platinum Flyer. Once, I had only my family to worry about. Today, there are close to twenty thousand people in the Blimpie system. These are the kinds of changes that seriously affect your life. It's important to regularly reexamine what you are doing to be certain that you are staying on track toward your goals.

When you take a step back, you give yourself the opportunity to re-examine your goals. If you do, you may find, for example, that your goals are oriented almost entirely toward money—rising to a high income level at your company, buying a much bigger house, and so on. You know it's going to be difficult to achieve your goal of maintaining an enriching marriage if you are a world-class investment banker who is expected to cancel a Christmas vacation with the family to get a deal done.

What about other quality-of-life goals? Is there a language you want to learn? Is there a worthy cause you would like to be involved with? How about your weight? Are there novels you would like to read? Movies you would like to see? Should you be spending more time with the family, taking more time off?

A good way to handle this is to draw an imaginary line right now and look at everything above that line as the completion of your life so far. It's the personal version of a corporation's annual report. The facts and figures in that report are over and done with. The company is now into a new year. It can't change what's done, but it can set new goals and pursue new paths for the future.

You have choices to make. Everything from the past—what you did well, what you didn't do so well—is, in fact, over. It's history. Starting today, you can choose to do, to be, something entirely different. All your experiences—as a child, a parent, a leader, a lover, a teacher, a student—and all the issues you've confronted in life and battles that you've fought, they're all part of you now. So, use them not to be stuck in the past but to help you set new goals and move into the future.

In a world that so highly covets progress and activity, sometimes the most productive thing you can do is stop and reflect. So, take a step back, give yourself some breathing space, collect your thoughts, reconfirm your goals or establish new ones, renew your passion, and move into the future.

5. Tension and Stress

During my father's forty-five years working for the New York Stock Exchange, he witnessed countless brokers, specialists, order clerks, and others suffering heart attacks or other medical problems during trading hours. They were all victims of stress. Dad used to tell me how stressful his own job was. He was a reporter, responsible for getting the details of stock transactions onto the

---

Decide how you want to grow. When you wake up five years from now, who do you want to be? What do you want your life to be like?

---

ticker, but I realize now that he really liked what he did and that when he spoke of his own "stress," he really meant "tension." There's a big difference. Tension is a form of excitement. It's what happens when you're about to close a big deal or when you are making an important presentation. Stress, on the other hand, is negative—a situation in which your emotions are in conflict.

People often ask me, "Tony, you've done well. Do you ever think of slowing down? Do you imagine retiring?" My answer is always a quick "no." And the reason is that I like what I do. I'm having fun. Oh, sure, there's a lot of pressure and tension in my day but, so what? It comes with the territory.

Stress happens when, for example, you're in a marriage that makes you unhappy or in a job you don't like. Stress is also caused by risk.

An understanding of your own risk tolerance is essential if you want to avoid stress. In any situation, there's no need to worry about what might go right. The right things take care of themselves. A cause for worry is what might go wrong. If the negative effects of what can go wrong in a risk situation are so great that they will cause you untold stress, then it's not worth taking the risk.

Let's say you really like the growth prospects of a certain company, so you decide to buy its stock—a lot of it. If the stock price declines and you realize that the hit you would take if the stock continued its decline would be more than you could handle, you get totally stressed out. You know you were too greedy. Sleeplessness invades your nights. Wear and tear is at your mind all day long. "Why did I ever do something as stupid as this?" you say. "The stress just wasn't worth it."

Stress will take a toll on your immune system. It will make you sick. It will kill you. As you face challenges of growth in all aspects of your life, properly assess the risk and assume only as much of it to ensure that you avoid stress.

6. Surprises

Growth often springs surprises—both positive and negative—on you.

People in fast-rising companies can be surprised by the level of success and personal rewards gained over a short period of time. Even those who appear self-confident may be thinking, "Gee, maybe I am achieving success; maybe I'm actually doing a good job here."

More established executives, on the other hand, are likely to experience negative surprises—the loss of friends, demands on time, the toll on their families, not having enough time to get the job done.

Donna Karan, chairwoman and founder of the design company that bears her name, puts it this way: "I think it takes an enormous personal toll on one's life to be successful, absolutely. People say the glamour; it's not there. The pain is definitely there. The insecurity, the pressure."

An important way to avoid negative surprises is to keep a watchful eye on the balance in your life. Allstate Insurance's CEO, Ed Liddy, who serves with me on the Board of Governors of the Boys & Girls Clubs of America, says: "I've got a wife, three kids, and a dog. I work hard at getting home for dinner. Sometimes it's a late dinner and I typically do a fair amount of reading after nine o'clock at night to keep up, but I think well-balanced people are better executives."

7. Momentum

Momentum makes an interesting study. Take the momentum of a moving car, for instance. My car, a Jeep Grand Cherokee, has one of those computers that show the amount of gas consumed as you drive. From a standstill, you see fuel consumption skyrocket as all that weight begins to move forward. More energy is expended in the first few seconds of acceleration—the first mile of motion— than over many miles thereafter. Then, once the car is speeding along, it takes serious braking to stop it. Once stopped, all that energy must be used to again achieve forward momentum.

The stock market provides a good study in momentum. The bull trend, which took the Dow Jones Industrial Average from less than 1,000 to more than 10,000, was a freight train that couldn't be stopped. One need only look back in history, however, to witness what happens when it does stop: the crash of 1987, the devastating bear market of the 1970s, the Great Depression of the 1930s.

At Blimpie International, we've certainly had our experience with momentum. Our euphoric start in the mid-1960s turned into

---

If you experienced extraordinary growth in the short term, don't automatically think that you have arrived. To do so may be a little like playing Russian roulette:

---

a nightmare in the late 1960s and early 1970s; turned upwards in the late 1970s and early 1980s, collapsed in the mid-to-late 1980s, zoomed forward for nine years until 1996, only to flatten out afterwards. One thing that always seems to hold true, though, is that once a trend is in place, major energy must be expended to turn it around.

Why is that? It has to do with psychology. In 1974, when the Dow was below 600 (hard to believe now), you couldn't *give* stocks away. People were convinced that capitalism was finished. Gloom and doom were everywhere. In retrospect, that's what had to happen—there had to be a bottom, a point where things could only get better. And the same thing could work with a high stock market. The point is, whether you're talking about investors, corporate people, ballplayers, members of the Boys & Girls Clubs, or your own family, the more the participants act as a team, the faster momentum will be reversed.

I noted with interest that there was only one New York Yankees player on the 1998 starting All-Star roster, only one player from one of the winningest teams in baseball history. On the other hand, the top home-run hitters—Mark McGwire, Ken Griffey Jr., Sammy Sosa—were all on teams that were out of pennant contention.

In other words, it doesn't matter how great one player performs; it takes a team to create winning momentum.

Franchising is, by design, highly interdependent. Each of the organization's components, independently, can accomplish things, but as a team, much, much more can be accomplished than anyone, even someone at his best, could accomplish alone.

In an organization, reversing momentum requires that everyone get on board toward the organization's goals and push in a positive way. The longer it takes to get people on board, the longer it will take to reverse the company's fortunes.

The word *team* today is so overused, yet there seem to be so few real teams anymore. A real team has the same goals, the same heartbeat. A real team doesn't necessarily have any guaranteed Hall of Famers. A real team just wins.

8. Keeping the Right Attitude

A great example of a guy who has been Building on the Best is Luke Thompson, a Blimpie International owner-operator. Luke purchased the Blimpie franchise for the Newnan, Georgia, restaurant, which had been owned by one of our chain's most successful franchisees. In the year before Thompson's acquisition, the store had reported sales that ranked among the best in the chain, making it one of the chain's best franchises. Understandably, the sale drew concern from Blimpie International executives, as well as the subfranchisor. An operator can make or break a location, and the last thing we needed was to have this store get broken.

It didn't take Luke long to allay our fears. He set a goal that didn't merely call for him to maintain sales levels but to exceed them. After a year, the results came in. Luke had taken the best and had made it better, building sales by 10 percent.

In 1999, he decided to open a second store, securing a site on the other side of Newnan. Significantly for us, he co-branded his Blimpie franchise with one of Blimpie International's new concepts, Smoothie Island. Shortly after opening, I visited Luke. As we stood in the parking lot outside his location, perched on a hill, Luke pointed into the distance.

"There's a Brewster's Ice Cream place over there, and a Steak and Shake on the other side," he said. They both sell shakes, so I figure there's a lot of people around here that I can get to have a Smoothie." Wow! Think about how many people would look at that situation in the opposite way. What if Luke had said, "There's an awful lot of competition around here; there's no way I'm going to open a Smoothie concept"? It would be hard to argue with that logic, because obviously there *is* a lot of competition there. Luke saw that competition as positive, while others, with lesser attitudes, would see it as negative.

If you are strictly a numbers kind of person, you will find it difficult to understand why some people can be so successful at something while others will fail at the exact same thing. It has to do with attitude.

Spend a little time with Luke Thompson in one of his Blimpie outlets and it's easy to see why he is so successful. When he shakes the hand of a deliveryman, answers the phone with "Good afternoon, Blimpie," or offers to help a customer make a menu

---

One of the most valuable things you can do in life, particularly during a period of growth, is to periodically take a step back. Any kind of growth can change your life, and you need to get some perspective on that.

---

decision, he's telling those people, with words and actions: "I like you. I'm glad you're here. This is a happy place. You're important to me."

The right attitude is a positive, optimistic attitude, even in the face of adversity. While you may not be able to control what happens to you, you *can* control how you react to it. Consider the words of Pat Riley, one of NBA's all-time greatest coaches: "After we lost in '84, I went through torment that summer, being publicly mocked and humiliated by the media. But then I realized that it didn't make any difference what had happened. What matters is how you deal with it. It's how you take it. It's how you come back from it."

It's more important to have the right attitude with the bad stuff than the good. Anyone can handle the good. People who do the best with their careers and lives are those who know how to deal with adversity.

Four Ways to Change and Improve Your Situation

For more than fifteen years, the CNN show *Pinnacle* has profiled CEOs of successful and growing companies. In May 1994, I became one of the select few to be profiled.

Sometimes exhausting, often nerve-wracking, and always exciting, the program's filming began with me at my desk in New York City, then to a Blimpie restaurant, and finally to my home in upstate New York.

In order to be in upstate New York for a morning shoot, the show's host, Beverly Schuch, and the TV crew planned to arrive in town the night before and meet me at a Mexican restaurant for dinner. Over a few burritos, we discussed the upcoming filming.

"My house is on the top of a mountain. It's beautiful there. We really should shoot outdoors," I said.

The producer was quick to retort: "Oh, no. We can't do that."

"Why not?" I wanted to know.

"Well, you see, it's the lighting. Then there are insects and bugs. Outdoors presents all kinds of problems."

I assumed these folks knew what they were talking about, so the conversation ended there.

Bright and early the next morning, Beverly walked and talked with me in the town center as cameras rolled. When enough footage was generated, everyone got into their vehicles and followed me up the mountain to my house. It was only April but, when we reached the top of my driveway, the day was sunny and warm. The views were magnificent. As soon as the crew and producer stepped out of their cars and trucks, they began to scan the landscape. In less than a minute, they had made a decision.

"The interview will take place outdoors," was the command. To this day, whenever I meet someone who has seen my *Pinnacle* show, they always comment on the beautiful mountain scenery.

Before they arrived at my home, the CNN crew was acting exactly the way people behave when they have preconceived notions about things. They were acting out of habit. Their experience dictated that filming indoors was the best option. Of course, once they actually saw an alternative, they could visualize how much better their production could be if the shoot were outdoors.

Ironically, when I first built my home there, I acted the same way, except that I carried it on for five years. I guess it had to do with spending so much time in New York City—you know you never want to kill anything that's green. So, when I built my house in the country, I removed only the trees necessary to create the space in which to fit the house. I was living in the woods and I was happy with that. My goal had been successfully accomplished.

After a few years, though, Building on the Best fever set in. Having always been someone who seeks to make things better, I set out to improve my house. One day, I decided to open up more

---

The most productive thing you can do is stop and reflect. So, take a step back, give yourself some breathing space, reconfirm your goals or establish new ones, renew your passion, and move into the future.

---

space on the landscape. With chainsaw in hand, I cut down a few trees. Suddenly through the forest, I could see far into the distance. Hmmm, I thought. If I cut down that pine over there, that spruce, and that oak, I may get myself a view. Sure enough, the more trees I removed, the better the view became, so much so that I hired a professional to clear a wide area.

Behind all those beautiful trees was something even more beautiful: A panoramic view of the sky and the mountains. In this case, a "Building on the Best" approach not only changed and improved my view and my environment, but it probably added substantial value to the investment I had in my home.

A couple of years ago, I spent three days in Fort Lauderdale with our National Franchisee Advisory Council. Now, the idea to a New Yorker of spending three days in Fort Lauderdale in the middle of February is pretty appealing. But, while our meeting was in a very nice hotel in a beautiful Florida resort, it actually took place on the hotel's bottom floor. For three days, we met, talked, and planned in a small, dimly lit room with no windows.

On the last day, when our meetings were almost finished, one of our franchisees said: "You know, it's really beautiful outside. We should have held these meetings outdoors, in the sunlight. We could have accomplished the same things, but we would all be feeling a lot better right now."

Of course, by then, our meetings were almost over. It was too late. "Well," we said, "maybe next time."

The realization that we could have spent the same amount of time doing the same business but doing it in a much more favorable environment got me thinking: Isn't this much like what we do in our daily lives? Don't we get up every day and go about our business without ever thinking too much about the fact that maybe, just maybe, we could create a better environment for ourselves? Isn't it possible that we could improve our lives if we simply had the vision to change our environment? Isn't it so, that if we continue to do the same old thing day after day, that we will wind up with the same old results, day after day?

I'm always trying to explain this to Blimpie franchisees who need a change: "You don't need a change in the concept, nor a change in the way you make your sandwiches. You may not even need a change in the amount of hard work and effort you put into running your business. What I'm here to propose is that you change your vision so that you can change your environment."

The best way for a Blimpie franchisee to experience a change in environment is for her to do something that resulted in higher top-line sales and greater net profits. That would make operators feel better about themselves emotionally and, obviously, financially. Higher sales and profits will boost the value of their franchises, the net worth of their businesses, and the pride they feel in their association with the Blimpie team.

For a Blimpie operator, a way to change things may be to renovate. Or perhaps he can do some aggressive promotions—such as having the local radio station run a series of remote broadcasts from the Blimpie restaurant.

If I were to ask every Blimpie franchisee, "Do you think you are going to do better this year than last?" I'd almost certainly get this response: "Yes."

Then I'd follow up with a second question: "What are you going to do differently?"

Think about that for a moment. If you expect to achieve better results this year, you've got to do something different, right? After all, doing the same thing over and over and expecting different results is, well, the definition of insanity.

In our daily lives, there are numerous things we can, and maybe should, change. The trick is to figure out which ones. Here are four ways to take one thing and convert it into something else.

1. Throw It Away

I did it with my first marriage, my college education, and my job. In the late 1980s, I did it with Blimpie's marketing and accounting departments. I've seen people throw away jobs, careers, relationships, and religions. If it has to be done, so be it. It's not always the best way. Financially and emotionally, it can be costly. And the grass doesn't always turn out to be greener. I got lucky in that things usually worked out for me, but I've seen people get hurt very badly when they tossed something that they should have held on to.

2. Ignore It

In the backyard of my upstate New York home, the stump of a cut-down tree began to sprout leaves. Soon, the leaves turned into branches. I had already cut down the original tree, so I knew I didn't want another tree there. Yet, despite walking past the newly growing plant a million times, I ignored it, figuring I'd get around

---

The right attitude is a positive, optimistic attitude, even in the face of adversity. While you may not be able to control what happens to you, you *can* control how you react to it.

---

to it sooner or later. Well, I should have got to it sooner, because when I finally went to cut it down, it had become not one, but four, trees. And they were large enough that, fearing I might damage the house, I called in a professional woodsman. No, ignoring a growing tree, a leaky roof, an infectious disease, or an arrogant boss is not smart. And don't try ignoring a bad marriage, either. Your spouse will eventually change, too—into a divorce lawyer.

3. Improve It

Greg Brenneman, a partner in Bain & Company, a consulting firm specializing in corporate turnarounds, was involved in one of the great improvements in American history, that of Continental Airlines. In the *Harvard Business Review,* Brenneman explains:

> In my six-odd years of working on turnarounds at Bain, I had never seen a company as dysfunctional as Continental. There was

next to no strategy in place. Managers were paralyzed by anxiety. The company had gone through ten presidents in ten years, so standard operating procedure was to do nothing while awaiting new management. The product, in a word, was terrible. And the company's results showed it. Continental ranked tenth out of the ten largest U.S. airlines in all key customer-service areas as measured by the Department of Transportation: on-time arrivals, baggage handling, customer complaints, and involuntary denied boardings. And the company hadn't posted a profit outside of bankruptcy since 1978.

Eventually, Continental, under the leadership of CEO Gordon Bethune, again became a winner, and it wasn't brain surgery: clean planes, on-time arrival and departure, good food, no lost bags, and reasonable ticket prices.

Improvements should not be limited only to situations or things that are not working. In an interview in *Business Week,* listen to what Bill Gates says about "Building on the Best":

> Companies fail when they become complacent and imagine that they will always be successful. That's even more dangerous in a world that is changing faster than ever, especially technologically. So we are always challenging ourselves: Are we making what customers want and working on the products and technologies they'll want in the future? Are we staying ahead of all our competitors? What don't our customers like about what we do, and what are we doing about it? Are we organized most effectively to achieve our goals? Even the most successful companies must constantly reinvent themselves.

Unfortunately, so many of today's business leaders will be blinded by their successes and fail to change to accommodate the marketplace. It happened to Levi's, and its share of men's jeans dropped from 48 percent in 1990 to 25 percent in 1998. It happened to Apple and IBM, and both almost went out of business. It will happen to any organization that is guilty of arrogance in assuming that just because it has a well-known brand that its product will remain preeminent. Moore's Law, the process first described by the co-founder of Intel, Gordon Moore, says that, every eighteen months, chipmakers will be able to double the number of transistors on a given sliver of silicon. How about that for generating the need for change?

While the pace of change is predictable, however, charting the direction is still a form of art. As former British Prime Minister Harold Wilson once observed: "He who rejects change is the architect of decay. The only human institution which rejects progress is the cemetery."

4. Seek to Understand

My friend Tom Catherall is one of the best restaurant operators in Atlanta. Prime, Tom Tom, Indigo Coastal Grill, and Noche are some of his highly successful dining places. Tom's success can be attributed to his understanding of the food-service business. It is this understanding that led him to take simple foods—steak and sushi, for example—and meld them together into an interesting

---

If you expect to achieve better results this year, you've got to do something different, right? After all, doing the same thing over and over and expecting different results is, well, the definition of insanity.

---

blend. Who would have thought that a steakhouse like Prime could sell a boatload of sushi and have a cigar-smoking bar at the same time? It confirms the German saying: "Discovery is seeing what everybody has seen and thinking what nobody has thought."

Building on the Best requires that we believe in improvement. Whether it's your waistline, your retirement plan, your tennis swing, or your business, things can always be improved.

Blimpie's New Wave . . . Toward a New Century

I'm proud to say that Blimpie International did achieve success, but the world never stops turning, and that means that success is never final. To continue to achieve success, a brand or a company must periodically reinvent itself, just as an individual must periodically reinvent herself or himself.

If we think about it, we've all achieved the Best in some way. And, of course, at Blimpie, we have laid claim to the Best sandwich. But if our attitude is "I achieved results once, and I'm done," then Building on the Best is something we need to address. Continuous improvement must be a way of life for us because our competition (either business or personal) is improving all the time.

People naturally resist change—especially when it comes to changing something that is apparently working. One of the artifacts in my office is a typewriter manufactured by the Woodstock Typewriter Company of Woodstock, Illinois. The logo on the carriage reads "Ball-bearing-Standard-Single-Shift." It must have been produced in the 1930s or 1940s. And it works! But if I were to ask my assistant to start using it, she would look at me as if I had two heads.

I keep this antique as a reminder that, just because something is working, doesn't mean it shouldn't be changed.

At one time, this typewriter was the Best. It represented the best product, the best technology, the best training program, and so forth. Then someone came along and said, "It's perfect. Try to improve it. Make it more reliable, more efficient, more convenient." Had the prevailing attitude instead been "It ain't broke, so don't fix it," our MIS Director would be repairing typewriters instead of building computer networks.

Rather than thinking the Best, which promotes complacency, "Building on the Best" makes you think, "How can I make it, or do it, better?"

I remember when I was afraid to touch a computer and when I looked at a fax machine with great skepticism. I've since learned that a rapidly changing world demands a high level of adaptability. If we react to things the way we used to react not long ago, we will face nothing but problems.

At a town meeting at the Blimpie convention in Las Vegas in the mid-1990s, a franchisee stood up and said to me, "When is Blimpie International going to stop changing things?" My reply, of course, was, "Never." Our company, our chain, our brand, our concept—they are always going to change. They must, or we will not survive and prosper and build on the best.

It's pretty obvious that an organization that changes rapidly will wreak havoc with some of the people in that organization. Some changes can be difficult and unpleasant—or, at least, might be perceived that way. Not realizing that change is an evolutionary process and that there is not always a clear path to follow because circumstances change, franchisees have accused us of having a private agenda, but we haven't always had all the answers, so how do you give the answers when you don't have them?

There's a lot more evidence today to suggest that organizations that are slow to change are headed for the most trouble. Sure, we can minimize the pace of change for today, but what will we do to ourselves in the long term?

Certainly an employee doesn't have to change just because his company does. An employee can decide, either consciously or without really stopping to think about it, that she'll resist, either by fighting openly and loudly or maybe silently and behind the scenes. People stress themselves out more and waste more emotional energy by desperately hanging on to the old habits and beliefs than they would by simply embracing the changes. In any case, don't go around complaining. If you don't like what's happening, help fix things or get out.

The best-run organizations are going to change—and change rapidly. Does it make sense to assume that you can remain effective without changing, too?

Change often makes people crazy. I remember watching a special television program on the 1950s, a story about Elvis Presley and some of the other rock 'n' roll performers of that time, and how people were reacting to this new kind of music. Politicians, media people, business people, church people, and people who

---

One of the artifacts in my office is a typewriter manufactured by the Woodstock Typewriter Company of Woodstock, Illinois. The logo on the carriage reads "Ball-bearing-Standard-Single-Shift." It must have been produced in the 1930s or 1940s. And it works! But if I were to ask my assistant to start using it, she would look at me as if I had two heads. I keep this antique as a reminder that, just because something is working, doesn't mean it shouldn't be changed.

---

might otherwise have been considered intelligent were denouncing this music, saying it should be banned, predicting that it would destroy our country.

Obviously, they weren't prepared to accept that an important change was occurring. Instead of trying to stop this change, they should have approached it more positively, perhaps by seeing the opportunities. They could have gotten into the recording business or bought stock in a music or entertainment company.

Blimpie International is always being reinvented. In 1997, a new initiative called "New Wave . . . Toward a New Century" was introduced. New Wave is all about change, a change so profound, so sweeping, that Blimpie will never be the same. It consists of five components.

1. A Portfolio of Brands

The essence of New Wave is that our company is evolving from Blimpie International, the brand, to Blimpie International, the brand-franchising company. Our plan is to not only build and franchise the Blimpie brand but to do the same with a menu of other brands as well.

In addition to Blimpie, our portfolio now includes several other brands. Maui Tacos is a small chain of quick-service Maui/Mex restaurants that started in Hawaii and has since opened locations on the mainland, for which we acquired the brand and development rights. Pasta Central offers eat-in, takeout, and home-meal-replacement Italian food. Smoothie Island is a juice-and-smoothie concept. And BI Concept Systems is a company offering equipment-and-design services to our own brands, as well as to companies outside the Blimpie International family.

For most of our existence, we viewed the Blimpie brand as our main asset. "New Wave" dictates that our main asset becomes franchise competency. We now see ourselves as brand builders, not just sandwich people.

2. New Leadership Organization

Less than a year after New Wave was introduced, one of our employees remarked to me: "So many people have left Blimpie International recently, it's scary." Well, I can see why some employees might be concerned, but not only was the staff exodus not scary to me, it was expected—and maybe even desirable.

We went through a change this dramatic, maybe even more so, once before. It was in the late 1980s, and we refer to it as the Rebirth of Blimpie International. The changes in Blimpie International staff at that time were much greater than those for New Wave. It's just that back then, Blimpie had a much lower profile. There were only about three hundred locations, the brand wasn't known nationally, and our stock was not listed on a major exchange. We didn't have to worry about the *Wall Street Journal* reporting lower earnings.

If you think that doing something like removing all accounting functions from your back office in New York and starting a new department with a new controller in a city one thousand miles away was not unsettling, think again.

I happen to be one of those people who thinks change is good and change is necessary. Some folks don't agree, or they discover that they cannot or will not adjust to the changes. For example, work flow may become greater or different for a person, perhaps only temporarily, yet that person doesn't adjust to the new schedule. Or a change in leadership or management means that an employee reports to a different person, and that doesn't sit well with the employee. Sometimes, an employee completely understands why it's in the company's best interest to make changes, but just doesn't want to be part of the changes.

Here's the good news. Eventually, the turmoil of change ends and what remains is a revitalized staff coupled with a group of new, motivated people who bring new experience, new knowledge, and new attitude to the company. That's when the magic begins.

In a perfect corporate world, everyone who gave so much to our company in the past would reinvent themselves to become the change that we need instead of fighting the change or running from the change. That obviously was not going to happen. That's why we bring in new people who breathe new life into the organization.

3. Global Development

Every well-known U.S. brand brings a bit of the American dream with it. When the brand is exported, the dream is exported. That's a wonderful asset for a company like Blimpie. Blimpie International's goal is to become a worldwide company with presence in the quick-service restaurant market in as many countries as is feasible. At the end of 1999, our chain had grown to have a presence in fourteen countries.

4. Alternative Financial Strategies

Some of the steps taken in this regard have been to repurchase some of the company's stock, acquisitions, and chainwide informational processes.

5. Expanded Communications

This plan includes efforts to increase communications in the following categories: internal, international, investor relations, corporate business communications, marketing, and public relations. The main purpose here, of course, is to get all stakeholders on board with our new initiative.

• • •

New Wave is a journey, not an event. It's a long-term, evolutionary process that we will use for Building on the Best. It's ideal for people who understand this vision and see the possibilities before they become obvious. Or, as NHL Hall of Famer Wayne Gretzky once put it: "I don't skate to where the puck is. I skate to where it's going to be."

Five Ways People React to Change

During a change, problems typically increase, and people are not as effective as they used to be. Here are some of the reasons.

- They feel awkward. People usually think that conditions will remain just as they are. They are comfortable tied to their daily routines so, when they are confronted with change, they feel awkward, out of control. They've grown attached to the structures, which have often achieved success for them—particularly if they were involved in creating those structures.

- They focus on what they are giving up. How many people have found so much more love and happiness in a second marriage, even though they were extremely unhappy, maybe even bitter, when the first one broke up? People need to be coached through a change and given a little time to digest it. They are afraid of the future, regardless of how much they may dislike the past. When we introduced our "New Wave" initiative, we announced to our staff: "No one is allowed to complain for four months."

- They seek revenge. "I'll get even," threatens the wife who resents her husband for leaving her. "I'll screw things up. I'll show them," thinks the employee who's upset with a company for making changes that he doesn't like. They take a stand against the change.

- One of the most important changes Blimpie International ever made was requiring all franchisees to bake bread fresh in their stores. At the time, though, some thought the company was making a mistake, and they fought the change. While their intentions may have been good, they hurt all franchisees because they delayed the process and made the company devote time and effort to forcing the change.

- They revert back to their old ways. Typically, when a change has to take place, the people instigating the change exert pressure on those who are required to carry it out. Once the pressure is off, though, the urge is to go back to the way things were. For change to last, it must be self-perpetuating. The changers must make it clear that there is no going back to the old days.

Change Is a Matter of Survival

The future belongs only to the people who see possibilities before they become obvious.

Do you watch *Party of Five* or *Buffy the Vampire Slayer?* Can you translate the words *phat* or *drop top?* Do you know the brands Mudd, Paris Blues, Invitro, Cement? Were you raised on Oprah, Geraldo, and MTV while under the threat of AIDS, and global warming? Well, the people who will be consuming things and running things in the future will answer "yes" to all of these questions.

Regardless of the successes we may have achieved in the past, if we are to "Build on the Best," we need to address the fashion, the music, the eating habits, and the lifestyles and issues of the current and future generations. We need to understand that change is not merely necessary to compete but is essential to simply survive. We must provide the training and the tools while searching for the brainpower and the creativity needed to compete. And we must make sure people understand the difference between management and leadership and unleash people's desires while promoting the leadership in them.

People tend to believe that whatever changes will affect their lives have already occurred. But Building on the Best is about tomorrow, not yesterday. The 3M Company says it doesn't know what products it will be selling in five years because they're yet to be invented. In the late 1970s, McDonald's founder Ray Kroc couldn't say what the best-selling food item would be in 2000, but unequivocally predicted that McDonald's would be selling it. Past experience is valuable only in that it provides a perspective on the future.

To the young generation, there is a constant drive to change the world. When you look at folks like Joe Kraus and his five college buddies who started the Internet company Excite in a garage and sold it six years later for $7 billion, you know that they are doing it. During a discussion about design of one of our new concepts at a Blimpie International board meeting, one board member said, "If it's presented to us and we like it, it's probably wrong. What appeals to young people today probably won't appeal to us."

At Blimpie International, we tap into the minds of people by asking them a few simple questions: What do you like most about the organization that you are involved with? What do you like least? What would you change if you could?

The answers we get from our staff often lead us on a path of positive change. Menu items, the store serving lines, our training programs—they have all experienced important changes that were generated because of advice from our staff. Suggestions about advertising sparked rethinking about how to promote the chain. We now view advertising as just a part of a larger marketing strategy, which includes things like outlets and signage at stadiums, ballparks, and arenas; movie tie-ins; our web page; packaging; our distinctive colors; Blimpie-labeled products (like potato chips and sweet and hot peppers); and our association with the Boys & Girls Clubs of America.

The key is to get the right people, give them the right opportunity, let them do what they do best, and coach and direct them to help them overcome the frustrations of their jobs. How can change truly happen if people don't buy into it? To get them to buy in, you have to listen to them and let them know that not only do you care about their ideas but that you welcome them and are serious about implementing them.

The world is changing so rapidly and so unpredictably today that it's almost a fact of life that if something works, it's probably obsolete and must be changed. And that invokes three things: First, the realization that there's always a better way to do things; second, an understanding that change must become the norm, so there's an ongoing search to do things better; and third, a dedication to the process of growing and executing—making change happen.

Shedding Our Shells for Growth

Blimpie International's executive vice president, Chuck Leaness, and his wife, Christina, have a beautiful summer home, off the coast of Portland, Maine. There's no way you can go to Maine and not eat lobster so, whenever Yvonne and I visit the Leanesses, we prepare to dine on some.

Usually, a one- or a two-pound lobster is my limit, but I've seen people eat three-, even four-pounders. For a long time, I never thought about how a one-pounder becomes a four-pounder. After all, even at one pound, the lobster is already confined in a non-expandable suit of armor.

Then, a marine biologist explained it to me. At some point, the lobster decides that it wants to grow larger, and it does something that I think is very brave. It travels out to a reef, sheds its shell, and exposes its naked self to all the dangers of the sea. It does this because it wants—it needs—to grow. So, immediately after shedding the old shell, it begins to grow a new one, a much larger one, a shell for the future. The creature may or may not survive the process.

To Build on the Best, each of us is confronted with similar challenges. If we want and need to grow, then we sometimes may have to shed our we've-always-done-it-that-way shells.

Old ideas are constantly crumbling around us. Shells are being shed by every forward-looking company and vision-inspired person in America. Those who continue to do something because "it's the way it's always been done" will, at best, remain confined to their worlds—or, at worst, become extinct. To quote Wayne Gretzky again, "You never make the shots you don't take."

Building on the Best requires that we make the decision to improve ourselves, to grow to a better place. To do that we must have the courage to shed our shells and expose ourselves to risk.

Ask, 'What if . . . ?'

I've always loved music and, for many years, I had wanted to play the piano. It all began one day in grammar school when a local music school was allowed to solicit students who might be interested in learning how to play a musical instrument. I looked at the brochure and was immediately intrigued by the thought of becoming a pianist. I ran home to get my parents' permission, but they gave me a dose of reality. First, a piano was expensive. They just couldn't afford it. And, second, there was no room in our house to put such a large instrument. "Let's sign you up for accordion lessons," they said. Typical Italians.

For about four years, I studied the accordion. Never happy with the squeeze-box image, however, I gave it up. My urge to play the piano never left me. Then, in the early 1980s, I took a new apartment in New York City. As I thought about furnishing the place, I observed that a baby grand piano would look great in a certain spot in the living room. Nah, I can't play the piano, I thought. But, what if I could play?

I began to imagine myself entertaining guests, singing with friends, or just enjoying myself—all with me behind eighty-eight keys. My urge to play became so great that, a few days later, while driving on a New Jersey highway, I spotted a piano store. Within a few minutes, I had bought a Yamaha baby grand.

Of course, there was no way I could look at a piano in my home every day without knowing how to play it. So, on the recommendation of the Blimpie sales director at the time, someone who happened to be an ex-jazz musician, I found Norman Gold, a jazz musician and piano instructor on West Fifty-eighth Street. My first conversation in Norman's studio went something like this:

"How much do you know?"

"As a kid I used to play the accordion."

"Can you read music?"

"Only the right hand."

"Play something."

"Now?"

"Yes, now."

I couldn't have played for more than fifteen seconds when I heard, "Okay, stop. I know what to do." I told Norman I wanted to learn jazz, but he said he wouldn't teach me jazz without classical. So, I got my first assignment, a Bach piece that I immediately took home and tried to play. I found that I couldn't put three notes together. "I can't do this." I thought. "This is crazy." I got up from the piano and went for a walk.

My thoughts turned to the previous year, when I had run the New York Marathon with a broken toe. "Wait a minute," I thought, "You can run twenty-six miles with a broken toe, but you can't learn to play the piano? Ridiculous."

I studied jazz, classical, and pop music for eight years, until business travel began to seriously impede my ability to take lessons and practice. Then, two years later, Norman passed away.

Ask, "What if . . . ?" Once I asked that question, I was able to make things happen for myself. The situations I imagined appeared exciting, fun, and entertaining. In my mind, the piano was transformed from a musical instrument to a catalyst for glamour and passion. Only after I got to that point was I able to apply myself sufficiently to be able to successfully learn to play.

Asking "What if . . . ?" is more important than ever in a world with an uncertain future. Big companies hire futurists to paint "What if . . . ?" scenarios so they won't be caught flat-footed. A company like IBM could have saved itself a ton of money and a trip to the brink of extinction had it pursued a "What if . . . ?" strategy about personal computers instead of deciding that they would never amount to much more than a toy.

When Blimpie franchisee Luke Thompson selected a location for his second store in Georgia, he decided that he wanted to dual-brand the space, that is, install a Smoothie Island franchise along with the Blimpie franchise using the same real estate. There was only one problem. When Luke approached the town where his store was to be located, he learned that the local code permitted only a certain amount of signage relative to the square footage of the front of his restaurant. The two signs combined would exceed the permissible code limit. Of course, a Blimpie sign was necessary, so obviously there could be no Smoothie Island sign and, consequently, no Smoothie Island franchise.

Luke Thompson doesn't give up that easily. He kept thinking of how much more business he could generate if he had two concepts instead of one. He was determined to figure out a way to make it happen. One day, while standing outside the building and staring at the location, Luke observed that if he walked out a couple of car lengths into the parking lot, he could see the extended roof that capped his store's portion of the building. And Luke asked himself: "What if . . . ?"

"What if I could get the town to agree that the roof over my store should actually be included when considering total square footage? After having his designer sketch a drawing of the location, Luke submitted it to the town. Sure enough, it was approved.

Most Limitations Are Self-Imposed

When I first got the idea for Blimpie, we knew no one else had created a national chain, or even a regional chain, selling only submarine sandwiches. That might have been enough to discourage us from pursuing our idea, but then we asked ourselves,

"What if . . . ?" What if we created a chain selling only sub sandwiches?

Our inexperience enabled us to see an opportunity where others saw only roadblocks.

In the 1980s, Blimpie International was losing money, our stock was selling for pennies, and we had a regional chain with only a couple of hundred stores—until we asked ourselves, "What if . . . ?"

- What if we grew to one thousand or more stores?

- What if we had a stock worth $10 or $20 a share?

- What if we built one of the best franchise systems in foodservice?

Until we asked ourselves those questions, our minds had been muddied up with all sorts of problems and mental roadblocks. We

---

Most limitations are self-imposed. But, when we ask "What if . . . ?" and imagine how something might come to pass, we are busting through those limitations, we're putting our problems aside and starting fresh, we're dreaming about what we can become.

---

couldn't get past the crisis of the day. But once we said, "What if . . . ?", well, there were no more roadblocks. Everything became possible.

Thinking about the future is the first step toward creating it. When John F. Kennedy talked about going to the moon, he was asking "What if . . . ?" When Dr. Martin Luther King, Jr. gave his "I Have a Dream" speech, he was asking "What if . . . ?"

Most limitations are self-imposed. But, when we ask "What if . . . ?" and imagine how something might come to pass, we are busting through those limitations, we're putting our problems aside and starting fresh, we're dreaming about what we can become.

A Journey That Never Ends

The last stop on a Mediterranean cruise that the H. J. Heinz Company sponsored, and that I had the good fortune to be invited on, was a small French village on the border of Spain called Port Vendres. When our ship entered the tiny port at nine on a June morning in 1999, people in this fairytale-like community left their residences and businesses so they could see the largest ship that had ever docked there. Stuck in my mind is the image of four butchers, shoulder-to-shoulder, aprons neatly draped over their bodies like uniforms, standing in front of a local charcuterie. Other merchants planted themselves similarly at their stores' doorsteps, while townsfolk peered through open windows from bright colored, neatly painted buildings that never exceeded three stories.

Our visit to Port Vendres and the neighboring village of Collioure was brief, but it was long enough to enjoy a wonderful lunch at a quaint, family-owned restaurant, buy a couple of paintings from local artists, and pick up some unique, priceless gifts. By 5:30 that afternoon, the ship was prepared for departure.

As we slowly moved away from shore, I watched the townspeople congregated on the docks and the city's sidewalks and all along the old stone walls that were fixed at the cliff's edge. Then, they began to wave—children, young adults, older folks—and took turns waving so that at all times many arms were extended as if to say, "Thanks for visiting our happy home."

At least a tinge of emotion had to overcome any passenger who chose to stand at the ship's deck rail that day. For me, it was more than that. Watching these gentle people who touched my life, even so briefly, fade away into the distance, I thought about all those who have come and gone in my lifetime, so many of whom made me laugh or brought me happiness or in some way helped me achieve my successes. And they, too, with the past, have faded away.

As the ship picked up steam, behind us, the little village of Port Vendres grew smaller and smaller until it was barely visible.

Meanwhile, I turned my attention to the front of the ship and the open sea. I looked long and hard into the horizon, as far as I could see. And I knew that when the ship got to that distant place, there would be a new horizon and a new distant place. And that the same thing would happen again, and again.

That's what Building on the Best means to me. It is a journey that has no end. There's always a new place to see, always a new place to get to. Because Building on the Best means there's always another challenge, always another reason to grow, always another dream that you can make come true.

CHAPTER 10

THE SANDWICH MAN'S RECIPES

My Mom loved to cook—but she also didn't have a choice. We were a family of four with a modest income earned by Dad alone. When Dad came home after work, he expected to have food on the table. Enjoying a meal at a restaurant was rare.

How things have changed. In today's fast-paced world, women are an important part of the workforce, men are often responsible for preparing food, and cooking is often seen more as a hobby than a necessity.

Cooking is also being influenced by growing sophisticated tastes. People eat out all the time now, and have gotten used to menu innovation, new variety, and all the concoctions dreamed up by celebrity chefs and product-development analysts at retail chains. So, when they prepare food at home, they are often interested in mimicking a restaurant dining experience or even one-upping the neighborhood chef. In doing so, however, they demand that it all be quick and easy.

What's quicker and easier than a good sandwich? Sandwiches have not only become more popular over the years, they have been gained more respect, too, popping up on the menus of some of the country's finest restaurants. People love sandwiches. They're easy to make, portable, eaten at any time of the day, and inexpensive. They can be made in a variety of ways with a variety of ingredients. They span all ethnic groups.

As founder and chairman of Blimpie International, Inc., marketer of one of the best-known sandwich brands in the world, I figured that I couldn't write a book without offering my readers a few of my favorite sandwich recipes.

On the following pages, you will find some Blimpie sandwich recipes as well as some of my other favorites, and sandwiches that should score a hit with a crowd.

It's All in the Bread

The Earl of Sandwich loved to play cards and, once he started to play, never wanted to stop—not even to eat. In that era, eating meant sitting at a table set with linen, plates, and silverware. The Earl had an idea. He summoned his servants to place a slice of meat between two pieces of bread and bring it to his card table. Thus, the *sandwich* was born.

The English may have invented the first sandwich, but the Italians invented the best sandwich. It all starts with the bread, and there's nothing like a loaf of good, fresh Italian bread. Grandma used to make the best bread. She'd do it from scratch, mixing the dough and placing it in a very large pan, which she covered with a blanket. After it had risen, she'd mold it into different shapes, then bake it. Taking a hunk of Grandma's bread hot out of the oven, adding some butter and taking a bite was like going to heaven.

Over the years, Americans lost the value of a good loaf of bread, often resorting to factory-made, supermarket-bought, bleached-flour varieties. Now, though, good bread is making a comeback. Small, artisan-type bakeries are leading the way as they spring up in all parts of the country. And, of course, even chains like Blimpie are baking fresh bread. Now, even the big bakeries and the big retailers are getting on the bandwagon. Today, you can buy really good bread just about anywhere. Also, of course, those mechanical bread machines make it simple to bake your own quality breads at home.

The very notion of what constitutes bread for a sandwich has changed. Tortillas have gone from a Hispanic staple to mainstream American as wraps, burritos, and roll-ups redefine the scope of sandwiches. This is happening not only because we have become accustomed to yeastless bread, but also because tortilla-style sandwiches can be neatly wrapped, enclosing any number of salad mixtures or hot, main-course-style fillings that would have been impossible to keep inside of traditional bread. Ideas flow like olive oil as a result of these sandwiches, with Mediterranean, Asian, and Mexican leading the list.

The bread for many of these sandwiches is a roll near to my heart that I call a Blimpie-style roll. That refers to a soft French-Italian loaf—the kind you'll see in every Blimpie store.

The Blimpie Best

Today, most of the original Blimpie menu is still served. But, in the early days, we found that by combining the #3 and #4 menu items, we could create the best sandwich. The Blimpie Best is still the greatest on the planet.

1 loaf Blimpie-style bread
2 ounces ham, in thin slices
3 ounces salami, in thin slices
1½ ounces prosciuttini, thinly sliced
2 ounces cappacola, thinly sliced
2 ounces provolone cheese, thinly sliced
Shredded lettuce
4 slices tomato
1 slice onion
Olive oil, to taste
Vegetable oil, to taste
Red-wine vinegar, to taste
Oregano, salt, and pepper, to taste

Slice the loaf of bread horizontally. On the bottom half, place, in this order, the ham, salami, prosciuttini, cappacola, and provolone. Cup each slice in the palm of your hand before placing it on the bread. Place the shredded lettuce over the cheese, then add the tomato slices. Separate the onion slice into rings, and place that over the lettuce and tomato. Drizzle on some olive oil, vegetable oil, and red-wine vinegar. Add oregano, salt, and pepper.

Serves 2.

The Roast-Beef American

Some of our best sandwich ideas have come from franchisees. This one was invented by Joe Maringano, who has been with the Blimpie chain since 1967. Joe and his partners operate three locations in the Union Square area of Manhattan.

1 loaf Blimpie-style bread
Butter
5 ounces roast beef, thinly sliced
½ teaspoon garlic powder
4 standard slices American cheese
Shredded lettuce
4 slices tomato
1 slice onion
Olive oil, to taste
Vegetable oil, to taste
Red-wine vinegar, to taste
Oregano, salt, and pepper, to taste

Slice bread in half, toast until golden brown, and coat lightly with butter. While the bread is toasting, prepare the meat. Place the roast beef on a microwave-safe plate, shake the garlic powder lightly over the meat, and place the cheese slices over the meat. Microwave on high power for 35 seconds, then place on the bottom half of the bread. Add the shredded lettuce and the tomato. Separate the onion into rings, place the piece over the lettuce and tomato, and drizzle on some olive oil, vegetable oil, vinegar. Add oregano, salt, and pepper.

Serves 2.

The Papa Tony!

While my daughter, Debra, was in labor with her second child, something wonderful and funny happened involving her first child, my grandson Nicholas. Debra's mother, Arlene (my ex-wife), said she was in the doctor's waiting room when Nicholas blurted out, "Papa Tony. Papa Tony." Arlene couldn't understand why he was saying that. "So I held him close and said, 'Papa Tony isn't here.' Yet he was persistent, 'Papa Tony, Papa Tony,' he kept repeating, until I realized that there was a TV in the room and he was looking at your commercial. Papa Tony was on TV." Wow, did that bring a smile to my face. It's great to be recognized.

> 1 loaf Italian-style bread
> Mustard and mayonnaise (enough to coat the bread)
> 2 ounces ham, thinly sliced
> 2 ounces turkey, thinly sliced
> 2 ounces American cheese, thinly sliced

Slice the bread in half horizontally. Smear the bottom half with mustard, then cover it with the ham, turkey, and cheese slices. Coat the top of the bread with mayonnaise and place over the ingredients.

Serves 2 kids (just ask Nicholas).

CRISPY TORTILLAS

Tony's Taquitos

When we owned the Border Café in Manhattan, I worked on and off in the kitchen for a few months. Besides gaining a lot of respect for the chef and other kitchen personnel, I also learned how to cook a thing or two, including one of my favorites, which the chef, Bobby Schnurr, was kind enough to name in my honor.

> Peanut oil, for sautéing
> 1 pound raw, chicken breast, sliced
> 2 tablespoons ground cumin
> 3 tablespoons chopped onion
> Salt and pepper, to taste
> 4 6-inch flour tortillas

Pour enough peanut oil into a 12-inch sauté pan to just cover the bottom. Place the pan over low heat and add chicken and onions, and sauté for 3 minutes. Add the cumin and continue to cook for 3 to 5 minutes, until the onions are translucent. Season with salt and pepper.

Briefly warm the tortillas in a low oven or a microwave oven. When the tortillas are warm, divide the chicken mix in four portions, and place one portion in the center of each tortilla. Fold over the end of the tortilla, and roll it around the chicken mix. Secure with a toothpick in the middle, and repeat with the remaining tortillas.

Fry the tortillas in a skillet over high heat with additional peanut oil until the tortillas are a light golden brown. Remove from the pan, and drain on paper towels for 1 minute. Serve with salsa, guacamole, and sour cream.

Serves 4.

Nick Conza's Passion

Dad had a passion for hot peppers. Fresh, fried, dried, crushed, in vinaigrette—he searched them out and made sure that Mom served them at every meal. He also loved to put them into his sandwiches.

> 1 loaf hard-crusted Italian bread
> 5 ounces prosciutto (the real stuff, imported from Parma, Italy), thinly sliced
> 3 ounces fresh mozzarella (the kind kept in water), sliced thick and drained
> Hot Italian peppers (fresh or dried)
> Extra-virgin olive oil
> 6 whole basil leaves

Slice the bread in half horizontally. Cover the bottom half of the bread with prosciutto, and layer the mozzarella slices on top. Fry a few peppers in the olive oil, and remove the stems. Add as many as you can stand. Top with basil.

Serves 1 (if you have my father's appetite).

The Pomodoro

Pomodoro means tomato in Italian, and there's nothing more basic to a good sandwich than tomato. My sister Carol uses tomatoes with pastas, on fish, fowl, meats, vegetables, and of course, sandwiches like the *Pomodoro.*

1 loaf Blimpie-style bread
2 to 3 red, ripe tomatoes
2 black calamata olives
2 cloves garlic
4 leaves fresh basil
Extra-virgin olive oil, to taste
Oregano, salt, and black pepper, to taste

Cut the bread in half, lengthwise, then cut each piece in half horizontally. Chop the tomatoes, olives, garlic, and basil. In a bowl, combine the chopped ingredients with the olive oil, and spoon the mixture onto the bottoms of the bread. Sprinkle oregano, salt, and pepper on top.

Serve as two open sandwiches, or slice into bite-sized pieces and serve as what my Mom would refer to as "a little something."

Serves 2.

Muffuletta

If you travel to Nawlins, you've got to have a Muffuletta. Alternatively, make one like we served as a special for a while at Blimpie.

1 8-inch round of soft French/Italian bread
3 ounces ham, thinly sliced
1 ounce salami, thinly sliced
1 ounce cappacola, thinly sliced
1½ ounces provolone, thinly sliced
4 ounces green olive tapenade
Shredded lettuce
5 slices tomato

Cut the bread in half horizontally and place the ham, salami, cappacola, and Provolone slices on the bottom half, in that order. Spread the olive topping over the meats and cheese, and add the lettuce and tomato slices.

Serves 2.

The Squeeze Box

I always loved music and, for almost as long as I can remember, I wanted to play the piano. But my parents, dissuaded by the cost of a piano and the space it demanded, decided to sign me up for accordion lessons instead. I took lessons for four years but eventually stopped playing. I was just never happy with the squeeze-box image. But, while reminiscing about my accordion, I recalled a sandwich that needs a good squeeze before serving. I call it "The Squeeze Box."

    4 panini (crusty Italian rolls)
    2 cloves garlic, peeled & chopped
    ¼ cup extra-virgin olive oil
    2 tablespoons chopped fresh basil
    4 tomato slices
    ¼ cup black calamata olives, pitted
    1 teaspoon capers
    1 yellow pepper, cored, seeded, and sliced across
    ½ cup cannellini beans
    2 teaspoons balsamic vinegar
    Salt and pepper, to taste

Slice each roll in half horizontally, and spread the chopped garlic over the bottom halves of the rolls, then drizzle with the olive oil. Add the basil, tomatoes, olives, capers, pepper slices, and beans. Drizzle again with olive oil, then add vinegar, salt, and pepper.

Place the top half of the rolls over the filling, and place a heavy can or pot on top of the sandwiches, and "squeeze" them for about 30 minutes.

Serves 4.

¡CARAMBA!

Hecho in Havana

I love Miami, particularly South Beach. The weather is great, the people are as beautiful as the beaches, there's lots to do, and you can get there easily and cheaply from New York. You also don't need a car to get around, something New Yorkers appreciate. Miami, of course, is also known for its wonderful restaurants, many of which are Latin. If you can't make it to South Beach, turn on a CD by the Buena Vista Social Club and play it loud. It will help you enjoy these sandwiches. *Hecho,* by the way, means made, and this sandwich is a personal favorite.

> 4 panini or Portuguese rolls
> ½ cup vinaigrette dressing
> 8 thin slices of green tomatoes
> ½ pound ham, thinly sliced
> ½ pound muenster cheese, thinly sliced
> 8 thin slices of dill pickles
> 1 cup sliced, pickled cherry peppers (hot or sweet)
> Olive oil, for toasting

Split the rolls horizontally and brush vinaigrette on all the inner surfaces. Arrange the tomato slices, ham, cheese, pickle, and peppers on the bread. Brush a warm griddle or pan with the oil and toast the outside of the bread, top and bottom, with a pan on top for weight. When the bread is golden brown and the cheese has melted, you're ready.

Serves 4.

Wrap-and-Roll Veg

This one is straightforward, light, and healthy—probably that's why it's one of my favorites.

1 10-inch flour tortilla
¼ cup shredded lettuce
2 slices tomato
½ large green peppers, cored, seeded, and sliced into thin strips
4-5 fresh mushrooms, thinly sliced
Small handful Alfalfa sprouts

Cover the tortilla shell with shredded lettuce. Add the tomato slices, peppers, mushrooms, and sprouts. Fold about 1 inch of the right side of the tortilla shell over the filling. Starting from the bottom, roll up the tortilla tightly enough to hold the ingredients together. Refrigerate before serving.

Serves 1. (If you have a big appetite, you might have to follow up with a Blimpie Best.)

Jalapeño Chili Burger

Before I met her, my wife, Yvonne, who is mostly Irish with a little Scandinavian thrown in, had never cooked a meal in her life. Then, one day, she woke up and said, "I had a dream, a dream that I made Moroccan Lasagna. I'm going to make dinner tonight." "Er, a dream? And what kind of lasagna?" I asked. Well, she made it, and it was great, and she's been cooking dream-inspired meals ever since. I think she came up with this one during that siesta she took with a sombrero over her face.

> 4 pounds ground buffalo meat (okay, if you're scared, use ground round beef)
> 6 tablespoons snipped fresh chives
> 2 teaspoons chili powder
> ½ teaspoon salt
> 1 teaspoon black pepper
> 1 tablespoon chopped fresh cilantro
> 2 teaspoons oregano
> 2 fresh jalapeño peppers, cored and seeded, membranes removed, and chopped

In a bowl, gently combine the meat, chives, chili powder, salt, pepper, cilantro, oregano, and chopped jalapeños. Divide into 8 portions and form into thick patties. Broil, or grill outdoors, for 5 to 6 minutes on each side.

Serves 8.

The Thai Fry

There's no question that you can cook up some rice and serve this recipe on a plate for dinner, but it sure does make a wonderful sandwich.

½ cup water
1 medium carrot, cut in 3-inch slices
1 head broccoli (florets only)
¼ cup canola oil
2 whole boneless, skinless chicken breasts, cut into bite-sized pieces
10 white mushrooms, stems removed and sliced
1 yellow pepper, cored, seeded, and sliced
2 tablespoons chili oil
½ teaspoon ground cumin
½ teaspoon dry mustard
½ teaspoon ground ginger
1 small clove garlic, minced
Paprika
Cayenne pepper to taste (optional)
2 loaves Blimpie-style bread

Combine the water, carrots, and broccoli in a bowl and microwave on high power for 8 minutes.

Heat the canola oil over medium heat in a large skillet. Add the chicken, mushrooms, pepper, and chili oil. Cover and cook over medium heat, stirring occasionally, for about 10 minutes. Add the broccoli and carrots, and the cumin, mustard, ginger, garlic, paprika, and cayenne. (Remember that cayenne pepper is very hot, so add it a little at a time, so you can gauge how hot you would like it.)

Cook, covered, for 10 more minutes.

Serve on Blimpie-style bread (or on a tortilla).

Serves 4.

Joe Conza's Pasta Fagioli

Here's the perfect side dish for every sandwich. And, it's my brother's special recipe. This alone is worth the price of this book!

5 cloves minced garlic

2 tablespoons olive oil

2 19-ounce cans cannellini beans (drained)

2 8-ounce cans tomato sauce

1 quart water

½ cup chopped basil

Salt and pepper to taste

½ pound elbow macaroni

In the bottom of a large pot, sauté the garlic in the olive oil. Do not let the garlic brown. Add the beans, tomato sauce, and water, and cook for 2 hours on low heat. Just before serving, cook the pasta according to package directions, add the basil, salt, and pepper, and add to the beans and sauce.

Serves 6 to 8.

Final Thoughts

Throughout this book, I've talked a lot about entrepreneurship, about opportunity and failure, about hard work and sacrifice, about maintaining a positive attitude, and about taking a common-sense approach toward achieving success in your life.

More than anything, however, what I want you to take away from what I've written here are these two overriding messages:

First, success is not about making money. It's about enjoying life. Money may help you be more comfortable; it may bring you recognition or prestige. It may enable you to buy or do the things you desire. But you will never be able to measure your happiness by what's in your bank account.

Second, think hard about your dreams, then pursue them with a passion. Enjoyment in what you do comes from a love and passion for what you do. The desire for success will not get you the passion. But get the passion and you'll be successful.

And success, well, it's a beautiful thing!

INDEX